Praise for

A Crucial L

Local Peace Committees and National Peacebuilding

"Odendaal impressively distills a wide variety of experiences with local peace committees and explains the complex interplay between national and local, formal and informal actors in an environment where conflicting groups can work together to forestall violence and take the first steps in what will be a lengthy peacebuilding process. He rightly stresses the importance of ownership of peace processes at the local level as a key condition for success and provides ample evidence for how this local ownership can be achieved. *A Crucial Link* is a must-read for peacebuilding practitioners and policymakers."

—**Nicole Ball,** Center for International Policy

"Odendaal draws on his deep experience as well as broad comparative research to identify lessons about when and how local level peace committees contribute to national level peacebuilding. This book is an important resource for practitioners and researchers alike working to improve the effectiveness of peacebuilding."

—**Diana V. Chigas,** The Fletcher School, Tufts University

"Exploring the connection between frameworks for peacebuilding at both the government and local levels, *A Crucial Link* underscores the importance of understanding peace processes as multilayered and complex, cross-cutting all levels of society. A valuable addition to course reading lists, this volume rightly emphasizes the need for grassroots ownership of peacebuilding processes and provides examples of successes where governmental bodies have collaborated with NGOs and local entities for greater overall effectiveness."

—**Landon Hancock,** Center for Applied Conflict Management,
Kent State University

"Odendaal's well-conceived and well-crafted book on global experiences with local peace committees presents cutting-edge comparative knowledge and practitioner lessons on local-level conflict resolution. This balanced and carefully researched book makes the case that international conflict resolvers must focus intently at the local level for conflict prevention in volatile transitions. This book is highly relevant for practitioners, scholars, and students of conflict resolution at a time when so many countries experiencing volatile transitions are in deep need of comparative lessons and international support for local-level processes to prevent violence and build peace."

—**Timothy D. Sisk,** Center for 21st Century Global Governance, University of Denver

"A convincing case for the centrality of local peace initiatives in securing the sustainability of national peace agreements. Odendaal provides a lucid practitioner's perspective on the process of local peacebuilding and critically reflects on the interconnections between the local and national peace processes. He combines personal experiences as a peacemaker with a thorough review of comparable international experience to provide both a conceptual mapping of the challenges of local peacebuilding and nuanced assessment of the practical lessons that can be drawn from these varied experiences."

—**Hugo van der Merwe,** Centre for the Study of Violence and Reconciliation

"This comparative study comes at the right moment, as many countries simply lack the capacity, structures, and mechanisms to deal with increased violent conflict. Through experiences from dozens of countries, Odendaal convincingly describes how local peace committees have contributed to preventing violence and promoting peaceful coexistence. An essential lesson is that local peacebuilding should be an integral aspect of a national peacebuilding strategy, and *A Crucial Link* optimizes the linkage between local and national levels and between stakeholders that are prepared to give peace a chance. This book deserves to be read by many, while the described approach deserves a fair chance in many more countries."

—**Paul van Tongeren,** International Civil Society Network on Infrastructures for Peace

A Crucial Link

A Crucial Link

*Local Peace Committees and
National Peacebuilding*

Andries Odendaal

UNITED STATES INSTITUTE OF PEACE PRESS
WASHINGTON, D.C.

UNITED STATES INSTITUTE OF PEACE
2301 Constitution Avenue, NW
Washington, DC 20037
www.usip.org

First published 2013

Printed in the United States of America

The paper used in this publication meets the minimum requirements of American National Standards for Information Science—Permanence of Paper for Printed Library Materials, ANSI Z39.48-1984.

Library of Congress Cataloging-in-Publication Data

Odendaal, Andries.
    A crucial link : local peace committees and national peacebuilding / Andries Odendaal.
        pages cm
    Includes bibliographical references and index.
    ISBN 978-1-60127-170-9 (pbk. : alk. paper)
    1. Peace-building. 2. Nation-building. 3. Peace-building—Social aspects—Case studies. 4. Nation-building—Social aspects—Case studies. I. Title.
    JZ5538.O32 2013
    303.6'6—dc23
                                                2013011722

For Martie.

Dankie, liewe vrou, vir die saamreis van baie jare . . .

Contents

Acknowledgments

This book has grown over a couple of years, progressing through a number of mutations. In 2008, I was commissioned, with colleague Retief Olivier, by the Academy for Educational Development (AED) in Nepal to write a comparative report on local peace committees. Following this report, the Bureau for Crisis Prevention and Recovery (BCPR) of the United Nations Development Programme (UNDP) requested that I expand the study by documenting eight country-specific case studies. It led to the publication in 2010 by UNDP of "An Architecture for Building Peace at the Local Level: A Comparative Study of Local Peace Committees." In 2009–10, I was a Jennings Randolph Senior Fellow at the United States Institute of Peace (USIP), where this book took form. I am grateful to these institutions for making the successive stages of the study possible and, in particular, to USIP. Without their assistance, both financial and editorial, this book would not have been possible.

A number of people have provided much valued support. These include the very able and helpful staff of USIP Jennings Randolph Program, Chantal de Jonge Oudraat, Ginny Bouvier, and Lili Cole, as well as research assistants Devin Finn and Annie Killefer. A particular delight of the fellowship at USIP was the collegiality among the fellows. I benefited a great deal from numerous informal discussions but am particularly grateful to Bill Long, George Lopez, and Marc Sommers, who commented on earlier chapters of the manuscript and provided much-needed advice.

It is an opportune moment to acknowledge and thank my comrade-in-arms, Chris Spies. Since the late 1980s, we have strategized, worked, and reflected together, and shaped each other's thinking and practice. I owe so much of my understanding of peacebuilding to him and am grateful for his feedback on the manuscript. Thank you also to Retief Olivier, who has been instrumental in my exposure to the field. Many others have shaped my understanding of the topic—too many to list. But Clever Nyathi, Ozonnia Ojielo, and the late Dekha Ibrahim Abdi deserve specific mention because of their pioneering work and inspiring example.

I wish to thank the anonymous peer reviewers. Their comments helped me to address specific shortcomings. Thank you also to Jannie Botes, who helped to get the manuscript's introduction right. I am indebted to Valerie Norville and her professional staff at the United States Institute of Peace Press and, in particular, to Kurt Volkan for his expert editorial attention to the manuscript.

Introduction

When Tommy Africa asked for a meeting,[1] I prepared myself for trouble. It was late 1993, and South Africa was in the throes of its uneasy and often violent transition from apartheid (the policy of racial segregation) to democracy. Tommy was the chairperson of the "civics" of George in the Southern Cape region of South Africa. Civics was the name given to residents' associations in black and colored townships that were formed in opposition to the local government structures of the apartheid government.[2] During the 1980s and early 1990s, the civics were in the forefront of the struggle against apartheid. Their tactics ranged from boycotts of all government institutions, consumer boycotts, protest marches, and sit-ins. Many of these events resulted in violence between the police and civic members because it was the police's duty to break up these events—a duty that they were often accused of performing with excessive force. People were seriously wounded and, in extreme cases, killed. Much damage was done to property, especially buildings and vehicles. The release of Nelson Mandela in 1990 and the onset of negotiations did not really change the dynamics of these confrontations. If anything, they became more intense and violent as negotiations at the national level dragged on.

Between 1993 and 1994, I was a regional coordinator of the Western Cape Peace Committee, a body established by virtue of the National Peace

---

1. Not his real name.

2. It is always problematic to use racial categories when discussing South African politics. At the time, though, the official racial categories were "white" for the descendants of European settlers, "black" for indigenous Africans, and "colored" for the descendents of the indigenous Khoi-San and people of mixed race. The fourth official category was "Indian."

Accord of 1991.[3] My responsibilities included establishing and supporting local peace committees. The peace committees' overall task was to prevent violence and promote peace. Whenever the civics were therefore planning a protest march or a boycott action, they had, in terms of the National Peace Accord, to inform me or my colleagues about it. It often meant that we had to spend tense and difficult hours facilitating negotiations to resolve the dispute, monitoring the event, and preventing violence, at times by physically positioning ourselves between the police and the civics.

So when Tommy told me that he wanted to see me, I braced myself inwardly. His request, though, was peculiar: "We want you to organize a meeting between us and the police and to facilitate the meeting. Please make sure that the top commanders of the local police are there." He did not want to say more, which left me in an awkward position. How was I to convince the police to attend a meeting without a known agenda? My gut feeling was that this was serious and important. Fortunately, the police accepted my assessment and agreed to attend.

On the evening of the meeting at our offices, the civics representatives arrived early—which was a surprise. I tried to usher them to where I thought they should sit as a group, but they defied me. They sat down, clearly with deliberate intent, in every second chair, leaving a chair empty in-between. When the police arrived, they had to sit down, rather sheepishly, between the civics members. It was an interesting sight—the police, all white males, in their blue uniforms with the symbols of their rank (colonels, captains, and lieutenants) on their shoulders. Between them sat the civics—men and women, "colored," according to their official racial designation, and dressed in overalls, the uniform of the working class.

I opened the meeting and asked Tommy what he wanted us to discuss. "Reconciliation," he said. "We as the civics, through our engagements with the peace committee, have decided that the time has now arrived for us to make peace with those who were our immediate enemies—the police. This is the reason why we want to sit between the police, not opposite to them."

I don't remember much of the proceedings of that meeting, only that it was rather haphazard and awkward. But at the end of it, they all shook hands with a commitment to work toward a more constructive relationship. After they had left the room, Patrick Davids, my young colleague, himself "colored," with distrust of the police almost bred into his bones, shook his

---

3. The National Peace Accord was signed in September 1991. For a more detailed discussion of the accord, see chapter 2.

head in disbelief. "I never thought in my life that I would experience anything like this."

This small bit of history illustrates a concept that is often used in peacebuilding literature—that of consolidating peace by anchoring it at local levels. By the time this unusual meeting occurred, the political elites had made substantial progress in negotiating an interim constitution for South Africa. Though still decidedly shaky and fragile, peace was in the air. Tommy and his comrades felt that they needed to make their own peace. They dealt with their own internal resistance to the very idea of reconciliation with their enemy and engaged in their own difficult, complex internal processes to reach consensus on the step. They made a very brave decision, implemented it, and thereby offered themselves, the police, and all of us an opportunity to break through barriers previously considered impenetrable. When, many years later, I read Elisabeth Wood's description of *pleasure in agency* as a factor in explaining the behavior of El Salvador's insurgents, I thought of the civics of George. As she explains, pleasure in agency is "the positive affect associated with self-determination, autonomy, self-esteem, efficacy, and pride that come from the successful assertion of intention" (Wood 2003:8). This positive affect was particularly relevant when accompanied by the sense that one was contributing to positive change in your own destiny. Tommy and his colleagues had a lot of that pleasure in agency. They had made their own peace.

However, the event was not completely serendipitous. By his own admission, the catalyst for Tommy's initiative was the presence and work of a local peace committee in town. Without diminishing the quality of their pleasure in agency, the behavior of both the civics and police was made possible, first, by the existence of a National Peace Accord, and, second, by the mechanism (a "peace infrastructure") that had been put in place by the National Peace Accord to facilitate local peacebuilding.

This formula—a national mandate for local peacebuilding plus local mechanisms to facilitate implementation in a manner that values local agency—is intriguing. It is a formula that is finding increasing application. Examples come from across the globe: South America, Europe, Africa, and Asia. In Northern Ireland, for example, the Good Friday Agreement of 1998 identified the transformation of policing as a peacebuilding priority. Consequently, in all the districts of Northern Ireland, District Policing Partnerships have been established to facilitate dialogue between local communities and the police. Their task has been to build consensus on local policing priorities in light of the severe distrust of the police that existed particularly in republican communities. Note the following description of such a meeting in West Belfast:

> There is something of a quiet, largely unseen revolution, taking place inside the republican community and the PSNI [Police Service of Northern Ireland], as each comes to terms with the other in their joint task of creating a new policing service for a society emerging from war and conflict. I got an insight into that quiet revolution last Thursday night at a meeting of the West Belfast District Policing Partnership. The first of its kind in nationalist West Belfast, the meeting brought together the protagonists in the conflict. There was a surreal atmosphere in the room in Beechmount's leisure centre. It was another one of those "pinch yourself moments" that have accompanied the peace process. On one side those with a long history in the IRA [Irish Republican Army] and Sinn Fein and their community. On the other those once with the RUC [Royal Ulster Constabulary]—the armed wing of unionists. . . . There were others representing the SDLP and independents but the fascinating experience was in the occasion itself which brought together those in conflict with each other for decades—representatives of an old enmity and ancient conflict, now firmly on the cusp of change beyond imagination. . . . The meeting was a constructive and critical encounter. The cut and thrust of the exchange reflected clear progress being made in tackling anti-community crime (Gibney 2007).

As is clear from the quote, the progress "in tackling anti-community crime" was surface matter. At the heart of it, progress was made in restoring the confidence of a community in the legitimacy of the state and its institutions that, in the community's experience, only meant it harm in the past.

A last example—for now—comes from a completely different cultural and political context: Sierra Leone. Few countries throughout history have ever experienced the violence of civil war in such devastating manners as Sierra Leone. In 2007 and 2008, Sierra Leone held elections—presidential and parliamentary elections in 2007 and local elections in 2008—their third set of postconflict elections since the end of the ten-year civil war and the 1999 Lomé Peace agreement, but this time with only limited support from the United Nations (UN) and no international peacekeepers around. In spite of great concern in the international community that the elections might be a catalyst for returning to war, these elections were not only relatively peaceful but also witnessed a successful transition of power—a still somewhat rare feat in Africa. Many factors contributed to this situation, but according to observers, the district committees put in place to monitor the code of conduct played an important role (European Union Election Observation Mission 2007; Nyathi 2008; Wyrod 2008; Ohman 2010). The code of conduct was a document negotiated between all political parties and monitored through a national committee consisting of the political parties, statutory bodies, and civil society. The national committee was replicated at district level. These local committees took responsibility for peace in their districts.

It occurred in a context where state institutions were almost completely incapable of providing for law and order at the local level. They mediated in at least forty-six cases of disputes with potential for violence (Ohman 2010). They not only prevented violence, but their fragile networks were also the only expression of social cohesion in an environment fraught with distrust and desperate competition.

These three examples of effective peacebuilding initiatives, created by the combination of a national mandate for local peacebuilding and the mechanisms necessary to implement it, demonstrate how peace can be anchored at the local level. The systems or procedures that were created are referred to, in current literature, as "infrastructures" or "architectures" for peace. The implicit assumption underpinning the establishment of such infrastructures is that local peacebuilding matters. A peace agreement between political elites, by implication, is a necessary but not sufficient condition for building peace. Peace needs to be anchored at the local level.

Why This Book?

The value of infrastructures for local peacebuilding is increasingly acknowledged, as demonstrated by the growing rate at which they are established in different arenas of violent conflict. The first example of this peacebuilding model occurred in Nicaragua in the late 1980s. In this book, I refer to eleven examples, with further reference to seven contexts with noteworthy developments that do not (yet) meet the requirements for being considered formal infrastructures (see appendix). In the meantime, many more countries are considering the option, specifically in Africa. The United Nations, for example, in collaboration with the Global Partnership for the Prevention of Armed Conflict (GPPAC), organized an "experience-sharing seminar" on "building infrastructures for peace" in February 2010 in Kenya that was attended by twelve African countries.[4]

However, as much as the trend in establishing such infrastructures is noteworthy, the absence of scrutiny and comparative assessment is worrying. The UN seminar in Kenya in February 2010 expressed this ambiguity (UNDP 2010). While supporting, in general, the strategy of establishing peace infrastructures, participants called for more research. Why, for example, are infrastructures in some countries more successful than in others?

---

4. Chetan Kumar (2011) mentioned that the United Nations is currently supporting the establishment or functioning of peace infrastructures in thirty countries. He used a broader category of peace infrastructures than used here.

How does one address the difficult practical dilemma of the role of such infrastructure vis-à-vis the state? What is the link between these infrastructures and development? And what is it that these infrastructures do that cannot be done by normal government and civil society institutions?

These and other questions need answers. At the moment, though, the phenomenon is escaping the attention of researchers. This need became clear when, in 2006 and 2007, I was working as a consultant with the Nepal Transition to Peace Initiative and the Ministry of Peace and Reconstruction of Nepal to develop an implementation plan for local peace committees. The ministry was required to implement such committees as an outcome of the peace agreement between the government and the Maoist insurgency. At the time, I was frequently asked whether I could point to some comparative study of local peace structures—a study that had identified best practices. None, however, was available.

My motivation in writing this book is to begin addressing the deficit in attention. It is also primarily pragmatic. With all the energy and resources already spent on infrastructures for peace, and given that this is a growing trend, it is certainly time to step back, assess progress, and identify some of the emerging lessons. I therefore hope to add to the "generic knowledge," which means "the study of past experience that identifies the uses and limitations of each strategy and the conditions on which its effective deployment depends" (George 1993: xvii). While it may still be too early to lay down definitive guidelines for the implementation of infrastructures of peace, it is not helpful to keep on reinventing the wheel. There are some clear lessons that have emerged from experience thus far, and these need to be identified.

Conceptual Building Blocks

Before turning to the main questions and arguments that are the substance of this book, it is necessary to explain in more detail what is meant by the two key concepts that are used: *local peace committees* and *infrastructures for peace*. In addition, I have to state my basic assumptions regarding *peace* and *peacebuilding*.

A Local Peace Committee (LPC) is an inclusive forum operating at the subnational level (district, municipality, town, or village) that provides a platform for the collective local leadership to accept joint responsibility for building peace in that community.

"Local peace committees" is an umbrella term. In practice, a variety of names are used, such as District Peace Advisory Councils, District Multi-

Party Liaison Committees, Village Peace and Development Committees, Committees for Inter-Community Relations, etc. The word *committee* is widely used to describe these bodies, but it is actually a problematic label. Committee conveys the image of a formal, authoritative decision-making body, which, as I shall explain in detail, is precisely what these bodies should not be. The bodies are actually forums, spaces for dialogue and consensus building. Any action that they take flows from consensus and not from wielding any coercive authority. However, the label most commonly used for these bodies is "peace committees," and in order not to cause unnecessary confusion, I shall continue to use this label.

Chapter 2 will describe the contexts wherein LPCs have been used in more detail and will provide concrete examples and a rough typology. But, in short, an LPC typically consists of representatives from all political parties, especially those that have been involved in conflict; representatives of civil society, such as religious institutions or business networks; and relevant local government officials, including the police. It is therefore a forum that typically brings the political sector, government, and civil society together with a joint peacebuilding mandate (see figure 1).

LPCs have various tasks, depending on the context, which fall into two broad categories: establishing a sufficient level of social cohesion or reconciliation to enable collaboration on urgent tasks, and preventing violence. They are therefore not alternative local government structures but forums that build consensus by facilitating dialogue and by mediating in specific disputes.

An *infrastructure for peace* (also at times referred to as a *peace architecture*) is a system for coordinating and supporting a peace process. LPC's are an aspect of a peace infrastructure; the infrastructure, however, is the complete national system that has been established to assist the peacebuilding process. It consciously links the local and national spheres, as well as the formal and informal sectors of society. The infrastructure entails structures and procedures to enable the task of building peace, as well as the capacity to access and leverage relevant networks and resources both within that society and externally.

Chapter 2 also describes infrastructures for peace in more detail with reference to practical examples. What is important is that these infrastructures have all been officially mandated through an inclusive national agreement, such as a peace accord, and often ratified by law. Typically an infrastructure will consist of: (1) a national multistakeholder body that exercises oversight of the infrastructure, facilitates communication with and between peace committees, and provides political support to peace committees; (2) an ad-

Figure 1. Local Peace Committee

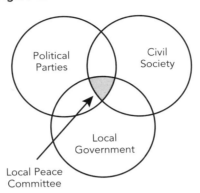

ministrative department that provides logistic and financial support to peace committees (which, in some cases, have been formalized into a dedicated government ministry); and (3) peace committees at various levels: national, provincial, and local. The existence of an infrastructure further facilitates the flow of reliable information between these levels.

The focus of the book is on LPCs as an aspect of a formal infrastructure for peace. There are many examples of LPCs that operate informally and without linkage to each other or to national processes. Here the focus will be on those LPCs that form part of an official infrastructure for peace.

Regarding the assumptions underpinning the use of peace and peacebuilding in this study, the following brief notes are in place. Without engaging the debate in any depth, my understanding of peace is, for the most part, influenced by scholar-practitioners, such as Adam Curle, Johan Galtung, and John Paul Lederach, which puts me squarely in the "sustainable peacebuilding" camp (Paffenholz 2010; see also Kleiboer 1996:378–85). Galtung (1996:9) has described peace as the context for conflicts to unfold nonviolently and creatively. Peace is therefore not the absence of conflict; conflict is necessary for the ongoing transformation of society. Peace, however, is the absence of violence, whether physical or structural. In the ideal world, peace means the collective ability to find constructive solutions to serious problems in a manner that is respectful of the rights and needs of all concerned.

As much as peace is a philosophical and ideological question, it is a complex practical matter. I was in Uganda in 2007 when mediation between the Lord's Resistance Army (LRA) and the government of Uganda was in full process. The indictment by the International Criminal Court (ICC) of the

LRA leader, Joseph Kony, and three other senior LRA leaders was a hotly debated issue, veering between the need to stop impunity and make the entrepreneurs of violent conflict accountable for their deeds and the desperate need for peace in Acholiland, the northern region of Uganda that had been brutalized by the war. Which voice was more important: the one clamoring for justice (put Kony in jail), or the one begging for peace (grant Kony amnesty so that the violence may stop)?

These questions were certainly relevant for the thousands of Acholi that have been living as internally displaced persons in refugee camps for more than twenty years. But for them, peace also evoked other questions: Will we get back the piece of land that we had to evacuate twenty years ago? How will we respond to those who now claim that the land is theirs? How will we survive when we return to our land? How will our children respond to the life of subsistence farming after having lived on handouts in a dense refugee camp all their life? How will women and the youth revert to a life under male patriarchy following their exposure to different roles in the refugee camp? How will we reintegrate the returned child soldiers into our families and communities? How will we deal with our community members who had denounced us to either the army or the LRA? And, ultimately, how will we trust a government that, in our understanding, has been complicit in our suffering and neglect?

Peace, for local communities, invariably means more than the settlement of the major national issues. It does not mean that local communities are disinterested in national issues; rather, it means that local, concrete issues coupled with day-to-day survival and coexistence are more immediate. Peace is therefore inextricably linked to the absence of violence, economic survival, the healing of family and community, the settlement of local disputes, and the reliability of government institutions.[5]

As far as LPCs are concerned, the peace that they can realistically contribute to relates to an end to the violence suffered in the past, a prevention of the occurrence or recurrence of violence, an acknowledgment that local patterns of exclusion and discrimination have to be transformed, a commitment to collaborate in that transformation, and joint action in dealing with the most threatening and urgent problems facing the community.

---

5. In an interview with the author on February 3, 2010, Dr. Shirley DeWolf, veteran pastor and peace activist in Zimbabwe, described, the expectations of local communities in Zimbabwe: "People at local level have lost confidence in political processes as such. They may link up to each other and create local initiatives, but they fear that politics will once again destroy these processes. Peace for them means the possibility to go and hoe their plots without interference."

Put differently: Peace can be built by LPCs if, in a specific context, incidents of violence are reduced or stopped, and if former protagonists collaborate in local initiatives to stabilize, rebuild, and transform their communities. Peace will also be achieved when governance and development can take place free from the debilitation of excessive social or political polarization.

The concept of *peacebuilding* was first used by Johan Galtung (1975) but popularized by the former secretary-general of the United Nations, Boutros Boutros-Ghali (1992). Boutros-Ghali distinguished peacebuilding from preventive diplomacy, peacemaking, and peacekeeping—four activities that had a distinctly chronological sequence in his thinking. Peacebuilding followed peace agreements and the cessation of violence. It has to "consolidate" or "solidify" peace and "advance a sense of confidence and well-being among the people" (1992:32). Peacebuilding has subsequently been understood as having two key objectives that are distinguishable but interdependent. The first is to prevent a relapse into violence, and the second is to foster and support sustainable structures and processes that strengthen the prospects for peaceful coexistence (Boutros-Ghali 1992; Bush 2004:25; Smith 2004; OECD-DAC 2008:8; Paffenholz 2010).

As with all concepts, there are a number of theoretical difficulties with peacebuilding,[6] including its association with "liberal peace" and top-down or externally imposed "state building" (see Richmond 2011). The assumption that underpins the use of peacebuilding in this study is that sustainable peace requires sufficient ownership at the local level. LPCs are important building blocks for peacebuilding because, in theory, they provide a platform at the local level for engagement, dialogue, and a local determination of the need for and nature of peace. Lederach (2005) has emphasized that a peace accord did not represent the end of conflict but rather created a social and political space where negotiations continued. The accord has to usher in a period of constructive social change that "must build responsive processes that address the deep challenges rooted in the relational context" (2005:48). These processes cannot be determined by external ideological constructs such as "liberal democracy" but have to be guided by the concrete needs and aspirations of a society.

The recognition of the long-term need for peacebuilding has informed the establishment of the Peacebuilding Commission by the United Nations. The rationale for the commission, as explained by Secretary-General Ban

---

6. For some of the theoretical considerations, see Paffenholz (2010).

Table 1. Convergence/Divergence between National and Local Aspirations for Peace

	National elites agree to peace	National elites do *not* agree to peace
Local communities agree to peace	(1) National peace accord sufficient	(2) Local peacebuilding disconnected from national strategies
Local communities do *not* agree to peace	(3) Local conflicts destabilize national peace process	(4) Civil war

Note: The author is indebted to Christopher Mitchell, who made these distinctions in a personal communication to the author on June 14, 2010.

Ki-moon (Secretary-General 2009), is that when large-scale violence ends, the challenges facing the leadership and people of the country are enormous. The situation is fluid, and peace is often very fragile. "We have learned that continued fragility and considerable volatility often accompany evolving peace processes. . . . The end of conflict does not necessarily mean the arrival of peace: a lack of political consensus and trust often remains and the root causes of the conflict may persist" (Secretary-General 2009 par.8). Sustaining or consolidating the peace therefore requires as much attention as making peace. These efforts require, in fact, much attention at the local level where peace has to be rooted

The Organization of the Book

The purpose of this section is to provide a rough guide for the following chapters, explain the logic of the book's structure, and provide a brief summary of the main arguments that are being pursued.

There is a significant difference between preagreement and postagreement local peacebuilding. The difference has much to do with whether local communities and national actors agree on the conditions for peace (see table 1). The second window portrays the situation where national actors still pursue military options. In this context, local peacebuilding is left to civil society organizations (CSOs), facing the mistrust, and often active opposition from, armed groups. Local peacebuilding under these circumstances is an extraordinarily difficult and, at times, heroic task. The third window describes the situation that will be the focus of the book, when a national peace agreement is in place but is still resisted by some actors at the local level or ineffectively implemented at the local level.

The objective in chapter 1 is to provide an explanation for the disconnect that often exists between peace at the national and local levels. The assumption that once national actors have agreed to peace it will smoothly descend onto the rural districts is too often not correct. Much as the production of violence requires alliances between national and local actors, the making of peace requires similar alliances. Put differently, preexisting conflicts at the local level acquire enhanced meaning and intensity when plugged into the national conflict and its violence. When the unplugging commences once an agreement has been signed at the national level, the situation at the local level does not automatically return to normal. Local conflict systems are not merely neat replicas of the "master cleavage"—that is, the dominant source of conflict at the national level. While they are indeed expressions of national tensions and structural causes, local conflict systems exhibit their own complexities and ambiguities due to their specific conditions, histories, personalities, and interests. Local conflict systems have sufficiently demonstrated the capacity to disrupt or disturb national peacebuilding processes. Furthermore, where violent conflict has taken place, three conditions often characterize the situation at the local level: (1) the persistence of violence at the local level in the context of weak state control; (2) the deficit in social cohesion, which blocks constructive collaboration in urgent tasks of reconstruction; and (3) the high emotional and personal quality of local conflicts, which complicates efforts to achieve reconciliation and collaboration in polarized communities. These conditions call for an approach that respects the specific and peculiar dynamics of local conflicts and that sees local peacebuilding as an integral and necessary aspect of a national peacebuilding strategy.

An LPC is a specific mechanism to facilitate local peacebuilding that is being used across the world in quite divergent contexts. Chapter 2 makes a basic distinction between informal and formal LPCs. Informal LPCs are usually established by CSOs. They do not enjoy official recognition by the state. Formal LPCs, however, are part of an infrastructure for peace that has been established through some form of national consensus (e.g., a peace agreement or legislation with bipartisan support). The focus of the book is on formal LPCs. The chapter contains two case studies. The first describes a bottom-up process of building a peace infrastructure, referencing the manner in which the Wajir LPC in Kenya stimulated nationwide developments. The second case study focuses on South Africa's infrastructure for peace (1991–94) as an example of a top-down approach, where the peace infrastructure was the result of a national-level peace agreement. The appendix provides an overview and summary description of the formal infrastructures for peace that have informed this study.

How do LPCs actually function? What methods and approaches do they use that are effective? And how important is the infrastructure for the functioning of these committees? These questions are discussed in chapter 3. From the evidence currently available, formal peace infrastructures support LPCs in four ways: (1) by *legitimizing* the pursuit of peace at all levels, including the local level; (2) by allocating *responsibility* for violence prevention and peacebuilding to a specific collection of people, including individuals trusted across a broad spectrum of society; (3) by ensuring that LPCs have access to *specialist support* in facilitating dialogue and violence prevention; and (4) by ensuring that sufficient *linkage* takes place between relevant stakeholders (government, political parties, and civil society) and resources at the different levels.

Furthermore, LPCs have been most effective when they rely on a consensus-seeking approach to respond to tension and conflict. For a variety of reasons, LPCs should not rely on coercive measures to enforce peace. Their primary role is to facilitate and mediate—not to arbitrate or compel.

Peacebuilding is, of course, a deeply political activity. Local peacebuilding depends on and is vulnerable to political conditions at the national level, yet its success depends on a high level of local ownership. The question is how best to safeguard enough independence for LPCs to perform their task. Chapter 4 addresses this issue by analyzing experiences from a number of countries. It discusses the three factors that have had the most direct impact on the political legroom that is available to LPCs. First, there is a real danger of "political capture" whereby one of the political actors seeks to gain control of the infrastructure. A precondition for the effective operation of a peace infrastructure is sufficient political will at the national level to pursue the peacebuilding objectives that have been agreed to in a collaborative manner. The best expression for such shared political will is the existence of a multistakeholder forum at the national level, where political oversight of and bureaucratic support to the infrastructure is exercised jointly.

Second, there has to be clarity on the manner in which the infrastructure for peace fits into the framework of public institutions as well as its role and functions. LPCs have been criticized for hindering the long-term goals of statebuilding by encroaching onto the terrain of statutory bodies, such as the justice system or the local government. From the case studies, three distinct models of the relationship between LPCs and the state have emerged. There are contexts where LPCs clearly performed a transitional role with no intention to inhibit statebuilding. A much more complex situation develops when state institutions are so weak or dysfunctional that LPCs have no choice but to get involved in governance and enforcement matters. It raises valid concerns, yet there are no easy answers. In a number of countries, though, LPCs have been permanently institutionalized with their role well defined through legislation. In all these cases, LPCs have no executive authority but are required to facilitate dialogue, advise, and mediate in community conflicts. This latter arrangement is a strong pointer in the direction of the most acceptable role for LPCs within the larger framework of the state.

Third, in most contexts, LPCs relied on some form of international support. While indispensible, international support may have a negative impact on the quality of local ownership. International actors invariably exert influence on the design and operation of a peace infrastructure through their funding priorities and the substance of their technical support. International actors often contribute largely to the efficiency of a peace infrastructure, but potentially at the cost of damaging local ownership—the most indispensible condition for local peacebuilding. The success of international support is therefore ultimately determined by the manner in which it galvanizes and enhances local ownership.

The next two chapters discuss the impact of LPCs. Experience with LPCs thus far indicates that they contribute to the two main objectives of peacebuilding: promoting peaceful coexistence and preventing violence. Chapter 5 considers the first of these objectives. It analyzes the success of LPCs in promoting social reconstruction; focuses on the ability of LPCs to facilitate dialogue and the impact it has on social cohesion; and discusses LPCs' role in promoting reconciliation, with specific attention to the complex interdependence of justice and reconciliation. Chapter 6 looks at the contribution of LPCs to violence prevention. LPCs do not enforce peace and are therefore limited in their capacity to prevent all forms of violence. However, by relying on their ability to build consensus and mobilize the collective ability of a community in pursuing peace and by mandating and supporting mediation in cases of local conflicts that have violence potential, they contribute to violence prevention. The role of LPCs to prevent elections-related violence receives particular attention.

Chapter 7 contains the conclusions. The overall conclusion is that local peacebuilding has to be an integral part of a national peacebuilding strategy and that infrastructures for peace contribute substantially to the effectiveness of local peacebuilding. However, the nature of my investigation of this matter is preliminary, meaning that a range of questions remain unanswered and require further research.

1

Why Local Peacebuilding?

One of the first and most dramatic lessons that I learned as a budding peacebuilder was never to assume that I have sufficient insight in a local conflict just because I understand national issues.

During the Easter weekend of 1993, Chris Hani was assassinated by white right-wingers. Chris Hani was, next to Nelson Mandela, the most charismatic and popular leader in the liberation movements of South Africa. It was the most dangerous moment in South Africa's transition process. The LPCs, established in terms of the National Peace Accord, were put on alert across the country and requested to do whatever possible to contain the violence that was expected to explode on the day of his funeral. In one specific town of the Southern Cape, I spent a long day facilitating a meeting between the local leaders of the African National Congress (ANC)—the main liberation movement—and the police to forge some agreement on how to contain local eruptions. The essence of the agreement was that the ANC would take responsibility for maintaining order, while the police would keep a low profile. The problem was that the mere sight of the police could trigger violence.

Two days later, I received a very early morning call from the police. The local black township was exploding in anger. Government buildings were being torched, nearby farmhouses were under attack, and general mayhem existed. "The ANC has broken its promise," the police captain informed me. "We have no other option now but to intervene." I hastily went to the scene and made contact with the ANC leaders. We agreed that the ANC leadership should try to get everyone to converge at the local football stadium where they would be addressed and calm would hopefully be restored. All of us got into a minibus to drive to the largest trouble spot in order to urge the people to go to the stadium. On our way, however, we were stopped by a group of very agitated men. There was a heated exchange of words, and then stones started raining on the minibus, shattering windows. Some of the men began to rock the vehicle, presumably to overturn it and put it alight. The driver of the vehicle managed, just in time, to reverse the vehicle and drive us to safety. From there, these men proceeded to loot and burn down the shop of one of the ANC leaders.

It took me a couple of weeks to get to the core of the matter. The local community was deeply divided into two factions. Recent elections for the ANC leadership positions, which had elevated the incumbent leaders into their positions, were controversial and hotly contested. So when the opportunity of violence presented itself as it did on the day when Chris Hani's death was mourned, the group of men seized the opportunity to settle their score with the incumbent leadership. My assumption that all people would be united in their grief for a genuinely popular leader and would heed the calls of the local leadership was patently naive and almost cost me my life.

My naivete was my own fault, of course, because the very reason for negotiating a peace accord was the fact that local conflicts were spinning out of control—in spite of the various attempts by national leaders to contain the situation. Even the iconic Nelson Mandela, leader of the ANC, was not able to convince all of his followers all of the time that they should not resort to violence; neither did President F. W. de Klerk's professed commitment to peace deter sections of his security forces from stoking and committing violence. The areas around Johannesburg and the KwaZulu-Natal province of South Africa were particularly prone to violence because of the conflict between the ANC and the Inkatha Freedom Party (IFP)—a more conservative, ethnic-based party.[7] The political elites were clearly unable to contain the violence. In January 1991, for example, the ANC and IFP concluded a bilateral peace agreement to stop the violence. Thousands of copies of the accord in English and Zulu were distributed, and flyers announced "Leaders Make Peace." On the day after the agreement, six people were hacked to death in KwaZulu-Natal, and another twenty-seven were killed as a result of ANC-IFP strife in the Johannesburg area.[8] At the local level, people were

---

7. Hugo van der Merwe (2007) described the violence in the Duduza and Katorus townships, east of Johannesburg. The master conflict clearly had a major impact: the politicization of relationships between ethnic Zulus and others and the instigation and manipulation of violence by the state apparatus. But he concluded that the communities experienced various dimensions of conflict: between the community and the state, between political parties in the community, within political parties, and among community members who no longer trusted each other because of rumors, suspicions, and generalized fear.

8. Timothy Sisk concluded (1995:123): "As has been demonstrated with respect to other conflict situations, political elites can easily mobilize their constituencies to demonstrate their power in society but they are unable to demobilize them when the moment of peace arrives. This inability to demobilize

clearly not ready for peace. Local dynamics played a role in how these conflicts played out; Bill Berkeley (2001:151) referred to the KwaZulu-Natal situation as a "mosaic of discrete miniwars."

Conversely, but similarly confirming the importance of local agency, the Mpumalanga community in the same province demonstrated that they were able to make peace in the midst of the raging violence. Mpumalanga had been embroiled in intense violence between 1986 and 1990 and was known as "Little Beirut." Over two thousand lives were lost. Because of an entirely locally driven peace process, in 1990 they resolved to end the violence and succeeded in maintaining peace while, all around them, the fires kept burning for at least six more years (ACCORD 2009).

Local dynamics and local agency, therefore, have an impact on the manner in which both violence and peace unfold. Understanding the importance of local dynamics and the nature of the interaction between national and local dynamics has important consequences for peacebuilding.

Peacebuilding in the Interaction between National and Local Dynamics

There is sufficient evidence of local conflict systems that are resistant to national peace agreements. Séverine Autesserre's (2010) study of the violence in the Democratic Republic of the Congo (DRC) provides ample proof of the significant contribution of local conflicts to the ongoing national crisis—in spite of the signing of a peace agreement in 2002 and the inauguration of a democratically elected government in 2006. In chapters to come, I describe in some detail how potentially destabilizing local conflicts in Ghana and Kenya have been defused by processes that respected local dynamics and worked from the bottom up. In Nepal, the political solidarity generated by the struggle to bring the Maoists into peace negotiations and to overthrow royal autocracy was soon threatened by the different perspectives of numerous marginalized communities "who felt their sidelining all the more intensely as peace agreements appeared to sidestep their concerns" (Chalmers 2010). It resulted in violent incidents, such as in Gaur and Kapilvastu in 2007, and the serious destabilization in 2007 and 2008 of the Terai region bordering India that posed a threat to the sustainability of the peace agreement.

---

is especially true of midlevel elites and local party leaders, whose claim to represent grass-roots opinion are strongest (but not necessarily true). . . . In many ways, the National Peace Accord is a pact to acknowledge that very problem."

The city of Jos in Nigeria is another case study of a resilient local conflict system. In spite of the consensus in the ruling party between northern (Muslim) and southern (Christian) elites that power is shared, for example, by regularly rotating the presidency, Christians and Muslims in Jos have been killing each other over the past decade in an increasingly vicious cycle of violence. National attempts to deal with the conflict have been ineffective. Between 2001 and mid-2004, no less than ten official commissions and committees were appointed to investigate and recommend policy. None of these were ever made public or acted upon (Ostien 2009:15). Analysts point to a potent mix of religion, ethnicity (indigenes versus settlers), local history, local politics, and local actors in a context of elite exploitation and unhelpful government responses (Danfulani and Fwatshak 2002; Danfulani 2006; Ostien 2009; Adebajo 2010[9]; ICG 2010a).

In order to discuss the relationship between national and local dynamics and its importance for peacebuilding, a brief detour through the literature may be helpful. As in most matters, a wide spectrum of opinion exists in this respect. On the one end are those that are influenced, in Stathis Kalyvas' words, by an "urban bias." "The urban bias is a serious problem because it distorts data and conceptualizations of civil war dynamics; it tends to privilege written sources, 'top-down perspectives', ideological or normative motivations of participants, and fixed, unchanging identities and choices over oral sources, 'bottom-top' perspectives, nonideological motivations of participants, and fluid identities and choices" (Kalyvas 2006:42). In other words, local dynamics are not valued by those who hold the view that state actors, political elites, and conflict entrepreneurs are the sole determinants of violence and peace. Local communities, in their view, come into focus only as resources for mobilization and information (by political actors), as victims, and as objects of humanitarian aid—not as agents and coproducers of both violence and peace.

At the other end of the spectrum are the proponents of "peacebuilding from below." In its more extreme form, it is offered as an alternative to top-down peacebuilding. Bronwyn Bruton (2009), for example, has argued for a grassroots approach to peacebuilding in Somalia. She is very critical of top-down impositions, especially from the international community, and included top-down impositions of local structures in her critique. As an alternative, she sought support for genuine community-based develop-

---

9. Adekeye Adebajo referred to the estimated twelve thousand people who have died in internal religious and ethnic feuds in Nigeria's recent history. These conflicts over land, religion, resources, and chieftaincy titles mostly had local roots, but "pyromaniac politicians" exploited them for their own ends.

ment and reconciliation efforts, a real grassroots rather than an "astroturf" approach, and pointed to several such initiatives in Somalia that held more promise than current efforts to artificially keep a national government in place. The position that peacebuilding in Somalia should be a bottom-up process (rather than the mediation of an agreement between warlords) was in fact supported as early as 1992 by then special representative of the secretary-general of the United Nations, Mohamed Sahnoun, with the support of the Life and Peace Institute. His position lost out to an approach that wanted to accommodate the warlords (Paffenholz 2003). The process observed in Somaliland (the autonomous region whose independence has not yet been recognized by the international community) started with numerous local peace conferences that built up to the Grand Borama Peace Conference. It brought relative stability to Somaliland (Lederach 1997:53; Paffenholz 2003; Weinstein 2005). It is, to date, the best illustration of a bottom-up peacebuilding process.[10]

The dominant position in mainline peacebuilding literature is that local peacebuilding processes are seen as complementary to top-down work. Oliver Ramsbotham et al. (2005:215–16) have offered a summary of current thinking in this respect. According to them, "a clearer understanding" regarding the role of local peacebuilding has emerged in three areas. First, the barriers to constructive intervention in conflict areas are more formidable than previously assumed. Embedded cultures and economies of violence are not easily transformed by "simple, one-dimensional interventions" (such as the mediation of elite pacts or the deployment of peacekeeping forces). Second, formal agreements need to be underpinned by understandings, structures, and long-term development frameworks that will erode cultures of violence and sustain peace processes on the ground. Third, local actors and the nongovernmental sector are significant, as are the links between national processes and local knowledge and wisdom. Sustainable citizen-based peacebuilding initiatives should be enhanced, and participatory public political spaces opened up (see also Prendergast and Plumb 2002:327; Fisher and Zimina 2009).

This clearer understanding has been influenced largely by the concept of sustainable peacebuilding as developed by Adam Curle, John Paul Lederach, and others (see Ramsbotham, Woodhouse et al. 2005; Paffenholz 2010). According to this view, the structures of parties and relationships may be imbedded in patterns of conflictual relationships that extend beyond the ac-

---

10. As another example Ben Reilly (2008:168–71) mentioned Bougainville, where an extended period of local-level peacebuilding preceded the first postagreement elections in the now autonomous region of Papua New Guinea. In his view, it contributed to a remarkably successful peace process.

tual site of conflict (Miall 2004). Put differently, while an agreement may be reached on specific issues at a given moment, the underlying structures and relationships that initially caused the conflict may remain in place. The conflict should therefore be transformed, meaning that a comprehensive process of transforming relationships, structures, discourses, and interests that support the continuation or reemergence of violent conflict should take place. It is a process that, by its nature, should involve a broad network of people and institutions within society over an extended period of time. It is not a task that can or must be done by outsiders; rather, it refers to the work that people within a conflict system must do to address the underlying causes of their conflict, both structurally and in terms of relationship systems. This task includes the involvement of local communities, and thereby local peacebuilding enters the agenda of peacebuilding.

Lederach (1997: xvi) has probably done more than anyone else to influence thinking in this respect. He had called for a "long-term commitment to establishing an infrastructure across the levels of society, an infrastructure that empowers the resources for reconciliation from within that society and maximizes the contribution from outside." His integrated peacebuilding framework envisaged functional interaction between all levels and sectors of society, including the local level.

The recognition that local peacebuilding can make an important contribution has received substantial, though indirect, support from the current research focus on the role of microdynamics in the production of violence. Kalyvas (2006) has developed a theory in this respect that has major implications for local peacebuilding. His key finding is that the violence of civil war can only be explained by acknowledging that "the loci of agency spawned by civil war are inherently multiple" (2006:365).[11] Local actors are not passive spectators or mere victims of violence; they have agency. Selective violence in particular is produced *jointly* by local and supralocal actors. Selective violence is different from indiscriminate violence in that it relies on denunciations by fellow community members of their neighbors. Selective violence is the violence that either the rebels or government inflict on a population to gain access to information and prevent defections. It is normally controlled and targeted. Because it relies on denunciations, selective violence results from "the *joint action* of local and supralocal actors, insiders and outsiders, civilians and political actors. It is the outcome of an *exchange* between them" (2006:336).

---

11. Kalyvas's main field research was the Greek Civil War (1943–49), but he referred to evidence from sixty-seven civil wars ranging from the Peloponnesian War (431–404 BC) to current civil wars in Afghanistan and Iraq.

Much of the selective violence is a product of malicious denunciations, that is, individuals who exploit the opportunity offered by civil war to settle personal scores or promote personal interests. More important for our topic is the role of local cleavages and conflicts in the production of violence. The general assumption is that mobilization happens in a top-down manner on the basis of an assumed shared ideology or collective interests. Kalyvas, however, proposed that there is another explanation for successful mobilization, that of *alliance*. "Alliance entails an interaction between supralocal and local actors, whereby the former supply the latter with external muscle, thus allowing them to win decisive local advantage; in exchange, supralocal actors recruit and motivate supporters at the local level" (2006:365).[12]

Civil wars, he argued (2006:371), "are imperfect, multilayered, and fluid aggregations of highly complex, partially overlapping, diverse, and localized civil wars with pronounced differences from region to region and valley to valley, reflecting the rupture of authority into 'thousands of fragments and micro-powers of local character' [quoting Ledesma]." Furthermore: "The fusion and interaction between dynamics at the center and the periphery are fundamental rather than incidental to civil war, a matter of essence rather than noise" (2006:365; see also Klopp and Zuern 2007:137).

It is therefore a contentious assumption that local populations give their support to political elites because of a shared enthusiasm for "the cause," whether identity based or ideological. The master cleavage of national conflict does not replicate itself neatly into identical local copies. Instead, through the mechanism of alliance formation, preexisting and contemporary local dynamics help to shape the developing patterns of allegiance and violence.[13] For example, the different sides in a local conflict often take opposing sides in civil war.[14]

---

12. In an article that argued for "autonomous recovery" rather than "aided recovery" in post–civil war contexts, Jeremy Weinstein (2005) described experiences in Uganda, Eritrea, and Somalia. His case studies provide an interesting description of the alliances that the civil war victors had formed with the newly governed at the local level and the nature of their interaction and interdependence.

13. The report of the Truth and Reconciliation Commission of Sierra Leone (2004) contains case studies from seven districts. The case studies clearly demonstrate that when the rebel army, the RUF, entered the districts they found ready collaborators, motivated by specific histories of grievance and unresolved disputes. In each district, a unique configuration of political, economic, and ethnic factors existed, much of it related to chieftaincy issues, personalities, political competition, and patterns and degrees of exclusion. Far from being a national battle imposed on homogeneous and peaceful districts, the conflict continued and exacerbated existing local conflict fault lines.

14. Antjie Krog (2009:8–17) described the violent conflict between the ANC and a notorious local gang in Kroonstad, a town in the Free State province of South Africa. The animosity began when the leader of the gang caught the ANC chairperson in bed with his wife. The gang leader consequently facilitated (with the help of the security police!) the establishment of a branch in Kroonstad of the IFP, a party with whom the ANC was engaged in a low-level civil war in KwaZulu Natal and the Johannesburg area. He then had himself elected as its chairperson.

The recognition of local agency in violence and peace, and the insight that violence is produced through an alliance between multiple actors, both at the national and local level, have a number of implications for our understanding of local peacebuilding. At the most obvious level, the destabilizing potential of local conflicts should be recognized, as well as the contribution of local peace initiatives to greater national stability.[15] "Disruptions from below" increase insecurities, exacerbate differences, challenge capacities for security, and reinforce intolerance (Risley and Sisk 2005). More fundamentally, though, is the implication that peace, as violence, is produced through alliances between local and national actors. It means that peace cannot be produced solely through the imposition of an elite pact, but neither can it be produced through isolated bottom-up processes. "Reducing violence requires as much local action as action at the center" (Kalyvas 2006:391). It actually requires a great deal of *joint* action.

Possibly the strongest application of this line of thinking to our understanding of peacebuilding is the study of Autesserre (2010). The subtitle of her book reads: *Local Violence and the Failure of International Peacebuilding*. International peacebuilding failed in the DRC, she concluded, because the reigning peacebuilding culture precluded attention to local conflicts. The dominant paradigm emphasized top-down interventions at national and regional levels and viewed local conflicts simply as a consequence of weak state authority. The organization of elections, therefore, was the prime peacebuilding and statebuilding mechanism—in spite of overwhelming evidence that the unresolved nature of local conflicts would preclude a functioning multiparty democracy. Autesserre provided a passionate and convincing argument for local peacebuilding as an essential ingredient of a comprehensive peacebuilding strategy.

The burning question is, of course, how effective is the contribution of local peacebuilding to the larger task at hand? Do we have evidence that local peacebuilding projects contribute to national stability and peace? The simple answer is that we do not really know, because no sufficiently rigorous research has been done in this respect. Much of the assessment of the impact of local peacebuilding has been merged with an assessment of the role of civil society in peacebuilding—for the obvious reason that most local peacebuilding work is performed by CSOs. It does not help,

---

15. The International Crisis Group (ICG 2010a) pointed out the threat to peaceful elections in Nigeria in 2011 from the eruption of local conflicts in Northern Nigeria. At the same time, it indicated that existing local-level dialogue and conflict resolution efforts contribute to a complex picture whereby Northern Nigeria is not just a potential cauldron of violence but also a surprisingly peaceful place given the complexity of causal factors.

though, to confuse the importance of local peacebuilding with the efficiency of CSOs.[16]

The work of Mary Anderson's Reflecting on Peace Project (RPP) is perhaps the best barometer we have at the moment (Anderson 2004). Her work relies on in-depth self-reflection processes conducted with civil society peacebuilders across the globe. She has found, inter alia, that the assumption that localized interventions will eventually add up, much like many small streams converging into a mighty river, is false. They do not necessarily add up, unless there is a more concerted effort to align local initiatives with the larger peace objective or "peace writ large." Hers is not an argument against local peacebuilding, rather an argument in favor of a more concerted focus on strategic linkages (see also Chigas and Woodrow 2009). The success of local peacebuilding, in this light, depends on the extent to which individual initiatives are able to link up with a wider peacebuilding process, adding value not necessarily by its size but by its ability to address, in linkage with others, some of the underlying drivers of conflict behavior.

The issue of successful linkage is, to my mind, of critical importance. Infrastructures for peace are relevant and important precisely because of their potential role to provide linkage between local and national levels and between the government sector and civil society. From the examples that we have of formal infrastructures (i.e., infrastructures that enjoy an official status and are recognized by the state), it is clear that their impact can be related to their success in providing strategic linkage between those institutions and individuals that are necessary participants in peacebuilding. Conversely, many local peacebuilding projects have failed to make an impact on transforming underlying drivers of conflict because of their inability to link their efforts with other strategic processes and actors, in particular state institutions and actors.

The verdict on the necessity of local peacebuilding therefore still hinges on one's intellectual paradigm. However, within those circles that accept the premise that local peacebuilding is necessary, awareness is growing of the necessity of strategic linkages. It is an awareness that converges with Kalyvas' finding that alliances between local and supralocal actors determine the patterns and nature of the violence of civil war. If these alliances are necessary to produce violence, they are certainly as necessary to produce peace. In this

---

16. Paffenholz (2010:58–60) bemoans the lack of a research agenda that matches the rapid growth of civil society peacebuilding. Many of the existing studies, however, are critical of CSO peacebuilding initiatives—despite positive achievements. The critique relates largely to their unrepresentative nature, their lack of transparency, their being instruments of a liberal peacebuilding agenda, and the use of strategies that are not sufficiently strategic.

light, local peacebuilding is not an optional appendix; it is a necessary aspect of a national peacebuilding agenda.

Characteristics of the Context of Local Peacebuilding

In the section to follow, I highlight three particular characteristics of local contexts following a peace agreement. The underlying argument is that the nature of the postagreement context at the local level requires that specific attention be given to peacebuilding at that level. The three characteristics are the persistence of violence at the local level in the context of weak state control, the deficit in social cohesion, and the high emotional quality of local conflicts.

Violence in a Context of Weak State Control

After peace agreements have been signed, conditions at the local level are often characterized by ongoing violence. The relative absence of strong control by the state or rebel movements and ongoing political volatility are major causes of this violence.

The reason a peace agreement is signed is because belligerents acknowledge, however grudgingly, that they are unable to win the war. By signing, they implicitly admit the limitations to their ability to exercise sufficient control over the whole population. Of course, this situation does not apply when an outright military victory has been achieved. In all the contexts that I look at in this study and where peace infrastructures have been established, outright victories were not achieved. The postagreement context is a transitional period where an official agreement to stop the violence is in place but central political authority is weak and in flux (Sisk 1995:117–18; Secretary-General 2009).[17] In particular, control over former combatants is weak and policies to reintegrate them into society are often nonexistent (Toft 2006:34–35). It is a context ripe for violence. There is a strong correlation between the lack of control and violence (Kalyvas 2006; Tilly 2003; Mkutu 2008:33–38). When control is weak or contested, actors will resort to violence in order to gain control. Where control is effective, the incidence of violence is low. In postagreement contexts where interim governance measures are in place with

---

17. Concerning the transition period in South Africa, Sisk said: "Although many complex causes were present, the upsurge of political violence was directly related to the much broader issue of the absence of a defined set of political rules during the course of transition. There was, during the uncertain interregnum, a power vacuum. . . . Simon Bekker accurately characterizes this interregnum as plagued by 'widespread confusion over how politics [is] to be conducted.'"

little authority, legitimacy, or capacity, the only bulwark against violence is the muscle of the peace agreement.

In reality, however, peace agreements rarely put an immediate stop to violence. Violence invariably continues after the deal is signed because of its enduring legacies, because of uncertainties inherent in the transition process, and because the opening up of political space creates new opportunities and incentives for violence (Höglund 2008:83–84). At the local level, the inherent political volatility of the transition period and weak central control enable a number of factors to contribute to enduring violence.

First, violence may take place in a local community because it serves the political purpose of external or elite actors. In the Lebanese city of Tripoli on June 17, 2011, seven people were killed during riots following an anti-Syrian demonstration. Local leaders from all persuasions were, however, unanimous in their analysis that the reason for the violence had little to do with intracommunity relations in Tripoli and more to do with sending a national political "message."[18] The newly appointed prime minister, Najib Mikati, who came from Tripoli, was to address a public meeting in the city that week to celebrate his appointment. The message, apparently, was that his appointment was not equally appreciated by all. This message, written in blood, is unfortunately not an isolated one. Across the world political elites instigate violence at the local level to serve their purposes, whether to strengthen their hand during negotiations, undermine their opponents, or support their election strategy (Sisk 1995; Van der Merwe 2001, Klopp 2001, Klopp and Zuern 2007).

Second, violence occurs at the local level because of the intensity of local conflicts. Such violence may occur because of an external trigger, such as the above example, or may be entirely caused by a local trigger. Local communities are never without internal tensions. Local actors invariably pursue contradicting interests. Violence, therefore, may occur at the local level in a postagreement phase primarily because of local conflict dynamics. Some of it may in some ways be a residue of the national conflict. John Darby (2001) has referred to the replacement of political violence by confrontational violence—the face-to-face violence as communities and individuals pursue the unfinished business of civil war at the personal and community level. But it may also be primarily local and only loosely connected to the national conflict. Put differently, local actors are willing to pursue violence, either by forming alliances with external actors or by acting on their own. Such violence may take place for various reasons, such as competition for control of resources (e.g., land or water use), to achieve dominance (e.g., chieftaincy

---

18. I was in Tripoli at the time as a consultant with the United Nations Development Programme (UNDP) and had interviewed civil society leaders from across the political divide.

issues) (Kalyvas 2006:364–76; Autesserre 2010; Mkutu 2008), because of the deep emotional trauma associated with their conflict histories (Stover and Weinstein 2004; Autesserre 2012), or because of the absence of credible conflict management institutions, whether political or cultural, that heightens the attractiveness of violence (Walter 2004).

Third, violence may have an opportunistic character. An International Crisis Group report (2010b) on Nepal refers to perceptions of threatening anarchy and a collapse of political order in the postagreement phase because of an increase in the use of violence for political and criminal purposes. The report concluded that the violence was not a threat to the integrity of the state but rather an expression of opportunism in a context of low-risk conditions. "Opportunism is the name of the game, and groups are making the most of the weak law and order situation during the transition." Tilly (2003:34–41) referred to "violence specialists"—people who pursue predatory violence for commercial purposes and who may or may not form discreet alliances with politicians. In the pastoralist areas of Kenya and Uganda, for example, such violence specialists have perverted the traditional culture of cattle rustling for commercial purposes (Mkutu 2008:32), thus complicating an already complex conflict situation. Opportunistic violence, therefore, serves the narrow interests of violence specialists who exploit the absence of effective governance for their own sectional benefit.

Fourth, postagreement contexts are often characterized by a high level of social restlessness that manifests in an extraordinary number of public protest events. The use of Tahrir Square in post-Mubarak Egypt is an example. In Nepal, public boycotts and protests across the country became almost endemic in the postagreement phase, and the same was true in South Africa. These public events—protest marches, rallies, political meetings, and even funerals—are all potentially violent not because of any deliberate plan to use violence but because tempers flare. Violence is therefore sporadic (Klopp and Zuern 2007). Charles Tilly (2003:15) used the concept "brawls" to describe this type of violence. It may be restricted to two or three people in a bar; but more significantly it may take place during a public event with very destructive consequences for communal relationships.

These types of violence all take place in a context of weak state control. At the local level, the weakness of state control is often acute. State institutions, such as local government, the police, and the judiciary, are dysfunctional for a number of reasons: the aftereffects of violence that destroyed physical infrastructure and human resources, the lack of political legitimacy (such as when these institutions have been misused by the previous regime for its own purposes), or the lack of resources and capacity because of poverty.

The challenge to local peacebuilding, therefore, is to find ways to prevent violence given the weakness of state institutions. Kalyvas (2006:391) has suggested that the best way to achieve local peace in the short and medium term was "tinkering with local control" rather than "investing in mass attitudinal shift." The ability to tinker with local control, however, is precisely the problem. Unless use is made of international peacekeepers, it is not clear who should do the tinkering because local state actors lack the capacity and/or the legitimacy to do so. A more constructive approach would be to seek the resolution of local conflict through credible, inclusive processes. This approach will indeed not be equally effective in dealing with all forms of violence. Local communities will remain particularly vulnerable to external manipulation and violence specialists. However, by strengthening the capacity of a local community to deal constructively with their own conflict, their resistance to those bent on the use of violence is similarly strengthened. It is this approach that informs the strategy to establish LPCs.

The Deficit in Social Cohesion

The argument for local peacebuilding further relates to the deeply disruptive and transformative impact of violence. Preexisting local conflicts are magnified when they get plugged into the master cleavage. The use of violence deepens existing polarization immensely. But war and violence also create new ruptures as new alliances are forged and new traumas created. The outbreak of violence and war at times takes people by surprise. The polarization is abrupt and unexpected, and the violence totally baffling. Civil war, therefore, also produces its own deep social cleavages.[19]

The point, however, is that violent conflict, regardless of whether it is rooted in prewar cleavages or is war-induced, disrupts, often irreversibly, the social fabric of a local community (Stover and Weinstein 2004; Steenkamp 2005[20]; Branch 2008). It is difficult, if not impossible, to return to prewar social and cultural mechanisms for conflict management because of fundamental shifts in social values and relationships that have occurred. In South Africa, for example, not only was the racial social hierarchy irreversibly challenged but the role of the black youth in leading local insurrections fundamentally transformed cultural assumptions concerning respect for elders

---

19. "Acknowledging that both violence and polarization can be endogenous to war implies a strong qualification of the view that violence arises exclusively from prewar cleavages" (Kalyvas 2006:83).

20. Chrissie Steenkamp discussed the phenomenon of high levels of crime and personal violence in postagreement contexts and concluded that war has such a large impact on society's norms and values that a greater social tolerance of individuals' violent behavior developed. A "culture of violence" becomes embedded in society, replacing previous peaceful norms and values.

and associating age with leadership and wisdom. In Nepal, the Maoist in-surgency directly challenged ancient assumptions regarding the role of caste in the management of society. In all these societies, the postagreement phase requires new roles and procedures of decision making. In FYR Macedonia and Serbia, certain sensitive municipal decisions are now, by law, subject to the criterion of ethnic consensus.

In an interesting study of the internally displaced community of Gulu, the main town of Acholiland in Northern Uganda, Adam Branch (2008) described the manner in which the war between the government and the LRA disrupted traditional lifestyles and perceptions. For the displaced rural dwellers, life in Gulu meant a dramatic introduction to the all-important need to earn money (as opposed to subsistence farming), creating both hard-ships and opportunities. It meant, in particular, new freedoms for women and the youth from the harsh rule of men under the patriarchal system. The prospect of a return to village life evoked ambivalent emotions and expecta-tions. The men looked forward to reasserting traditional authority by undo-ing the newfound power of women and the youth. At least some women were determined not to give up what had been gained. If a strategy to fa-cilitate the social reconstruction of postwar village life were to depend on "traditional reconciliation," it would be problematic in three respects. First, it was questionable whether the elders and chiefs still commanded suffi-cient authority for this role. Second, tensions between male lineage-based authorities and armed youth have been one of the main causes of war in Northern Uganda over the past two decades. A new assertion of that author-ity was unlikely to be successful. Third, there was a real possibility that such traditional authority might create new exclusions: that of foreign women, independent or assertive women, people with uncertain ancestry, and ex-LRA combatants. Such exclusion effectively meant blocking access to land; a matter with serious social and economic implications. A return to prewar cultural patterns therefore seems unlikely. Life will not be the same as before the war. Paradigms have shifted.

The dysfunction in social systems is a characteristic of peacebuilding phases. The presence of violence points to the inadequacy of existing mech-anisms to prevent or contain the violence. The "old way of doing things" may, in fact, be part of the reason for the violence. Legal, social, and cultural mechanisms used in the past to manage conflict may become illegitimate or fall into disrepair. Formerly excluded groups now demand inclusion; formerly oppressive mechanisms, whether political or cultural, have to be transformed. Opposing factions that share a joint history of bloodshed and trauma now have to collaborate. In a vacuum created by flux and with relative weakness at the center, local communities have to find ways to manage their affairs at a time when both traditional and constitutional mechanisms may suffer from a lack of legitimacy.

The challenge to local peacebuilding, therefore, is to find an appropriate mechanism or social space to facilitate a sufficient level of social cohesion and agreement that would enable the necessary transitions and transformations to take place.

The Emotional Content of Local Conflict

Local conflicts have a particularly emotional quality. Kalyvas (2006:330–63) talks about the "intimacy" of civil war violence—the "privatization of politics" rather than the politicization of private life. Malicious denunciations are mostly driven by private feelings of jealousy and revenge. The fact that neighbors turn against neighbors and that families are torn apart by violence reflect the "dark face of social capital"—the shocking underbelly of what is often romantically viewed as the positive, close-knit quality of village life. The causes of local conflict cycles are at times lost in the mist of history and driven more by the forces of social comparison and competition for dominance in conditions of dense social interdependence. The violence of civil war can only add exponentially to the strong undercurrents of hatred, fear, resentment, and distrust. Conflict cycles with such deep emotional content are not easily amenable to resolution through the imposition of peace conditions that have been negotiated by political elites.

This does not mean that national level conflicts are devoid of emotional content or that local conflicts do not develop on substantive material issues. The difference is in degree. National elites are often relatively unaffected by the violence personally. At the local level, violence is experienced personally—often linked to or executed by people intimately known to each other.

Following the historic elections of 1994 in South Africa, I was involved, along with my colleague Chris Spies, in a three-year project for the Centre for Conflict Resolution in Cape Town to continue some of the local peacebuilding work done under the now-defunct peace committees and to experiment with various training and empowerment models (see Odendaal and Spies 1998; CCR 1998; Dressel and Neumann 2001). One of the key findings of the project related to the high emotional content of local conflicts. Our assumption was that local peacebuilding should be facilitated by inclusive teams of local actors, and we consequently paid careful attention to the selection of team members and their training needs. We were, however, consistently struck by the manner in which the violence of the past, both in its physical and structural forms, had damaged not only social relation-ships but also individuals' emotional capacity to exercise empathy. In terms of the mediation model that we have used, empathy was a necessary quality in mediators. Empathy referred to the capacity to understand the behavior of others in terms of their own motivations and not in judgmental ways. The mediation model therefore required that mediators be able to demonstrate empathy toward the parties they were working with. The project found that team members were indeed able to play various constructive roles in dealing with conflicts, but the ability to achieve the deeper level of empathy required for mediation was a much more complex and difficult task than we assumed. It required that members develop empathy with the issues and needs of identity groups other than their own, an objective that many found extraor-dinarily difficult to achieve. In addition, in many of the local disputes that we became involved in, the direction of negotiations were not determined so much by the substantive points on the agenda but rather the underlying stream of anger, resentment, distrust—and shame.

Consider, for example, the challenge faced by local communities in the eastern DRC. In terms of the Tripartite Agreement between the govern-ments of the DRC and Rwanda and the UN Refugee Agency (UNHCR), signed in February 2010, fifty thousand Congolese refugees will return from refugee camps in Rwanda to the DRC. Their reintegration into society will be facilitated in part by LPCs called Comités locaux permanents de concili-ation (CLPC) (UNHCR 2009; Hege 2010; Olson and Hege 2010). These committees will also be used in more general terms to promote reconcilia-tion and support the mediation of highly complicated issues of land owner-ship. LPCs are very appropriate in a context such as the eastern DRC, but there should be no underestimation of the challenges they face. One of the challenges is political—given that the tripartite agreement has, in the view of some observers, not sufficiently dealt with some of the main issues (Olson and Hege 2010). However, the biggest challenge may be managing the emo-tional content of local disputes. Just to mention one aspect, the use of rape as an instrument of war has reached unprecedented proportions in the DRC. John Holmes, UN under-secretary-general for humanitarian affairs, called the sexual violence taking place in the eastern DRC the worst in the world: "The sheer numbers, the wholesale brutality, the culture of impunity—its ap-palling" (Gettleman October 7, 2007). The thought of local people, many of whom have been affected either as victims or perpetrators of rape, meeting in a forum to facilitate reconciliation is sobering.

The task of reconciliation at the local level in the face of deep fissures in local communities and extraordinary levels of trauma is therefore a daunting one. Furthermore, reconciliation is not a once-off event. It requires a sustained effort. Norbert Ropers (2008) has drawn attention to the fact that it is the *system* of relationships that needs to be transformed. The advantage of understanding relationships as systems—as opposed to understanding them as expressions of political convenience—is that the full complexity of human relations comes into focus. Relationships are not determined by once-off, single-plane, linear factors, such as the moment an agreement is signed. Relationships are rather sustained or destroyed by complex patterns of interconnected factors. In the language of system theory, feedback loops exist—that is, the capacity of the various interconnected factors to continue to reinforce or counteract good relationships despite the fact that at a given moment a specific decision has been made.

The transformation of relationships is therefore complex and a process that develops over time. Its success depends on whether the factors that push toward peace eventually outweigh the pull back into violence. In the context of traumatized communities, the question therefore is what structure would best serve the sustained effort required to transform the system of relationships.

The nature of local communities, given their high levels of social interdependence and the manner in which violence is experienced at the local level, produces, therefore, a peacebuilding context where sensitivity for the highly personal and emotional quality of conflict is necessary. Peacebuilding processes that are imposed from the top are usually highly insensitive to such local sentiments. Peacebuilding at the local level requires a process that will acknowledge the raw impact of emotions and that will be sufficiently adept at managing these emotions in constructive manners. It has, in the final analysis, to be a patient and sustained process because the objective has to be the transformation of relationship systems and not once-off reconciliation events.

The Imperative to Respect Local Dynamics

Local dynamics contribute to the production of violence and peace. Put differently, local conflict systems are an integral part of the equation that produces civil war. Their peaceful transformation contributes to peace at the national level. The relationship between national and local peacemaking dynamics is complex, and never in a simple one-way or top-down direction—in spite of the obvious power asymmetries. Local peacebuilding, therefore, matters and should receive significant attention.

Given the importance of linkages and alliances between the national and local levels, local peacebuilding should be a conscious interaction between these levels, where local actors have access to information, political clout, and technical support at the national level, and where national actors have access to local information, as well as to local constituencies in order to leverage local collaboration—this time in pursuit of national peace objectives.

In light of the particular challenges associated with local peacebuilding—the persistence of violence in a context of weak state control, the deficit in social cohesion, and the high emotional quality of local conflicts—the methods and approaches of local peacebuilding deserve particular attention. This matter will be discussed in detail in the chapters to come, but the fundamental principle that stands out from the discussion above is that the dynamics of local conflicts should be respected on their own terms. This statement cannot be overemphasized: Local conflict systems are not smaller clones of the master cleavage at the national level, even though they are never disconnected from the overarching social, political, economic, and structural dynamics that created the conflict in the first place. The practical implication for local peacebuilding is that it should deal with the national from the local perspective and not vice versa. Local histories, actors, issues, and systemic relationships must receive primary attention. The local circumstances should not be interpreted solely in terms of national discourses. Rather, the impact of the national discourse should be understood as it has been interpreted and applied by local actors. Local peacebuilding, therefore, means a primary engagement with the dynamics at the local level in order to ultimately build peace nationally.

2

Infrastructures for Peace
Illustrations and Distinctions

In a village called Kibimba in Burundi, during a particularly vicious attack by rebels in 1993, seventy secondary school children were burned alive at a petrol service station. As a consequence, the community divided along ethnic lines into two deeply polarized camps. In 1994, an LPC was formed, following some initial training by the Mennonite Central Committee. The LPC began facilitating communication between the different groups and eventually succeeded in returning some degree of normalcy to the heavily traumatized community. The reopening of the school and hospital—and the fact that both communities were using these facilities again—were important indicators of success. The LPC continued for the next seven years to mitigate some of the harshness of life under conditions of civil war and near state collapse and to restore some dignity and agency to the community (Ningbabira n.d.; see also The Advocacy Project 2009; Butt 2004).

The Kibimba LPC was an informal LPC. The distinction between informal and formal LPCs is important. Formal LPCs operate in the context of a national peacebuilding mandate that includes the consent of the state and the main political protagonists, whereas informal LPCs lack such a mandate. In this book, I focus on formal LPCs, but it is necessary to pay brief attention to informal LPCs.

Informal Local Peace Committees

There are many examples of informal LPCs from across the world (Van Tongeren, Brenk et al. 2005:50; Hancock and Mitchell 2007; Odendaal and Olivier 2008). They are normally the creations of CSOs. Often their operation is tied to the efficiency and financial lifespan of the CSO that is responsible for their establishment.

Informal LPCs have the capacity to fill some of the vacuum created by state weakness or collapse, as demonstrated in Kibimba. Relying on its capacity to restore relationships and mediate conflicts, the committees provide useful interim services that state institutions cannot or will not deliver. These efforts are valuable and should be judged for what they intend to deliver—the mitigation of some of the immediate social distress. In many of the almost anarchic contexts where LPCs are established, direct linkage with national actors is perhaps not that relevant. More important is their ability to engage with local-level armed actors—the local guerilla leaders or army officers (see Hancock and Iyer 2007:46).[21]

Examples of relative success come from all parts of the world, such as Nigeria (Otite and Albert 1999), the Democratic Republic of the Congo (Clarke 2008), Croatia (Bloch 2005), El Salvador (Hancock 2007), Nepal (UNDP 2004; Danida/HUGOU 2005), and Northern Uganda (USAID 2009). Informal LPCs, however, are most effective when they succeed in engaging government at the local and national level and mediate greater state responsiveness to conflicts of local communities. In the absence of state involvement, LPCs are unable to transform deep-rooted local conflicts because they lack implementing power. In Nigeria, for example, where CSOs have been active in establishing LPCs, a sustainable peace was in fact established when the government followed up on LPC recommendations (see Akinteye, Wuye et al. 1999). But the opposite is more the norm: Government's failure to implement and the LPCs' lack of clout to leverage implementation meant that little progress was made (Otite and Albert 1999; see also ICG 2010a).[22] When a disconnection develops between the track followed by the state and that of the LPCs, the impact of LPCs is likely to be confined to the mediation of conflicts without high political relevance (see Collaborative Learning Projects 2006:v).

LPCs in the Context of Infrastructures for Peace

In contrast to informal LPCs, formal LPCs enjoy state recognition and are normally part of a bigger process to achieve specific peace objectives. In these cases, peace infrastructures have been established, meaning that systems and procedures have been put in place to support the LPCs administratively, financially, and technically, as well as to provide political linkage and oversight.

---

21. Hancock and Iyer have based this observation on their study of the so-called Zones of Peace in the Philippines and Colombia.

22. This was confirmed in an interview with the executive director of Academic Associates Peace-Works, Judith Asuni, March 9, 2010, Washington, DC.

I have used two criteria to identify the formal peace infrastructures that are discussed in this book. First, there has to be an inclusive national decision or agreement on the establishment of a peace infrastructure. It may take the form of a peace agreement or a decision by a national institution (for example, a parliament or statutory body, such as an election commission) that enjoys the support of all the main political actors. Second, the infrastructure has to make provision for the establishment of structures at the local level to achieve the peace objectives agreed to at the national level.

In what follows, I discuss two examples of infrastructures for peace, in Kenya and South Africa. The main distinction between these two examples is the manner in which they have come to life. In Kenya, the still emerging infrastructure is a truly bottom-up process that started with a discussion by a group of women at a marketplace. In South Africa, the process was top-down. The infrastructure was designed at the national level when the National Peace Accord was negotiated and then taken down to the local level.

Kenya: The Wajir Peace and Development Committee

During the early 1990s, a highly destructive cycle of violent conflict raged in the district of Wajir between different clans of Kenyan Somalis in Kenya's northeast region, resulting in 1,213 deaths over a period of four years. The violent conflict had its roots in the centuries old custom of livestock raiding by pastoralist groups. However, in the context of a growing population, an influx of refugees from neighboring Somalia and Ethiopia, increasing aridity, the ready availability of small arms, the very weak presence of government in the district (resulting in the failure of state institutions to regulate conflict, provide security, and promote development), and heated electoral politics, the conflict became excessively violent and destructive (Ibrahim and Jenner 1998, Menkhaus 2008).

In 1993, a group of women met at the marketplace and started a discussion on ways to stop the violence. It blossomed into a process of peacemaking that is impressive by all accounts. The process basically entailed the formation of a group of civil society actors working together to sensitize the population to the need for peace. They engaged the elders of the different clans and set up a mediation process. After several meetings, the elders agreed to sign a code of conduct called the Al Fatah Declaration, which effectively stopped the violence. In this process, the civil society actors had worked with and involved representatives of formal authority, particularly the district commissioner and a member of parliament, but on a voluntary basis.

The initiative was therefore completely homegrown and locally owned. Two subsequent developments are noteworthy. First, it was soon realized that the LPC would need some form of formalization for two reasons: (1) to provide coordination to all the peacemaking and peacebuilding activities in the district; and (2) to ensure sustainability in the participation of figures with formal authority (Ibrahim and Jenner 1998:19). The manner of formalization was a problem, but eventually it was decided to integrate the peace initiatives into one structure within the district administration in Kenya that brought government, CSOs, and citizen groups together, namely the District Development Committee. In May 1995, the Wajir Peace and Development Committee was formed, with the district commissioner as chairperson. Members included the heads of all government departments, representatives of the various peace groups, religious leaders, CSO representatives, traditional chiefs, and security officers.

Second, the success of the Wajir Peace and Development Committee in bringing peace to the district and in maintaining that peace acted as a model to other districts in the northeastern part of the country. International donors, CSOs, and the National Council of Churches of Kenya became involved in facilitating and supporting the establishment of local peace committees. However, the process was uncoordinated and haphazard, leading in some cases to the establishment of several peace committees in one district (Adan and Pkalya 2006). National government soon took notice of the LPCs. In 2001, it established the National Steering Committee on Peace Building and Conflict Management with the objective to formulate a national policy on conflict management and provide coordination to various peacebuilding initiatives, including the LPCs. In the same year, it used the facilitation of LPCs in five districts to negotiate the Modogashe Declaration with the various pastoralist clans. The declaration essentially laid down ground rules for dealing with ongoing conflict associated with cattle rustling. The declaration was revisited in May 2005, amended, and renamed the Garissa Declaration. This declaration enjoys the formal recognition of the government (Chopra 2008a).

The Wajir Peace and Development Committee "was unquestionably instrumental in the remarkable turnaround of Wajir district from one of the most anarchic to one of the more stable border zones of Kenya" (Menkhaus 2008:27). Its success depended on its ability to engage both the traditional leadership and government and facilitate greater government responsiveness to the needs of the population. A result of its success was the formalization of its role. The process was taken a step further when, in the aftermath of the postelection violence that wracked Kenya in late 2007 and early 2008, the National Accord and Reconciliation Act of 2008 recommended the establishment of District Peace Committees in all of Kenya's districts, with priority given to the Rift Valley where most of the violence, had taken place. During this outburst of violence, the northeastern region was quiet and stable—to the surprise of many Kenyans (Wachira 2010). The infrastructure for peace formalized by the National Accord and Reconciliation Act therefore acknowledged the impact that local peacebuilding had thus far in Kenya and sought to build on it.

At the time of writing, this process is not yet complete. The formation of a National Peace Council has been agreed to in principle, but legislation is still pending.

South Africa, 1991–94

South Africa was, by the end of the 1980s, a very violent society. The bankruptcy of the ideology and policies of the ruling National Party was, by that time, clear not only to the opponents of apartheid but also to an important section of the ruling party. The apartheid policy sought to achieve the complete geographical, social, and political segregation of the various racial and ethnic groups in the country. In reality, it was an attempt to avoid black majority rule over the white minority, while keeping control of the main economic resources of the country in white hands. The uprising of black students on June 16, 1976, in Soweto (which at the time led to more than five hundred deaths) became a catalyst for a movement of civil disobedience and "ungovernability" that had built up a seemingly unstoppable momentum toward the end of the 1980s. Most of the governance structures in the urban black areas had collapsed by then, and most of the universities and schools in the black areas were spaces of intense resistance to government rule, while the production of factories and mines was increasingly disrupted by the politicization of black trade unions and negatively affected by international economic sanctions.

In short, at the start of the decade in 1990, the government of South Africa had not only lost its legitimacy to govern in the eyes of the vast majority of citizens but also much of its capacity. The consequence was a spiral of violence perpetrated by security forces on activists; by the armed wings of the liberation movements on security and, in some isolated cases, civilian targets; by communities on government institutions; and by community activists on those that they had perceived to be sellouts or traitors.

When President de Klerk, on February 2, 1990, announced to Parliament that all the liberation movements would be unbanned and that the government would engage them in negotiations for a "New South Africa," there was a general expectation that the internal violence would subside. That did not happen. Between 1985 and 1990, more than 6,000 people died because of political violence (a little more than 1,000 deaths per year, which is the commonly used yardstick to determine when a country is in civil war). During the period between September 1990 to August 1991, more than double that figure (2,649) died. This trend continued, with 3,404 deaths in 1992–93, and 3,567 deaths in 1993–94 (Gastrow 1995).

The escalation of violence post-1990 was baffling to most observers. In an illuminating essay, André du Toit (1993) attempted an explanation. He pointed to the commitment to the idea of a modernizing state that the black elite shared with white society. The master narrative of the black resistance movement since the beginning of the twentieth century had been to end the exclusion of blacks from the modern state—not its abolition and a return to precolonial arrangements. This shared commitment made the dramatic breakthrough to the politics of negotiation possible. The escalations of violence at the local level, however, were "anomalous developments for which the master narrative hardly allowed" (1993:28). He pointed to two possible explanations. First, the master narrative of the resistance movement did not necessarily "fully inform all the critical confrontations or many local struggles that developed on the ground." These local struggles often generated their own "historical self-understandings" and dynamics and created their own micronarratives and concrete symbolisms (1993:29). Second, the violence reflected the sense of exclusion of marginalized groups who anticipated that the modern state would not—for them—fulfill its promises.

It did not mean that all violence in South Africa was driven by local factors. Clearly national political developments had a major impact. Timothy Sisk (1995) has graphically demonstrated how incidents of violence in South Africa followed the ebb and flow of the negotiation process. At every point where the process was in crisis or when critical decisions had to be made, violence spiked. On occasion, protest action (which was always potentially violent) was sparked by national events, such as in April 1993 when Chris Hani was assassinated or when, following the Boipatong massacre in June 1992,[23] the ANC suspended negotiations and called for "rolling mass action." The bulk of activities that led to violent confrontations, though, was triggered by local dynamics: the decisions or behavior of local municipalities or businesses, local issues that acquired political significance, local personality clashes, local competition for economic advantage (such as between taxi associations or in cattle raids), and local intraparty struggles for power.

---

23. Forty-six residents of the Boipatong township were massacred allegedly through collaboration between IFP cadres and security forces

The national leadership clearly struggled to assert its authority over these, at times, baffling expressions of discontent.[24] No one, however, suggested that a complete disconnection existed between the local and national levels. Disparate as they were, the local conflicts were essentially political. They expressed local discontent with an overarching political and economic condition that was unacceptable—albeit in manners that were not necessarily sanctioned by the elite.

The deepening spiral of violence was of course worrying in itself, as was its increasingly brutal nature. But what created the deepest concern was the perception that the violence was having a negative impact on the prospects of a negotiated settlement. President de Klerk was the first to try and organize a peace conference to deal with the problem of violence, but it was rejected by the ANC, which then proceeded to organize its own peace conference. The political opponents were clearly not ready to cede initiative in this important matter to the other.

Civil society saved the day, in particular the churches and organized business. They brought the leadership of political parties together and—through the facilitation of Archbishop Desmond Tutu and John Hall, representing the churches and organized business respectively—a National Peace Accord (NPA) was negotiated (Gastrow 1995). It was signed at a public ceremony on September 14, 1991, by most political parties who had representation in the national Parliament or the Parliaments of the so-called homelands (quasi-independent ethnic states). It was also signed by the ANC as the main liberation movement and by government on behalf of the security forces. Though some smaller political actors on the left and right of the political spectrum refused to sign, all major players committed themselves to the NPA.

The National Peace Accord. The NPA (see Gastrow 1995 for full text) was not a political agreement. It did not contain a political settlement. Political negotiations were continuing in a stop-start manner in a parallel process. It was essentially a code of conduct that bound the government and its security forces, the political parties, and the liberation movements to a set of mutually agreed upon ground rules. Its specific objective was to contain the spiral of violence by regulating the behavior of all main actors while negotiating a political settlement.

---

24. A spokesperson of Zweli Mkhize, the current premier of the province of KwaZulu-Natal, recently offered the following explanation of the violence in that province: "This infighting started as minor feuds amongst factions within different clans, and resulted in political violence which was then fuelled by the apartheid machinery" (News24 2010).

The NPA included codes of conduct for political actors and the security forces, particularly the police. The NPA furthermore created a commission of inquiry into the prevention of public violence and intimidation (the so-called Goldstone Commission, named after Judge Richard Goldstone who was its chairperson). Important for our purposes are chapters 7 through 9 of the NPA. These chapters provided for the peace infrastructure: a national peace committee consisting of all signatories; regional peace committees (RPC) in eleven regions of the country; local peace committees in all affected areas; and, very important, a National Peace Secretariat under multiparty control to establish, coordinate, and administer the regional and local peace committees. It also stipulated monitoring and enforcement procedures such as "justices of the peace"—individuals empowered with legal authority to enforce compliance to the NPA—and an agreement on the use of arbitration in case of a dispute between signatories regarding a transgression of the NPA.

It has to be said at the outset that the national peace committee was largely ineffectual. It met only twice and was not a factor in the continued unfolding of the peace process. Also, no "justice of the peace" was ever appointed (more on this later on), and arbitration was never used to deal with any of the many transgressions of the accord. The impact of the NPA was confined to the work of the Goldstone Commission and the regional and local peace committees under coordination of the National Peace Secretariat.

The Peace Infrastructure. The National Peace Secretariat divided the country into eleven regions and facilitated the establishment of RPCs in these regions. Not all regions experienced the same levels of violence, though. The focus was on the most troubled regions, namely the Pretoria-Witwatersrand-Vereeniging (PWV) area (roughly correlating with the current Gauteng Province), KwaZulu-Natal, the Eastern Cape, and the Western Cape. The RPCs consisted of regional representatives of all signatories with a presence in that region, as well as other relevant civil society formations operating at the regional level, such as religious organizations, trade unions, business and industry, traditional authorities, etc. The police and military also had to be represented, as well as relevant government ministries, such as those tasked with the administration of black townships.

The RPCs coordinated the establishment of LPCs in towns and villages in the region, particularly those towns that had experienced violence. The composition of LPCs followed that of the regional committees, but it is important to emphasize that the focus was on inclusivity (Odendaal and Spies 1996; Collin Marks 2000). CSOs that wanted to be on the LPC had been welcomed.

However, it was soon realized, once the RPCs were established, that the task of establishing LPCs would not be a simple one. In some communities, the resistance to peace was strong (Odendaal and Spies 1996; Carmichael 2010). It was not going to be possible to impose LPCs on communities. In this light, RPCs, with the support of the National Peace Secretariat, made the decision to employ a full-time staff to facilitate the establishment of LPCs and provide them with ongoing support (Gastrow 1995; Collin Marks 2000).

As a consequence, the establishment of each LPC was a facilitated process, a mini peacemaking exercise aimed at securing the consent and active support of all local actors. The NPA guaranteed the legitimacy of such processes, whereas the full-time staff provided the facilitation services. It is noteworthy that in a number of locations local communities had refused to form an LPC. The refusal was respected by RPCs; and rather than coercing the community to form an LPC (which would have been meaningless), efforts were strengthened to facilitate mini peace processes within those communities. The refusal to form an LPC was seen as an indicator that much more preparatory work was needed within that community and that the local drivers of conflict had to be addressed. Most of the "pre-LPC" work was done by full-time staff.

Modus Operandi of LPCs. The LPCs were inclusive bodies, composed of community representatives that were still deeply divided amongst themselves. In fact, LPC members not only represented different sides of the forty-year struggle against apartheid but also a 350-year history of colonialism and displacement. The "peace" between members of the LPC was, at the best of times, fragile and extremely tentative.

The first critically important task of an LPC was to select its chairperson. Given the composition of the LPC, this was no easy task. The selection had to rest on consensus, implying that the chairperson would be someone enjoying trust across political and racial divides. In some cases, the LPC chose the option of two cochairpersons—one black, the other white—when they failed to find one suitable individual. These LPC leaders mostly came from civil society, especially the religious sector. The chairpersons, as supported by staff of the RPC, became the primary interveners in potentially violent situations and facilitators of negotiations.

The LPCs performed three functions (Odendaal and Spies 1996; Collin Marks 2000; Carmichael 2010). First, they prevented sporadic violence associated with protest actions. By virtue of its composition, the LPC had access to all the major political and social networks in the community. LPCs, therefore, were early warning mechanisms, aware of emerging situations with violence potential. The LPC, led by its chairperson or specifically mandated members of the LPC, would facilitate discussions between the relevant actors (many of whom were in fact represented on the LPC). Such discussions focused on strengthening a consensus to avoid violence and jointly design the most appropriate process to deal with the crisis. It included agreements on matters such as the route to be followed (in case of marches), proper monitoring, and the specific responsibilities of all actors, including the police. LPC-appointed monitors had, on various occasions, defused potentially violent standoffs that developed in the course of such events. The fact that they had a mandate from the community via the LPC to prevent violence lent substantial authority to their interventions.

Second, LPCs mediated local disputes that had violence potential. These disputes were varied. LPCs mediated disputes between local resident organizations (the civics) and municipalities; between the police and local communities; between local political groupings; between factions in intraparty conflicts; and even in such unpolitical matters as disputes between soccer clubs or religious groups. The outcomes of such mediations were always going to be preliminary and tentative, given that most solutions depended on national negotiations to succeed and the arrival of the new dispensation. But, when successful, they crafted short-term agreements on a way forward, thus defusing potential violence. In the process, they achieved another objective by introducing the "politics of negotiation" at the local level (Cilliers 2001:265).

Third, LPCs contributed to an emerging social cohesion. The LPCs were in most places the first platform that enabled all sections of a local community to engage in dialogue and joint problem solving. It has to be understood that, before 1990, no political space for local peacebuilding existed. Before 1990, the policy of the liberation movements was to promote civil disobedience and noncollaboration with government institutions. Meanwhile the government had banned the liberation movements, and any suspicion of collaboration was punishable with imprisonment. The NPA legitimized the pursuit of peace. The very decision to form an LPC was therefore, in the vast majority of cases, the first step that a local community took on the long road of reconciliation or social reconstruction. If only for this reason, it was so important that local communities were offered the opportunity to make that decision by themselves, thus claiming ownership of it. Furthermore, LPCs were communication centers that ensured improved communication between actors and, in general, spread a message of peace (Carmichael 2010).

They dealt with the very destructive force of rumors by being a mechanism to check and distribute correct information. They actively informed communities about the content of the NPA and all measures taken to promote it. All the activities of LPCs combined—taking the first step toward reconciliation, the dialogue and efforts at joint problem solving, the sharing and spreading of information, the active promotion of peace, and success in jointly defusing potentially violent standoffs—laid the foundation for an emerging social cohesion.

Impact Assessment. The NPA did not impress everyone. André du Toit (1993:10) expressed some of the reigning skepticism thus: "[The NPA] represented a not altogether concerted attempt, at once tentative and somewhat desperate, of some political and civil leaders to regain some measure of control over the proliferating incidents of political violence at the local and grassroots levels. The subsequent history of the Peace Accord has not been a major success story; more often than not the Peace Accord structures have failed to function effectively and to prevent or contain violent conflicts at local levels."

His skepticism was justified, of course, by the trend of escalating violence. The NPA was clearly not delivering very well on its key objective—to stop violence. Yet, such an unqualified dismissal of the NPA and its infrastructure is not correct. In numerous cases, LPCs had been able to prevent violence—at a time when nothing else was really proving effective.

A number of studies have made an assessment of the impact of LPCs (International Alert 1993; Nathan 1993; Shaw 1993; Sisk 1994; Gastrow 1995; Odendaal and Spies 1996; Odendaal and Spies 1997; Ball 1998; Collin Marks 2000; Cilliers 2001). By way of summary, four observations have been made. First, LPCs had different success rates in different parts of the country. The Western Cape, for example, was more successful than Kwa-Zulu-Natal—probably because the IFP had a weak presence in the Western Cape. But even within the same region, the performance of LPCs would vary. The reliance on local agency is a double-edged sword. It encourages local ownership of the peace process but also gives local actors the space to block the peace process. By its nature, therefore, a process that relies on local agency is bound to have varied results. Furthermore, the success (or failure) of a specific LPC depended on a variety of factors: the quality of support received from the National Peace Secretariat and the RPC; the presence in a community of people with the aptitude and commitment to fulfill peacemaker and facilitation roles; and the nature of specific configurations of local issues, personalities, and histories.

Second, it is extremely difficult to quantify the extent of violence prevention because we simply lack sufficient data. Success in violence prevention is an extraordinarily difficult matter to assess. There are three questions that have to be answered: first, could the nonoccurrence of violence be attributed to other preventive factors; second, would, in the absence of an intervention, violence have been inevitable; and third, was the intervention sufficient to explain the avoidance of conflict (Ramsbotham, Woodhouse et al. 2005:111)? However, the observers are unanimous in their view that LPCs had indeed contributed toward containing the spiral of violence—in spite of the fact that the number of violent deaths had increased during the lifetime of the LPCs. The minutes of RPC meetings and the National Peace Secretariat contained regular reports of successful LPC interventions. *The Star*, a leading Johannesburg daily, initially expressed skepticism regarding the NPA. An article published on September 15, 1992, however, included this statement: "Without an accord it would be easy for South Africa to be sucked up into a vortex of violence" (Gastrow 1995). In other words, violence had escalated, but the general consensus is that the escalation would have been far worse if it were not for the peace committees. LPCs therefore helped to restrain the escalation of violence but were unable to stop it.

Third, the impact of LPCs on establishing social cohesion is just as difficult to assess given the absence of quantitative data. Even so, their contribution toward introducing dialogue and negotiations to local communities as a primary conflict management approach was important. The fact that LPCs symbolized a community's willingness to consider peace and galvanized local agency in the pursuit of peace contributed to the overall legitimacy of the peace process. On the negative side, LPCs were powerless in the face of acts of deliberate violence or when political will was lacking. Local bodies that operated on the basis of facilitation and mediation were powerless in the face of planned violence. They were equally powerless, as in KwaZulu-Natal, when some local political leaders were clearly not committed to peace.

Fourth, and lastly, LPCs have, somewhat unfairly, been criticized for making "negative peace"—that is, reducing violence without addressing the root causes of violence (Bremner 1994). The root causes, however, could only be addressed through the negotiation of a completely new constitution, which happened in a separate process.

Nicole Ball (1998) has provided possibly the most apt summary assessment: "Viewed as a whole, the peace committees had a mixed record, and a definite assessment of their 'success' or 'failure' is impossible. Peace committees were unable to stop violence completely but often limited its occurrence. They were unable to end impunity on the part of the security forces, but they were able to help equalizing the balance of power between those in power and ordinary citizens and to strengthen accountability. Their ability to address the underlying causes of conflict was circumscribed, but even in the most violence-ridden areas peace committee staff were able to mediate conflict and create a safe space within which problems could be discussed. And though unable to transform the 'struggle mentality', they were able to help South Africans take their first steps toward understanding the value of negotiations and how to engage in them constructively."

The LPCs of South Africa, therefore, were not perfect. However, in a context where nothing else—neither political leadership nor coercive security measures—was effective in stopping the violence, LPCs provided communities with the option to work at their own peace. Many LPCs achieved surprising results. Moreover, it gave local communities the sense that they were participating in the national quest for peace, rather than being passive bystanders. Laurie Nathan (1993) used the metaphor of "imperfect bridges" to describe LPCs: When the bridge has been swept away by a torrent and makeshift bridges have to be crafted to reach the other side, the question is not whether the bridges are perfect but whether they enable the most rudimentary traffic between the two sides.

Observations from the Two Cases: Kenya and South Africa

The two case studies discussed in this chapter demonstrate two very different ways in which a peace infrastructure was established under widely different circumstances. In the majority of cases that will be discussed, a top-down approach was followed, but Kenya is not the only example of a bottom-up process. Ghana also followed the same route, while in Malawi the local bodies sustained the infrastructure even when the national body proved highly ineffectual.

In chapters to follow, the various key issues reflected by these case studies will be discussed in more detail and compared to other experiences. At this stage, three observations are noteworthy. First, there is evident advantage in the linkage between local and national levels and between the state and civil society actors. The existence of a formal infrastructure makes such linkage and coordination much easier, but a formal infrastructure is not a necessary precondition for effective linkage. At the time when the Wajir group did their most significant work, they did not enjoy the advantage of formal recognition.

Second, both cases illustrate the importance of political legitimacy. When still informal, the Wajir LPC had to negotiate its legitimacy. The only available instrument was the quality of its interaction with all the different stakeholders and the trust that the facilitators succeeded in generating. The South African LPCs enjoyed the legitimacy granted by a national agreement. Even so, this formal mandate did not relieve LPCs from the necessity to establish credibility in the eyes of local actors. Formal LPCs, therefore, enjoy a considerable advantage in terms of political legitimacy, but a national mandate is not sufficient to ensure local credibility.

Third, the strength of the Wajir LPC was the high level of local ownership it achieved. When attempts were made to replicate the successful model of Wajir in the wider region, the same levels of local ownership were not achieved because the primary initiative no longer belonged to the local community but to external actors. The South African experience also demonstrated that the success of an LPC depended on the extent to which a local community took ownership of the process. Perhaps the most important conclusion to reach here is that local ownership is not necessarily guaranteed by either its formal or informal nature but by the level of commitment of the collective local leadership to the process.

The existence of a formal infrastructure that provides political legitimacy and effective coordination is indeed a substantial benefit to local peacebuilding. Such an infrastructure also guarantees better continuation and sustainability as can be the case with civil society–supported LPCs. However, it would be a mistake to see a formal infrastructure as a *necessary* precondition for effective LPCs. Depending on their specific objectives and capacity, LPCs can be effective in the absence of such an infrastructure. Also, an assumption that the existence of a formal infrastructure would be a *sufficient* precondition for effective local peacebuilding would be equally wrong. The LPC must enjoy *local* legitimacy and ownership in order to be effective.

3

The Problem of Teeth
The Means and Instruments of LPCs

One of the most recurrent criticisms of LPCs in South Africa was that they were without teeth—like toothless bulldogs, all huff and puff, but with no ability to sanction transgressors of the peace accord. The critique did not only come from detractors of the NPA but also from sympathetic observers and participants. Peter Gastrow (1995:63), for example, himself a member of the National Peace Secretariat, referred to what he termed "one of the main weaknesses" of the accord—its lack of teeth for dealing with alleged contraventions of the codes of conduct (see also Sisk 1994; McCall and Duncan 2000:167). What these critics do not answer is where the teeth should come from and who should be fitted with them to do the biting. In such a highly polarized context where the very legitimacy of government authority was disputed, what type of body would have been sufficiently detached from the boiling cauldron of passions, fears, interests, and suspicions to be seen to adjudicate fairly and, more important, to apply sanction effectively?

Possibly the most important issue to understand regarding LPCs is that they lack coercive power. Indeed, they have no teeth—and should have no teeth. They rely solely on their ability to facilitate consensus-building processes. This is, clearly, a matter that requires more explanation.

The Three Approaches to Conflict

William Ury et al. (1988) have made the by now well-known distinction between three approaches to conflict: power-based, rights-based, and interests-based. The distinction points to three fundamental ways of approaching and managing conflict: using coercion in one of its many forms (power-based), applying arbitration or adjudication (rights-based), or seeking to solve the underlying problem in a manner that satisfies the interests of all parties to the greatest possible extent (interests-based). The first approach relies on political, economic, and military power; the second aproach relies on the justice system. Both of these approaches have teeth. They can bite those that refuse to collaborate. By contrast, the third approach, at its most effective, does not need teeth. It relies on a genuine search for mutually satisfactory solutions through a negotiation style that uncovers the real interests of all parties and crafts a solution taking all these interests into account.

This last approach has subsequently been popularized by Roger Fischer and William Ury (1991) in their best seller, *Getting to Yes*. Its publication took place at a time when a general sense of optimism existed that intractable conflicts could indeed be resolved, that "win-win outcomes" were possible. It was the time following the collapse of the Berlin Wall. A total of thirty-eight conflicts ended during the decade—an extraordinarily high figure (Toft 2006:9). Fisher and Ury's emphasis on an interests-based style of negotiation combined well with the dominant conflict resolution theory of the time, that of John Burton and his colleagues at the Institute for Conflict Analysis and Resolution at George Mason University. Burton believed that conflicts could be resolved once the underlying frustrated basic human needs were uncovered and a solution was forged that addressed those basic needs. His optimism was captured in statements like: "Conflict Resolution means *terminating* conflict by methods that are analytical and that get to the root of the problem" (Burton 1988; italics added). This optimism has been further communicated and spread by countless training workshops in conflict resolution across the world that emphasized the notion that all conflict could be solved through the right understanding of conflict dynamics and skill in using specific negotiation and mediation approaches.

The mood has subsequently sobered, and the optimism regarding conflict resolution and interests-based negotiations has been replaced by a more realistic understanding of the long-term, multifaceted commitment required to transform conflict and build sustainable peace. Violent conflict as a social phenomenon cannot be seen in isolation from the wider national, regional, and global sociopolitical and economic systems that co-determine conflict patterns and behavior. The transformation of conflict is therefore not solely a matter of a successful local negotiation session but of the systemic change of those political, economic, and cultural systems that encourage violence.

In addition, there is a growing realization that the concepts and skill sets of the conflict resolution field are imbedded in liberal Western cultural and ideological assumptions that do not necessarily transfer to other cultures (see Salem 1993) or socioeconomic contexts (see Ramsbotham et al., 2005:90–91).

However, greater soberness and humility about our collective capacity to solve deeply intractable conflicts do not negate the valuable insights and useful strategies that have been developed thus far. In postagreement conditions in particular, the approach that relies on finding inclusive, mutually satisfactory solutions to problems and that works with underlying needs and interests is not only viable but also deeply desirable and often the only practical option.

LPCs typically operate in environments where the first two approaches (that of power and rights) have limited chances of being successful for a variety of reasons.

Regarding the power-based approach, the application of coercion in a postagreement context is counterproductive and often dangerous. The reason a peace agreement was signed in the first place was precisely because none of the parties was able to win a decisive victory. Authority, in a postagreement context, is therefore uncertain and fragile. New authority structures have to emerge, but the old is not quite something of the past. It is a situation of ambivalence, flux, and weak legitimate force—not the context where coercion is effective or constructive. Not all political players necessarily acknowledge this fact. They may continue with efforts to manipulate the peace process and coerce others into compliance with their agenda. In reality, however, such attempts at coercive behavior are weak and ineffective because of the inability of one political party to impose its will on the others.

For example, in both South Africa and Northern Ireland, the security forces and the police in particular were seen by the liberation movements and the republicans respectively as the main instruments of their oppression. A priority task during the postagreement phase was to transform the security sector. The police, in other words, were no longer available as a mechanism to assert authority in matters that had political meaning. Therefore, when community conflict erupted, it could not be dealt with merely by sending in the police. The mere sight of the police was often the trigger for violent behavior.

Similarly, in weak state conditions, the use of coercive measures is often counterproductive because it cannot be sustained. It is not sufficient, for example, to send in the police to suppress dissent if the police are incapable of containing the situation for a sustained period. In the absence of inclusive political solutions, sporadic police action is rather likely to deepen resentment and complicate the problem.

In both postagreement and weak state conditions, therefore, coercive measures are ineffective in the absence of a credible and capable authority.

The efficient use of the judicial system, or of other forms of arbitration, similarly depends on both the legitimacy and capacity of the judicial system. In most postagreement situations, or in conditions of a weak state, the judicial system is compromised or inefficient, and therefore a weak instrument to use. There are actually three contexts when a rights-based approach to conflict is particularly difficult. The first is when the justice system is perceived as illegitimate—a compromised relic of the old dispensation. In South Africa, for example, the law was seen as the white man's law. For those in the liberation movement, it was a matter of pride to resist the law. Nelson Mandela himself spent twenty-seven years in jail because he was sentenced by a court of law. The formulators of the NPA were therefore quite unrealistic when they agreed that transgressions of the accord would be dealt with through arbitration. They specified that "justices of the peace" would be appointed at the local level to deal with transgressions and accusations of intimidation. In their task, they would apply natural law. In reality, no "justices of the peace" were appointed, and none of the many transgressions of the accord were dealt with through arbitration. Such measures would simply have lacked any authority or implementing power.

The second context where a rights-based approach is problematic is when the capacity of the justice system is so weak that it is incapable of delivering justice. In Sierra Leone, for example, the judicial system would not have been able to sanction any prominent political party during the election campaigns in 2007 and 2008. Not only was it compromised in light of the role played by the judiciary in the prewar situation (collaborating in the kleptomaniac pursuits of the elite[25]), but it also simply lacked the capacity, particularly in the districts, to exert its will. The justice system was just too weak to arbitrate in political conflict.

The third context where a rights-based approach is difficult is when there is a fundamental difference between the justice paradigm of specific communities and that of the state. This is the situation in countries like Kenya and Uganda where pastoralist communities operate with culturally determined perceptions of justice that are incompatible with that of the state. In addition, the state lacks sufficient coercive power to consistently stamp its authority on the situation (see Muhereza, Ossiya et al. 2008; Chopra 2008a; Chopra 2008b). It has resulted in patterns of violence associated with cattle rustling that the state has found very difficult to contain.

The interests-based approach, or, as I would rather call it, a consensus-seeking approach, is therefore the most appropriate one for a postagreement

---

25. TRC 2004, par. 420, 441.

context.[26] The heart of the approach is the facilitation of processes that are respectful of the specific dynamics of the conflict and that seek to find sustainable solutions that all role-players are willing to agree to. The approach is sensitive to specific cultural dimensions, to the emotional needs of participants, and to their substantial interests. It therefore relies on instruments such as the facilitation of dialogue, negotiation, and mediation. It deals with the dilemma regarding the legitimacy of power by seeking consensus, and then uses the consensus that was achieved as the guiding authority in implementing decisions.

This approach has considerable advantages. Most important, it strengthens relationships and social cohesion. It promotes collaboration and a deeper understanding of the demands of coexistence and interdependence. It is sustainable because it is based on the joint decisions of participants and not on imposed decisions. As such, the approach is highly relevant for the type of challenges that communities face in the postagreement phase.

But the approach also has limitations. In the face of those bent on using destructive violence, or in situations of power asymmetry, weaker parties remain vulnerable. They may feel coerced into agreements on the basis of a superficial consensus but with no guarantee or safeguard. Also, the process of consensus building is time consuming and requires extraordinary patience and skill—at a time when urgent action is needed. Yet both the unavailability of other options and the inherent advantages, specifically in postagreement contexts, render it the most desirable and practical approach.[27]

Therefore, for LPCs specifically, toothlessness is an asset rather than a weakness. The evidence from the field is consistent. LPCs are most effective when dealing with problems that are not solvable through the use of coercive or legal measures. LPCs are useful in contexts where normal processes of governance and adjudication are ineffective because of the lack of social cohesion or governance capacity.

---

26. The chairperson of the LPC in Chitwan, Nepal, expressed it thus: "We're living in a virtual stateless situation here. The administration and police cannot deal with many cases. Therefore people call us whenever there is some major problem. . . . In these transitional times, only negotiation and mediation work in many cases, not legalistic or administrative methods" (NTTP 2008).

27. There is, in the literature, an argument for "complimentarity" (Bloomfield 1995, Svensson 2007). In the context of the debate between a confidence-building approach or a power-based approach to mediation (Kleiboer 1996, Nathan 1999), the argument for complementarity states emphasizes that the context should determine what approach is best and that the one does not necessarily exclude the other. My argument on the primacy of consensus building is consciously in line with the confidence-building approach to mediation. While acknowledging the need for external pressure on parties, such pressure should not be exerted by the mediator (see Nathan 1999). In the case of mediation under the auspices of LPCs, the reliance on a confidence-building approach is, in my view, even more compelling for the reasons mentioned earlier.

Prerequisite Features of an Infrastructure

The basic task of LPCs, therefore, is to build consensus on the most urgent peacebuilding tasks facing a community. They have to facilitate agreement on the best ways to contain or prevent violence and to rebuild a sufficient level of social cohesion. They perform the task by using basic consensus-building instruments: the facilitation of dialogue, negotiation, and mediation.

The infrastructure for peace has to make it possible or easier for LPCs to perform this role. In this respect, there are four design features of an infrastructure that are particularly important. The success of LPCs largely depends on the way in which the design of an infrastructure meets these requirements in contextually relevant ways.

The four prerequisites are, first, that the formation, composition, and function of an LPC should all be geared toward achieving optimum legitimacy. Second, the structure of the LPC should enable the role of local peacebuilders. Third, LPCs should have access to specialized support. And fourth, the infrastructure should enable horizontal and vertical linkages.

A Legitimate Platform

By establishing an LPC, a platform is created for legitimate local peace-building. In a context where authority is weak and contested and the social fabric torn apart, the formation of an LPC means that all the relevant local actors have agreed voluntarily to collaborate in building peace. They do so, in addition, with an explicit mandate from the collective national leadership and with active support provided through the services that form part of the infrastructure.

Given the context of LPCs, it has to be understood that an LPC's legitimacy is and remains a fragile matter. It is subject to extraordinary emotional and political pressures that are inherent in postagreement contexts—the ongoing political struggle, the reemergence of violence, the impact of past traumas, competition for survival, and lingering anger and distrust. For this reason, very careful attention should be given to the manner in which its establishment is facilitated. A top-down instruction to establish an LPC defeats the purpose. The formation of an LPC should be anchored in the free commitment of local actors. Furthermore, at no stage can the legitimacy of an LPC be taken for granted. At every moment of crisis, it has to be reaffirmed or even renegotiated.

Peace accords, in reality, are elite affairs. Often, so are decisions to establish infrastructures for peace. They are created at the national (or international) level with little to no input from local communities. At the outset, therefore, the establishment of an LPC in terms of such an accord is hindered by the manner in which the national process has taken local communities for granted. This negative start can be offset, though, by the way in which the establishment of LPCs takes place. The formation of an LPC should be the result of a local consensus, based on sufficient information and adequate opportunity for discussion. It is a process that should be facilitated with extraordinary care and thoughtfulness. This process should include respect for the right of local communities to refuse to form an LPC. It is an important right because it signifies the difference between a top-down imposition and local ownership.

All of this assumes that facilitators with the necessary expertise are available. It is one of the most important responsibilities tied to an infrastructure for peace—to make expert facilitators available to support the establishment of LPCs. This matter will be explored in more detail below.

There are two additional design features that enable LPCs to be legitimate platforms for peacebuilding: *inclusivity* and *consensus*. George McCall and Miranda Duncan (2000:169) referred to South Africa's LPCs as "clumsy and inefficient contraptions, pretty much all wrong from the theoretical perspectives of group problem-solving and process-design." Yet they enjoyed "almost unprecedented legitimacy" because of these two design features (i.e., inclusivity and consensus).[28]

Inclusivity means that all relevant political and social groups should be represented on the forum. It is particularly important to include those groups that have been involved in the violent conflict and groups that have been marginalized or excluded in the past (such as women and marginalized identity groups). Furthermore, people who represent the peacebuilding capacity of a community should also be included (see next section). An LPC cannot be composed only of protagonists. An LPC has to be representative of the total capacity of a community to produce violence *and* to produce peace.

In practice, several dilemmas may emerge regarding the inclusion of groups that either continue to threaten the use of violence or are still actively involved in violent or intimidating acts (see Jarstad and Sisk 2008). In this respect, LPCs operate on two assumptions. The first is that organizations that participate in LPCs have willingly committed themselves to a joint

---

28. The "unprecedented legitimacy" that LPCs enjoyed in South Africa must be seen in context, though. It was indeed unprecedented in comparison with any previous attempt to legitimize peacebuilding, but that does not mean it was perfect. Sisk (1994) indicated the many concerns that existed at the time regarding its legitimacy, most important the top-down nature of the accord. The legitimacy was largely earned by the manner in which the establishment of LPCs was facilitated and the buy-in by local communities into the process. However, it still left many communities with a residue of resentment at being taken for granted.

search for peace. They participate in the LPC because they have, on their own volition, decided to give peace a chance.[29] In reality, such a commitment does not always prevent parties from threatening or using violence, but in such cases, the LPC as a collective has to deal with the culprit through ongoing engagement and peer pressure. The second assumption is that exclusion defeats the purpose of an LPC.[30] If a violent actor is excluded, who is not an opportunist with criminal motives but is representative of a section of the community, then this exclusion can only mean that the conditions for peacebuilding are not yet in place.[31]

One practical implication of the principle of inclusivity is that membership in an LPC should not be predetermined by a national formula. The problem with imposing a national formula is the threat to inclusivity. It is easily foreseeable that a group relevant to the local peacebuilding process may be excluded purely because the national formula forbids its inclusion. The exclusion of a relevant group will certainly undermine the legitimacy of the LPC in that specific location.

In Nepal, for example, the current legislation regarding the establishment of LPCs stated that each local committee should consist of twenty-three people according to a very specific formula: political parties will share twelve seats among them, the business community one, civil society four, "conflict-affected groups" four, and excluded minorities two. A third of the committee has to be comprised of women (MoPR 2009). The overall intention of this formula is praiseworthy. It is clearly intended to safeguard inclusivity. However, the prescription of such a strict formula adds unnecessary complexity to the process—and in one of the most diverse countries in the world. The composition of an LPC should instead follow an analysis of the local situation. Local dynamics and conflict patterns should determine the composition of the LPC. In some districts, for example, there may be more than four conflict-affected groups and less political polarization to justify twelve seats for political parties. In another district, the situation may be reversed. North-

---

29. The so-called Mitchell principles that were used in the Northern Ireland process made inclusion dependent on a commitment by parties to adhere to principles of democracy and nonviolence (Höglund 2008:96–97).

30. Höglund (2008:98) referred to quantitative research reports in support of the notion that when rebel groups are excluded from peace processes, a return to armed conflict is more likely. See also Jarstad (2008:23).

31. The World Bank uses the concept "inclusive enough," stating that the current evidence indicated that agreements seldom included all actors. Coalitions are "inclusive enough" when they include the parties necessary for implementing the initial stages of a confidence-building and transformation process (see World Bank 2011:12–13). While this distinction releases some of the excessive pressure on inclusion, which is useful, the challenge remains to ensure that there is sufficient inclusion to ensure the credibility and sustainability of the process.

ern Ireland and Sierra Leone also determined composition through a nation-ally determined formula. In contrast, in South Africa, the peace committees were open forums. Any social group wanting to join was welcomed.

The principle of decision making by *consensus* is equally important if the LPC is to operate as a legitimate peacebuilding platform. Note, however, that LPCs should not be required to make governance decisions. The type of decisions that LPCs should make refer to peacebuilding tasks: whether a specific initiative (such as organizing dialogues, preventing violence, or mediating in a specific dispute) is necessary, who should lead the initiative, and what process should be followed. LPCs, therefore, decide on whether and what type of intervention is necessary to defuse potential violence or to unblock local political deadlocks. In respect to the latter, they may initiate a mediation process under their auspices between political or government actors, but any decisions that will be made will be those of the political actors—not of the LPC.[32] They may also decide on confidence-building measures that should be taken, reconciliation strategies to follow, or public events to raise greater awareness of and buy-in into the agenda of peace. These decisions by the LPC have to be taken by consensus. The principle of consensus protects weaker or minority parties from being bullied. More important, a peacebuilding initiative that has been mandated by a consensus decision can truly claim to have a substantive mandate from the whole community.

In order to achieve inclusivity and consensus decision making that is qualitatively more than a mere bureaucratic exercise, careful attention should be given to the matter of the *facilitation* of LPC meetings. Inclusivity should mean more than window dressing, and consensus more than agreement between those with the loudest and most aggressive voices. The quality of inclusivity and consensus is determined by the extent to which the voices that had been silenced in the past are now heard. Inclusivity therefore means more than finding the right formula to have all groups represented. Successful inclusivity and consensus means that *all* the voices are heard by all: those that speak with pain and anger, and those that speak with fear or shame.

It is, therefore, very important to determine who facilitates meetings and in what style. It has to be done by a person with the personal aptitude and skill to facilitate communication—to make communication possible. In both Northern Ireland and Nepal, the enabling law stipulated that the chairperson of the LPC must be a politician. The decision in both cases was ameliorated by mandating regular rotation of the chair, but it remains an unfortunate decision. Despite the fact that some politicians may make good chairper-

---

32. See chapter 4 for a more detailed discussion of this aspect.

this decision does not serve the objective of open and honest dialogue. By virtue of his or her position, a politician will be tempted to be defensive, aggressive, or manipulative when the interests of his or her party are at stake. The same goes for any LPCs in which a government official is the chairperson, such as in Ethiopia. When the conflict is between a community and its government, as is often the case, it cannot be expected that a government official will facilitate open dialogue. It is therefore important to identify people who could serve as chairpersons or facilitators of meetings that have the stature and ability to facilitate open discussions and can be trusted not to be defensive or manipulative. In Nicaragua, Sierra Leone, and South Africa, the practice was to select a nonpolitician as chairperson, with good effect.

In summary, in a context where the legitimacy of authority is not shared by all the different sectors of a community, an LPC, if properly formed, provides a credible, legitimate platform to launch specific peacebuilding initiatives. Its legitimacy is based on its local ownership, inclusivity, and the fact that decisions on peacebuilding processes are made by consensus. Much depends, however, on the manner in which LPC meetings are facilitated and on whether the facilitator succeeds in mediating open, constructive dialogue where all voices are heard.

Local Peacebuilders

Each society is composed of hawks and doves. There are those who have an interest in pursuing the conflict even through violent means if need be (the hawks), and those whose interest is in a peaceful and stable community (the doves). The former are often the representatives of the different political or identity groups involved in the violent conflict, while the latter are often based in religious, cultural, education, or business sectors. They are invariably not neutral about the reasons for the conflict, but they believe that it is for the greater good to bring stability and peace to the community. As important as it is to have the hawks on the LPC, there should be doves too.

Sometimes within those circles where decisions are made regarding the establishment of infrastructures of peace, there is a naive belief that, in order to make peace, it is enough merely to bring former protagonists into the same room. This belief disregards the level of trauma, distrust, fear, and hatred that local conflict actors share. It assumes that the fact that national leaders have made peace is a sufficient reason for local leaders to put aside their own histories, emotions, and interests. Contrary to this assumption, concerted efforts should be made to ensure that the LPC operates as a space where dialogue and consensus building is indeed possible. There are two key measures to assist in this respect: the chairperson needs to first, ensure that the facilitation is done in a manner that makes it safe for people to express themselves truthfully and, second, make sure that there are people on the LPC who, in spite of the past, believe in the benefits of peace for the wider community and are motivated by a vision of an inclusive future. The doves, in other words, have to be the integrating center of the LPC, a force that holds the constituent parts of the community together to counter the centrifugal tendencies of the hawks.

Experience has also shown that tensions and even violence may erupt between parties that are represented on the LPC. The fact that people have agreed to be part of an LPC does not mean that peace has been achieved. It only means that there is consensus on the need to *build* peace. Without the presence of a group of people on the LPC that can effectively occupy the middle ground and mediate between parties when such tensions erupt, the LPC will most likely fall apart. Furthermore, the various tasks that have to be performed on behalf of the LPC—such as facilitating dialogues, mediating in disputes, defusing potentially violent situations, or networking—are best performed by this group of people. They have the vision, drive, and aptitude to take on such tasks. The fact that they have received a mandate from the LPC makes it possible to perform these tasks with credibility.

Paul Wehr and John Paul Lederach (1991) have referred to this group of people as "insider-partials." Their observations were made in the context of Nicaragua's peace committees. They noted that the people who had the biggest impact on the peace process did not operate from a position of impartiality—as some of the literature on mediation requires—but from a deep sense of connectedness. "The insider-partial is the 'mediator from inside the conflict,' whose acceptability to the conflictants is rooted not in distance from the conflict or objectivity regarding the issues, but rather in connectedness and trusted relationships with the conflict parties."

Insider-partials (also at times called "insider-mediators") are therefore people known and trusted in communities across a wide spectrum of opinion—despite the fact that they may belong to one or another political or identity categories (Elgstrom, Bercovitch et al. 2003; Mason 2009). They are able to operate as mediators or in various other peacebuilding roles because of the trust that they enjoy. I strongly advise that the chairpersons of the LPC should come from this group of people because they are more likely able to facilitate the type of open dialogue that is necessary. The chairpersons of the LPCs in South Africa (Odendaal and Spies 1996) and Sierra Leone (Nyathi 2009) fell in this category. In contrast, in FYR Macedonia, the Committees on Inter-Community Relations, in some districts, were composed of only one representative per ethnic group. The problem with such an arrangement is twofold: First, it makes proper inclusivity impossible because it assumes that one person can adequately represent an entire interest group (in this case, an ethnic group), including women and the youth; and secondly, and important for what I am discussing in this paragraph, such a composition invariably excludes the presence of peacebuilders. If only one person were to represent an interest group on such a body, it is likely to be the leader of that interest group or someone appointed by him or her. The result is an LPC solely composed of leaders of interest groups with no room for insider mediators.

It is interesting to note the growing institutionalization of insider-mediator capacity. The African Union, for example, established the Panel of the Wise in 2007. The panel is composed of five people who are highly respected individuals and who must not hold active political office during their tenure on the panel. Panel members advise on peace and security issues. They may also intervene as mediators or facilitators—under the auspices of the Peace and Security Commission. The Economic Community of West African States, West Africa's regional authority, has a Council of the Wise that has a similar function, while the Southern African Development Community, the Southern African community of states, is currently considering proposals to institute a panel of elders. It is too early to comment on the impact of these panels, but what it demonstrates is that the concept of wise people who facilitate peacebuilding on behalf of a representative forum is culturally and politically acceptable in Africa.

In summary, for an LPC to perform a peacebuilding function, it should include local peacebuilders who have the vision for peacebuilding, who enjoy the trust of their communities, and who have the aptitude to build peace. These are the people who will fulfill most of the peacebuilding tasks on behalf of the LPC, particularly those tasks that require some form of crisis intervention.

Specialist Support

There are notable examples of LPCs that have been established and that have functioned well without any external support. The Wajir Peace and Development Committee of Kenya is probably the most outstanding example. Its success can be attributed to the presence of exceptional local peacebuilders in the community.[33] On the whole, though, LPCs rely on specialist support.

Specialist support refers to support from those with knowledge of the basic principles of peace processes and skill in facilitating such complex processes. It also refers to the ability to transfer such knowledge and skill in

---

33. Dekha Ibrahim Abdi, who provided crucial leadership in this process, was awarded the Right Livelihood Award (the "alternative Nobel Peace Prize") in 2007 (see Mason 2009). She died tragically in a car accident in 2011.

culturally acceptable manners. The specialists needed are therefore conflict transformation practitioners that have professional skills in facilitation, mediation, and training.

Imagine, once more, the task of establishing LPCs in the eastern part of the DRC. The context is one of extreme brutality that has continued now for almost two decades, severe poverty and competition for resources, dismal performance on all the basic social indicators, deep ethnic distrust, and a fragile national and regional peace agreement that has not solved some of the most serious political issues such as citizenship and land ownership rights. The decision to establish LPCs is a sensible one, but only on the condition that sufficient specialist support is available. It is inconceivable that these local actors will be able to achieve the objectives set for them (e.g., the reintegration of refugees and mediation of land disputes) by pulling themselves up by their own bootstraps.

Specialist capacity normally resides in the UN system or in CSOs. In a few cases, such as South Africa, professionals were employed and located in the peace infrastructure. The manner in which the infrastructure for peace is set up should determine how LPCs may access the specialist support. There are a number of options: Professional facilitators may be appointed at the national level on a full-time or part-time basis to provide support to LPCs as needed; CSOs may be contracted to provide the support; or selected individual members of LPCs may be trained in the facilitation of dialogue and conflict resolution processes.

There are a number of specific functions where specialists are needed. First, as we have seen, the process to establish an LPC should be based on sound consultative processes and the facilitation of dialogue. The facilitation skills required to manage such a process do not necessarily exist in a community; or, if they do exist, there is no firm joint mandate yet for such people with those skills to take the lead. In some instances, therefore, the task to establish an LPC has to be performed by someone from outside with the requisite mandate and skills.[34] Second, the LPC may require specialist support in any of the peacebuilding tasks that it wants to perform, whether it is the facilitation of dialogue, violence prevention, mediation, or any other task. Third, LPCs need to be oriented regarding their role and task. LPCs are mostly established in contexts where an authoritarian or exclusivist political culture was in place. The role of an LPC is invariably new, as are its approaches and

---

34. An interesting example of external actors kick-starting local peace processes is from Bougainville, where, in some locations, international peacekeepers had set up the initial meeting and provided security. Deep-rooted fear existed that violence might erupt when local protagonists first had to face each other. The peacekeepers therefore acted as both facilitators and guarantors of security. See John Braithwaite et al. 2010.

methods.[35] LPC members therefore need to be engaged in thorough discussions regarding the role they must play. Fourth, it is often very useful to provide training to LPC members in basic conflict transformation skills (in facilitation and mediation techniques).[36] Of particular importance is to assist the local peacebuilders or insider-partials with information, appropriate skills training in mediation, and active support as appropriate.

Current evidence suggests that LPCs that have access to specialist support fare better than those without it. Where such support was lacking, LPCs did not reach their potential. Those LPCs with a better understanding of the consensus-seeking methodology and with greater skills in applying it appear to have been more successful. Local conflict transformation processes therefore benefit from quality professional attention. Local peace processes are inherently complex; their solution is certainly not easier than at national level simply because they are smaller in scale. It is unreasonable to expect local actors to have the capacity to deal with their conflict all on their own. The logic of an infrastructure for peace is that it locates ownership of local peace processes at a local level through the formation of an LPC but with expert assistance available to provide support as needed.

Linkages

An LPC is an amazing meeting point of a very broad spectrum of political and social networks in a community. Each person that serves on an LPC has access to one or more networks. Collectively, an LPC represents a spread of networks and resources that, if successfully mobilized toward the same outcome, has great potential.

The linkage that an LPC provides has a number of important benefits apart from the potential to mobilize a broad range of networks and resources in the pursuit of peace. It also ensures that an LPC is an excellent early warning mechanism. First, through its networks, an LPC should receive early warning of all imminent threats and potentially violent situations, allowing timely preventive action. Second, an LPC is a platform for sharing

---

35. In saying this, I do not imply that the use of a consensus-seeking methodology is culturally foreign to violence-torn societies. Many of the non-Western societies, in particular, where LPCs have been established, have been practicing consensus-seeking methods in dealing with conflict for many centuries. However, in the transfer from small-scale societies to postcolonial national states, the use of such consensus-seeking approaches has been lost at the political level. The new postcolonial political culture encouraged the centralization and imposition of authority, often in contrast to the traditional culture of consensus.

36. For an in-depth discussion of the most appropriate manner with which to conduct training in culturally diverse societies that is not an imposition to Western assumptions and cultural values, see Lederach 1995.

reliable information. Reliable information is extremely important in volatile contexts. Conversely, rumors are potentially very dangerous. A false rumor may easily trigger a violent episode. For example, I once received an early Saturday morning call from the chairperson of an ANC branch in a small town during the days of peace committees in South Africa. He told me that the "comrades" were worked up and preparing themselves for attack because someone had informed them that the police were lining up their armored cars to invade the township. Because there was a peace committee in that town, it was an easy procedure to link the ANC chairperson directly with the police commander, who provided the correct information—the police were moving their vehicles to a better parking spot. Without this information, any police officer's life would have been in danger in that township on that day. Sreten Koceski (2008) mentioned that in FYR Macedonia LPCs have been specifically successful in controlling rumors. The relevance of this fact for the prevention of violence cannot be underestimated. The insulated discourses that take place in identity groups that perceive themselves under threat are potentially toxic. LPCs provide a forum where reliable information can be shared, thus inserting a broader perspective and more reasonableness into the discourses.

Reliable information is also necessary for other constructive peacebuilding work. Civil society actors, for example, need reliable information on the priorities and strategies of government, while the government needs the same regarding civil society initiatives. Political parties need to know when and where rallies of their opponents are taking place, and the police and civil society similarly need to be alerted so that proper precautionary measures can be taken. Reliable information enables better collaboration and synergy.

LPCs provide not only horizontal linkage—that is, linking various actors at the local level—but also vertical linkage to national and international levels. When a functioning infrastructure is in place, LPCs should have access to political and administrative resources at the national level. One such resource is, again, information. Local communities are often starved of relevant information; and when information becomes available, it is often distorted by the specific channel and filters through which the information has been conveyed—whether it is a government department, a specific political party, or a civil society institution. LPCs—as a collective, representative body—have the capacity not only to access information from the national level but also to jointly collate and reconstruct the bits of information that are available and establish the relevance of the information for the community.

LPCs also have the capacity to access information at the national level that is necessary in order to address a specific crisis or dispute—for example, whether the government is indeed planning to close a certain school, as rumor has it, or whether the rebel movement is indeed planning to take up arms again, as another rumor suggests. The flow of information is not only top-down—it is in both directions. Through the infrastructure, decision makers at the national level have reliable information about dynamics at the local level.

Vertical linkage, just as in the case of horizontal linkage, also provides an opportunity for greater collaboration and synergy in dealing with local conflicts. The RPC in South Africa met every two weeks and discussed reports from the local peace committees. In numerous cases, the RPC then delegated someone from among themselves to provide specific assistance to a local committee. In Sierra Leone, both the National Monitoring Committee and the Political Parties Registration Commission, mother bodies of the LPCs, at times sent support to local bodies as requested. When local actors therefore got stuck and could not find a joint solution, an intervention from a higher level was necessary and often effective in unblocking the process.

The small town of Grabouw in South Africa provides us with a good example in this respect. A young man was shot and killed by the police. It took place in the context of a criminal investigation but was immediately politicized. It led to a strong outburst of public anger and the realistic fear of more violence to come. In response, the LPC decided to call a community meeting to try and defuse the situation and to invite the police to explain to the community the circumstances of and reasons for their action. Through the offices of the RPC, the provincial police commander was approached with the request that he should personally attend and address that meeting. The police commander, with the rank of general, first met with the LPC to discuss the situation, as well as the objectives and strategy for the mass meeting. In an ironic twist, the LPC guaranteed his safety during the course of the meeting. To his credit, the general agreed to the request. It was a risky decision, but all agreed that it was the most appropriate strategy to deal with the situation.

The evening of the meeting, the hall was packed. The general entered the meeting unarmed and without police protection but with LPC members surrounding him. There were tense moments, but the careful preparations of the LPC regarding the facilitation of the meeting paid off. For example, the LPC had only one microphone at the meeting, requiring all who wanted to speak or ask questions to wait their turn at the microphone. It slowed down the process and prevented sporadic, emotional outbursts. The critical moment was when the mother of the deceased took the microphone. Her son, she said, was her only child and breadwinner. However, she wanted peace. She did not want the death of her son to be the cause of more people dying. The only thing she asked was to know why it happened. The general responded with much sympathy and promised her that the matter would be investigated properly. On the whole, the event provided an opportunity for the community to vent its anger not in destructive violence but in dialogue with the relevant authority figure. It worked. Calm was restored to the community in anticipation of the legal processes that now had to take place (Spies 2010). The ability of the LPC to convince a police general to come down to the community level where the anger was boiling was a critical factor. The LPC could do that because of the linkage provided by the peace infrastructure.

South Africa also provides an example in which the linkage extended to the international level. Following the Boipatong massacre of June 1992—when forty-six residents of the Boipatong township were massacred, allegedly through the collaboration between IFP cadres and security forces—Nelson Mandela, leader of the ANC, asked the United Nations for a peacekeeping force. The United Nations responded by sending an observer team of sixty people called the UN Observer Mission in South Africa and asked other international organizations to also send observer teams. The Commonwealth, the European Community, and the Organization for African Unity complied, deploying about one hundred additional international monitors across the country. Their mandate specifically included collaboration with the Peace Accord structures and enhancing their monitoring capacity. They have, through their presence, contributed substantially to the role of LPCs (Sisk 1994; Gastrow 1995; Ball 1998). They have been particularly effective in strengthening the capacity of the peace structures to prevent violence through effective monitoring. Peter Gastrow (1995:73–74) mentioned the example of a large and peaceful Shaka's Day rally on September 24, 1992, in the KwaMashu township outside Durban. Shaka was the founder of the Zulu nation. Shaka's Day was therefore an important cultural event for the Zulu nation, but in the context of the politicization of Zulu ethnicity—in opposition to the ANC—it had huge potential for violence. The event was addressed by the leader of the IFP, Mangosuthu Buthelezi, and the Zulu king, Goodwill Zwelithini. The venue, which was in ANC territory and a no-go area for the IFP, had been the scene of many violent clashes in the past. The peacefulness of the event was made possible through the collaboration between local and regional peace committees and international observers. Those who were at the rally were almost unanimous in believing that the presence of the international observers played a significant role.

A major attribute of LPCs, therefore, is their ability to facilitate communication and collaboration between a broad spread of networks both horizontally within the community and vertically through their access to national and even international networks and resources. A formal peace infrastructure should intentionally facilitate effective linkage.

* * *

LPCs are not alternative local government structures or judicial mechanisms to ensure law and order. LPCs are formed when local actors take responsibility for the peace in their own community and decide to work jointly on the social reconstruction of their society. They do not enforce peace but facilitate consensus. They mobilize their respective networks and constituency bases to prevent violence and to support the jointly decided peacebuilding agenda. Where necessary, they mediate between local actors in order to unblock political or governance processes that are stuck in deadlock.

The contribution of an infrastructure for peace to the efficiency of LPCs is essential in supporting four critical tasks: strengthening the legitimacy of the LPC, galvanizing the role of local peacebuilders, providing access to specialist support, and facilitating effective horizontal and vertical linkages. To the extent that the formal infrastructure supports and enables these functions, it is relevant for local peacebuilding.

4

A Bit of Legroom
The Political Space for LPCs

LPCs always operate in a difficult and fluid political context. The national political consensus that is achieved when the decision to establish a peace infrastructure is made is never constant. Political agendas shift, new priorities develop, and the commitment to a joint peacebuilding process wanes. LPCs are vulnerable to the mood swings of national politics and the shifting modes of national political pressure on local conditions. Furthermore, most peacebuilding contexts are characterized by the strong presence of the international community and its engagement with the peacebuilding process. There are inherent tensions and challenges in this situation. International actors have competing agendas, and they seek to influence the peacebuilding agenda, at times in undue manners.

LPCs, therefore, operate in a context wherein a spectrum of national and international actors continuously affect their circumstances and their operations. This is par for the course, but it becomes a problem when national or international actors undermine the key ingredient of successful LPCs: local ownership. LPCs need some measure of independence to perform their role. They need a bit of legroom. If national or international political conditions cramp LPCs too much, they will smother them.

The ability of LPCs to operate with a measure of independence and efficiency is largely shaped by three questions: who exercises political control over the peace infrastructure, what place has been given to LPCs vis-à-vis the institutions of the state, and how local is the ownership of LPCs in the context of international support? The manner in which these questions are answered will establish, to a large extent, the legroom of LPCs to attend to local issues without excessive external manipulation or disturbance. These three matters, therefore, deserve our attention.

Multistakeholder Control

A peace process between former enemies cannot, by definition, be controlled solely by one of the parties. It has to be a collaborative effort. One-sided control of a peace infrastructure means that the basic intention of the peace infrastructure has been canceled out.

The effect of the reluctance to share control of the peace infrastructure is perhaps nowhere as clear as in Nepal. There are important lessons to learn from this context.

The search for peace in Nepal has been a multilayered and complex process. The most urgent task was to end the violence associated with the Maoist uprising in the country that led to almost thirteen thousand deaths between 1996 and 2006. The Maoists fought for a communist people's republic, which would bring about an end to the monarchy and its associated feudal system. However, it was not the armed insurgency that brought the rule of the monarch to an end but a massive popular demonstration initiated by civil society in April 2006. A subsequent peace agreement (the Comprehensive Peace Agreement of November 2006 between the Maoists and the established political parties) led to successful elections for a Constituent Assembly on April 10, 2008. The first significant act of the newly elected Constituent Assembly was to formally abolish the now-defunct monarchy and declare Nepal a federal democratic republic.

The Constituent Assembly has to negotiate a new constitution to give substance to the ideal of a *federal* democracy. Nepal, according to the census of 2001, has a highly diverse population, with 103 caste and ethnic groups and 92 living languages among a population of 22.7 million. Many of these groups had experienced marginalization under the monarchy, and their struggle for minority rights in the postmonarchy situation has at times been violent, especially in the Terai region during 2007–08. Progress in writing the new constitution has been frustratingly slow as deep levels of suspicion and a wide variety of seemingly incompatible agendas make the negotiation of an agreement extremely difficult. The collective political anxiety contributes to high levels of social disorder in society, with mass protests and strikes being the order of the day.

Of interest is the fact that Nepal has, fairly early in the peace process, recognized the need for an infrastructure for peace. The first structure, the Peace Negotiation Coordination Secretariat, was established as early as 2003. This structure evolved through various mutations to the establishment of a full-blown ministry in 2007, the Ministry of Peace and Reconstruction (MoPR).

One of the MoPR's key responsibilities, as stated in the Terms of Reference of the Ministry, was to provide administrative support to the implementation of LPCs (MoPR 2007). The decision to establish LPCs was first made in 2006 with the objective "to institutionalize the peace process at a local level" (Government of Nepal 2006). The decision was substantiated by references to the Janaandolan II (the popular uprising against the king) and the agreement with the Maoists at that stage (the so-called twelve-point agreement), which emphasized the need to ground the peace at the local level. However, the specific decision to establish LPCs was not, at the time, negotiated with the Maoists but was a unilateral move by the political parties then in government. Consequently, no progress was made. In 2007, the Maoists joined a unity government. The matter of LPCs was revisited, and terms of reference were adopted by the inclusive cabinet in August 2007. However, contrary to the recommendations for establishing LPCs that were contained in an implementation manual developed for the MoPR, the ministry issued a bureaucratic instruction in September 2007 to chief district officers to set up LPCs. This instruction led to the formation of more than thirty LPCs over subsequent months.

Soon after the instruction was sent out, the Maoists withdrew from government, leaving the newly formed bodies without political legitimacy. While in practice some LPCs continued to function (often including Maoists), the situation was far from optimal (NTTP 2008). Of importance is that one of the demands made by the Maoists as a precondition to return to an inclusive government was the establishment of what was called the High Level Peace Commission. The commission would be a multistakeholder body that would provide oversight of the peace process in general and the MoPR in particular. At that stage, the minister in charge of the MoPR was the secretary-general of the Nepali Congress, the ruling party. The Maoists were highly distrustful of this arrangement and believed the management of the MoPR were biased against them.

The stalemate continued until a new government was formed after the elections in 2008. The Maoists emerged as the strongest party much to the surprise of their political rivals and many political commentators alike. They immediately took control of the MoPR and made no effort to install the High Level Peace Commission. New terms of reference for LPCs were approved by the cabinet on October 16, 2008, and greater powers of control over LPCs were given to the MoPR—now under the control of a Maoist minister. Predictably, the opposition parties objected strongly, and in February 2009, a third draft of the terms of reference was accepted by the cabinet after the four major parties reached consensus on the details (Sapkota 2009). In May 2009, the Maoists withdrew from government in a standoff regarding the dismissal of the army chief. The control of the MoPR shifted hands again, this time to the Communist Party of Nepal (United Marxist-Leninist, or UML), the party that led the new government coalition. However, the terms of reference of LPCs remained unchanged, indicating that consensus around the framework remained intact.

The LPCs that were established in 2008 had to be disbanded and reconstituted when the second terms of reference—as drafted by the Maoist-led government—were approved. This process repeated itself when the third terms of reference were approved in February 2009. The appointment of secretaries (i.e., civil servants appointed to meet the administrative needs of LPCs) in itself indicated the level of political control over LPCs. The first batch of secretaries was recruited on contract in April 2009, and they were subsequently orientated and deployed. However, the secretaries' contracts were only valid until July 15—the end of the financial year. Most of the seventy-five appointees were Maoist cadres or sympathizers. Their contracts were not renewed by the MoPR now under UML control. A new recruitment drive was concluded in October 2009.

The detrimental impact on LPCs of the above history is all too clear. LPC members became frustrated and had low morale; communities were unaware of LPCs or unimpressed by them; and their impact was, in most locations, negligible (NTTP 2008; Chang 2009).

This sorry state of affairs should be viewed against the background of a country that presents the most compelling grounds for LPCs. It is a country with mind-boggling diversity. More important, every community portrays that diversity. Each district has its own distinct ethnic and caste composition, all with their particular histories and interests. Every community, therefore, is a very unique arena of conflict with its own deep-rooted identity issues and stark socioeconomic disparities. Furthermore, throughout the history of the kingdom, the elite in Kathmandu had neglected the rural areas, creating a deep center-periphery divide (Hutt 2004; Sharma 2006). In the postagreement phase, the lack of political stability at the center only served to deepen the isolation and neglect of the districts. The specific topography of Nepal—the extraordinary Himalayas with their deep valleys that leave many communities accessible on foot only after days of trekking—adds to the isolation of rural communities. The combined effect of these factors—district-specific diversity, very weak central authority, and the topography—necessitates a very specific focus on local peacebuilding.

There are, in addition, encouraging examples of the desire for and capacity to achieve local peace. Nepal has been a recipient of an extraordinary amount of attention by international peacebuilding CSOs. In 2005, for example, no less than seventeen organizations had offices and projects in Nepal. A significant amount of capacity building has therefore taken place. Much of these activities focused on human rights issues, strengthening the capacity to defend the human rights of threatened social groups. Even at the height of the military insurgency, these "human rights defenders" and "peace facilitators" were able to intervene effectively in specific crises.[37] They secured the release of hostages, facilitated agreements to repair damaged infrastructure, facilitated the effective resettlement of displaced persons, provided counseling to victims, and managed to reduce the number and extent of atrocities committed by security forces and rebels. They formed effective networks and established informal peace committees (UNDP 2004; Danida/HUGOU 2005). What was missing was a platform with sufficient political legitimacy that would enable the participation of all relevant local actors, including state officials and politicians. Also missing were productive linkages with national, political, and civil society resources (UNDP 2004:2).

Therefore, in spite of the compelling need for LPCs and the proven track record of competence in this respect at the local level, LPCs did not achieve their potential in Nepal for two main reasons. First, the failure to establish multistakeholder control of the infrastructure at the national level meant that the MoPR and the LPCs were but another pawn in the political chess game. The peace infrastructure was seen as an important political space to control, not a space for collaborative action to achieve the peace objectives that had been agreed to. Second, the manner in which the establishment of LPCs was reduced to a bureaucratic procedure did much harm. By reducing the process of establishing LPCs to faxed instructions, the creation of offices, and the appointment of secretaries, the peacebuilding potential of LPCs was seriously undermined.

It is not only Nepal where the urge to control the peace infrastructure has threatened its efficacy. In FYR Macedonia, some local councils appointed members to the LPC on behalf of ethnic communities, thereby depriving those communities of the opportunity to select persons that they trust to represent them. In Ethiopia, the country's president—a largely ceremonial position—chairs the National Peace Forum. Ethiopia, however, is still subject to a rebel military insurgency. In addition, the relationship between the ruling party and opposition parties is unhealthy to say the least. The most recent general elections in Ethiopia did not impress international observers (Gellaw 2010). In the context of a very dominant ruling party, the peace infrastructure in Ethiopia is clearly not meant to address political conflict;

---

37. INSEC (Informal Service Sector Center), a local CSO with offices in all the districts, has been at the forefront of most of these efforts.

rather, it is meant to deal with local-level interethnic conflict and "to eradicate harmful traditional practices" (Ministry of Federal Affairs 2010).

Fortunately there are examples of effective multiparty control of peace infrastructures. In Nicaragua, the National Reconciliation Commission consisted of four prominent individuals representing various sides of the conflict under the leadership of a cardinal who was a well-known government critic. In Northern Ireland, the Policing Board consisted of nineteen members: ten members of the legislative authority representing different political parties, and nine individuals from civil society elected for their specific expertise. In South Africa, the National Peace Secretariat, the body that in effect exercised the day-to-day management of the peace infrastructure, was chaired by a senior advocate. It furthermore consisted of five political representatives and a delegate of the Department of Justice. In Sierra Leone, the National Monitoring Committee consisted of all parties that were participating in the elections and representatives of the religious sector, civil society, the electoral commission, the police, and the statutory human rights commission. In Ghana, the National Peace Council consists mainly of eminent citizens elected for their gravitas and independence and is chaired by a highly respected cardinal of the Catholic Church.

These examples demonstrate the most appropriate option to structure the management of a peace infrastructure. The underlying logic is the same as that which guides the composition of LPCs, namely the insider-partial approach. It involves intermediaries from within the conflict setting who as individuals enjoy the trust and confidence of one side in the conflict but who as a team provide balance and equity (Lederach 1997:50). There are two models: The one composed of individuals who, by virtue of their personal stature, inspire confidence in them (as in Nicaragua and Ghana); the other including all protagonists but under the leadership of an independent and well-respected individual (as in South Africa and Sierra Leone). In all cases, decisions are made on the basis of consensus, thereby precluding the need to stack it with a majority of supporters.

Shared control of a peace infrastructure is therefore a necessary precondition for success. Conversely, one-sided control over and manipulation of the peace infrastructure is a sure cause of its inevitable failure.

Bureaucratic Support

Linked to the issue of political control is the manner of providing bureaucratic support to the peace infrastructure, including LPCs. Bureaucratic support has been organized in two ways. Some countries have set up their own systems, such as the dedicated ministries of Nepal and Côte d'Ivoire, or an alternative structure, such as the National Peace Secretariat in South Africa. In other countries, such as Ghana, Sierra Leone, or Macedonia, international organizations have provided the bulk of support.

There are two sets of problems associated with bureaucratic support. The first deals with the legitimacy of the service provider. If, as in Nepal, the service provider is seen as at the service of one actor, it is viewed with suspicion by the others. In South Africa, funding for the peace infrastructure came from the government budget. The money therefore had to be channeled through a government department—in this case the Department of Justice. It created a serious problem because of the deep distrust that the liberation movements had in government in general and this department in particular. The problem was addressed by a decision of the National Peace Secretariat, which was accepted by the government, to appoint its own staff and establish its own offices while retaining financial accountability to the Department of Justice. At a later stage, the task was transferred to the Department of the Interior, which was a less controversial department. In reality, therefore, the "peace offices" were physically and politically distinct from government but financially accountable to government. In the northern part of Nicaragua, similar issues of distrust existed regarding the role of the Organization of American States (OAS).

The second problem area is when bureaucratic decisions are insensitive to peacebuilding imperatives or principles. The example from Nepal is a good case in point—whereby the ministry sent out faxes to instruct the senior bureaucrats in districts to establish LPCs. In Côte d'Ivoire, some bureaucrats who supported LPCs approached conflict "in a bureaucratic manner," i.e., making decisions in authoritative and directive ways, with the interests of government and the ruling party close to heart (M'banda 2010). It effectively deprived LPCs of the ability to forge consensus.

In the design of a peace infrastructure, this matter should therefore receive careful thought. The legitimacy problem is best addressed by establishing multistakeholder control, as discussed earlier. The bureaucratic system, in other words, should be politically accountable to the multistakeholder body that provides political oversight, even if they were to be financially accountable to government or to an international organization. The manner of bureaucratic support is as important. Bureaucratic behavior in a peacebuilding context is not neutral. It either contributes to or distracts from the main task. It has to be channeled in ways that are acceptable to all parties and that are consistent with the peacebuilding objectives and strategies that have been agreed upon. In practice, it means that concerted efforts should be made to ensure that the relevant officials have a deeper understanding of the dynamics of the peace process and the challenges that are faced. Ideally, they should be engaged in orientations and discussions on the demands that the peacebuilding agenda places on their role.

LPCs and Statebuilding

The second issue regarding the political space available to LPCs is its relationship to other state institutions. How do infrastructures for peace and LPCs fit into the landscape of state institutions? Are LPCs adding to an already cluttered space of weak or dysfunctional committees? How is the expense of resources and energy on LPCs justified in light of pressing concerns to build the capacity of mainline state institutions?

It is, of course, important to avoid unnecessary duplication. In his report on peacebuilding, Secretary-General Ban Ki-moon (Secretary-General 2009, par. 22) stated: "Our collective task is to resist the temptation to create new mechanisms unless they are absolutely necessary. Rather, we should build on our experience of what works, and strengthen our capacities to ensure a more predictable, coherent and targeted approach to supporting countries as they emerge from conflict."

It is certainly not acceptable to establish a peace infrastructure with its supporting bureaucracy if there are existing institutions or mechanisms that can achieve the same objectives. The question regarding the usefulness of LPCs in the context of statebuilding, however, goes deeper than the need to avoid unnecessary duplication. Tanja Chopra (2009), in her assessment of Kenya's LPCs, went to the heart of the matter by asking whether peacebuilding contradicted statebuilding and whether LPCs were hindering the larger objective to ensure the effective functioning of the state's justice system.

The dilemma, Chopra said, is twofold. First, there are tensions between universal values (as pursued by international organizations) and local sociocultural concepts and practices. LPCs have been more effective than the state because the LPCs worked within and with local cultural paradigms. The values of local cultures, however, may contradict not only international values but also the constitutional values of the state. For example, in the pastoralist communities of Kenya, older men hold all authority, with women and the youth fulfilling subservient roles. The LPCs have largely respected these authority structures, although some LPCs, under donor pressure, included women representatives but with rather artificial results. The women attended meetings without participating in any meaningful way. To what extent, though, can the state compromise its constitutional obligation to ensure gender equity in order to appease local communities? Moreover, the practice of cattle rustling is culturally determined, as are the rules for dealing with transgressions. How far should the state go in accommodating practices that are clearly in violation of its own values and laws? The LPCs have achieved substantial success in mediating greater understanding between the state and these communities and in devising practical means to avoid further violence, but at what cost to the long-term integrity of the justice system?

The second dilemma is the possible contradiction between short- and long-term objectives. LPCs are effective because the state has failed in providing security and justice. LPCs, in this context, are ad hoc attempts to make up for the deficiencies of the state. The question is whether the success of LPCs adds to the further weakening of the state rather than to its strengthening. In the long term, the answer to the security and justice needs of a society cannot depend on ad hoc compromises at the local level. It has to be based on the constitution and the ability of the state to regulate conflict in terms of existing legislation.

These dilemmas deserve serious attention. There are, however, three types of contexts where LPCs have been employed where these dilemmas play out in different ways: LPCs in transitional contexts, LPCs in contexts of enduring diversity, and LPCs in the context of enduring state weakness.

LPCs in Transitional Contexts

In some cases, LPCs have been established as mechanisms to ease the transition to a new dispensation or as emergency mechanisms in the context of a weak state. They are therefore not envisaged as permanent features. They are part of the scaffolding of the peacebuilding period that should give way to permanent governance structures as soon as possible. In South Africa, the peace infrastructure was dismantled after the 1994 elections that put a legitimate government in power. In Nepal, the terms of reference of the LPCs specify that the LPCs will disband after the new constitution has been ratified and legitimate local governments are in place. In Northern Ireland, there are signs that its LPCs (the policing partnerships) may have run their course. In these contexts, LPCs have the task to ensure a sufficient level of social cohesion to enable local actors to collaborate in preventing further violence and dealing with the most urgent tasks of reconstruction. Once legitimate and capable governance has been restored, they will become obsolete.

LPCs in Contexts of Enduring Diversity

In other contexts, LPCs have been introduced as a permanent feature of the institutional landscape. In these cases, the objective has been to institutionalize a mechanism to facilitate, in an ongoing manner, matters of coexistence between diverse communities at the local level.

In FYR Macedonia, the Committees for Inter-Community Relations (CICRs) have been established through legislation. They form a subcommittee of the municipal council. Their task is to ensure that the council is sensitive to the needs of the whole spectrum of ethnic minorities. The council has the legal obligation to respond to the concerns of the committee. It is therefore obliged to take note of the impact that some of the council's actions may have on the relationships between ethnic groups. But the council is not obliged to act on the recommendations of the CICR. The role of the CICR is therefore primarily to facilitate dialogue between ethnic groups and to advise the council on the state of ethnic relations in the district.

In Serbia, there is a similar arrangement. The Law on Local Self-Government, 2002, authorized the establishment of CICRs "to deliberate issues related to the achievement, protection and promotion of national equality; and recommend to municipal council." The law further allows CICRs to challenge decisions of municipal councils before the constitutional court in cases where such decisions are deemed harmful for ethnic relations. The ability to take council to court gives these committees some teeth, but essentially they have an advisory role. The assumption, of course, is that such advice has been formulated through a consensus-seeking process between representatives of ethnic groups at the local level.

In Ghana, legislation was approved in 2011 to institutionalize a peace infrastructure by creating peace councils at national, regional, and district levels, as well as a bureaucratic and specialist support system. The decision to establish such an infrastructure came out of the nation's experience with local conflicts that demonstrated that there were shortcomings to the normal "law-and-order" approach. Such an approach did not fully resolve such conflicts (see chapter 6). The former minister of the interior of Ghana, in his motivation for an institutionalized peace infrastructure, referred to the fact that the government's law and order approach to community conflicts was not sufficient. "Our responses to these conflicts have at best been reactive. We have maintained a peacekeeping presence in the communities affected by violent conflict without being able to resolve the issues at stake." The security forces and the courts, in other words, have not been sufficiently successful in dealing with local-level conflicts. The vision with the infrastructure is to create "a dynamic environment where people can engage in their lawful activities confident that the institutions, mechanisms and capacities for mediating differences and grievance are effective and responsive" (Kan-Dapaah 2006). In other words, the emphasis is on creating mediation capacity to deal with community conflicts in light of the fact that mediation processes have shown greater promise.

In all three countries, therefore, the institutionalization of a peace infrastructure has not been an emergency measure or an ad hoc arrangement in the context of a fragile state. It has rather been a response to the demands that community conflicts place on the state system. In all these contexts, identity groups with a history of violent conflict have to coexist at the local level. LPCs are therefore a mechanism to facilitate coexistence and an alternative conflict resolution option.

The legal position of the LPCs has been well defined in all three cases. LPCs do not have any executive power or the power to arbitrate. Their role has been clearly defined as an advisory one. The LPCs are to facilitate dialogue, provide advice, and mediate conflict—in the context of the legal framework of the state. LPCs can therefore not override the constitution. They cannot forge agreements that compromise the rule of law. They seek solutions to complex issues of coexistence in contexts of diversity by primarily utilizing consensus-seeking methods.

The role of LPCs in these contexts can perhaps be best compared with alternative dispute resolution systems in civil litigation. The justice system of a growing number of countries recognizes and encourages the use of mediation to deal with certain cases of civil litigation based on the understanding that specific types of conflict cannot be dealt with effectively by a court of law or some other form of coercion. This is particularly the case where no criminal offence has been committed and where the conflict involves issues of relationships (such as in family disputes) and values (such as religious convictions). The understanding, furthermore, is that mediation will be the first step in efforts to resolve the conflict. When mediation fails, the matter may still be referred to the courts. The option of mediation does not preclude further access to the justice system.

The institutionalization of LPCs in these countries is therefore an interesting development that seeks to strengthen and widen the repertoire of state responses to community conflict. It recognizes the limitations of law-and-order approaches to certain types of community conflict, especially where issues of identity are at stake. It further acknowledges the relevance in such contexts of a conflict resolution methodology that seeks inclusive solutions on the basis of consensus.

LPCs in the Context of Enduring State Weakness

In Ken Menkhaus's (2008:29) analysis, peace committees, as in Wajir, "may be at the forefront of an emerging, largely unrecognized, hybrid form of statebuilding in weak states." The development in Wajir, he said, was an example of governance building in a "mediated state." Because of the lack of capacity of the state to govern its frontier regions, it was forced to rely on existing local traditional and civic institutions—that is, nonstate actors—to mediate its governance role. The government did not agree to this option because of a policy preference, but because it had no other choice. In essence, it meant "a forfeiting of a state's claim to 'omni-competence' within its borders; a new, flexible way to deal with the current 'messiness' that conventional inherited political structures have had great difficulty managing" (Menkhaus 2008:32).

In some cases of enduring state weakness, therefore, the role of LPCs has mutated into a hybrid form of governance. Kenya's peace committees in the northeast have indeed crossed over from being a mechanism for facilitating dialogue and mediating disputes to a mechanism that is ensuring compliance with the rules of the agreement. When the various declarations were negotiated, the LPCs acted as mediator, facilitating the agreement. They had no teeth at the time, but the agreement itself gave them teeth because it prescribed a role for them in the application of the rules that have been negotiated. From Nicaragua, there are also reports of LPCs that had to perform local government functions because of the weakness of the state (see next section).

Menkhaus (2008:34) observed that these are developments that citizens and international observers "may not prefer but which is not a matter of preference." There is, in other words, little choice in the matter. LPCs that play a governance role are the product of a reality that does not allow conventional remedies. I have argued that LPCs should ideally not exercise authority and that a clear role distinction should be maintained between LPCs as consensus-building mechanisms and as a governance mechanism. It may well be that in contexts such as the pastoralist areas of Kenya this distinction is far too academic, but I fear that the role confusion between facilitation and governance will hinder rather than help the peacebuilding process. There are worrying signs that, precisely because of the perception that LPCs wield important power, they have attracted power struggles and competition for control of key positions (Adan and Pkalya 2006; Chopra 2008a).

With reference to all three types of relationships with the state discussed herein, it is clear that there are unanswered questions and dilemmas. The question of whether LPCs should be involved in the act of governance in cases where there is no effective local government is certainly the most vexing. Regarding the question of the political legroom available to LPCs in their relationship to the state, the answer provided by countries where LPCs have been institutionalized is the most promising because of the clear description of the respective roles of the LPC and local government. Such role clarity guarantees, at least in principle, some measure of independence for LPCs from political manipulation.

Local Ownership and International Actors

The third issue to consider regarding the political space for LPCs is the extent to which they are beholden to international actors. Donor agencies, international nongovernmental organizations, regional organizations, and the United Nations have been involved in the promotion, establishment, and support of LPCs. Only South Africa and Northern Ireland did not depend on international funding or other forms of support to establish and maintain their peace infrastructures. In all the other cases, nonnational actors played important roles: for example, the Organization for Security and Co-operation in Europe in Macedonia; faith-based organizations and the OAS in Nicaragua; the United Nations in Ghana, Kenya, Côte d'Ivoire, and Sierra Leone; the Academy for Educational Development and the Asia Foundation in Nepal; the German Gesellschaft für Internationale Zusammenarbeit in Malawi; the International Foundation for Electoral Systems (IFES) in Sierra Leone, etc. These roles involved substantial inputs ranging from raising awareness about the concept of an infrastructure and promoting its benefits to the specific design of the infrastructure, capacity building for its implementation, and funding for its operation.

The role of international actors in peacebuilding in general poses a serious dilemma (Weinstein 2005[38]; Fortna 2008; Jarstad and Sisk 2008). Anna Jarstad and Timothy Sisk (2008) have referred to it as the "systemic dilemma"—the trade-off between efficiency and local ownership. International support enhances the efficiency of peacebuilding but dilutes local ownership. With the involvement of international actors efficient systems can be designed, set up, and funded. This contrasts with the indecision, confusion, and lack of capacity that often characterizes post-agreement contexts. Yet, as long as the critical decisions in peacebuilding are made by actors that

---

38. Jeremy Weinstein contrasted "autonomous recovery" with "aided recovery" and argued the benefits of the former. A key dimension of his argument is the importance of a social compact between leaders and the governed. Such a compact is successfully forged by strong victors of an armed conflict but is absent in contexts where the inviolability of boundaries and the dependence of leaders on international aid flows (and not taxation) preclude the need for such a compact. Building effective state institutions, he argues, entails much more than bureaucracy or a set of rules recorded on paper. Effective institutions "are the result of a bargain—a social compact between rulers and constituents—and it is the nature of that compact that shapes the existence, structure, and membership of the institutions of government" (2005:8). Such a bargain cannot be forged when the initiative for and control of institution building is externally located.

are not accountable to local citizens, democratization, and thereby the long-term sustainability of peace, suffers.

The problem is not that the broader international community does not recognize the value of local ownership. It has in fact been widely embraced (see OECD-DAC 2001; Nathan 2007; Secretary-General 2009; OECD-DAC 2010). The World Bank, in its *World Development Report 2011*, concluded that the most important strategy to address the combined impact of violence, insecurity, and poverty on large sections of the world population is to strengthen legitimate institutions and governance. The emphasis is on *legitimate* institutions. Consequently, there should be continuous interaction between confidence building and the transformation of institutions (World Bank 2011:12). The transformation of institutions, in other words, is not possible without sufficient citizen confidence in the institutions, actors, and the processes that are followed (see also INCAF 2010, OECD 2010). If the citizens do not own the transformation process, the results invariably disappoint.

While this growing international consensus is welcome, the problem is that, in the trade-off between efficiency and local ownership, efficiency often wins. The models and programs of the international community still at times end up being imposed in a manner that reflects "a mixture of arrogance and naivety" (Nathan 2007:2–3). Some of the reasons for the behavior of international actors include a sense of superiority; an underestimation of the difficulties of transformation, blaming setbacks on local incompetence; and the nature of the financial and bureaucratic systems of donors that require programs with a high level of predetermined detail, inhibiting flexibility and responsiveness to local circumstances (Nathan 2007; see also Bush 2004, 2005).

The same dilemma is also acute regarding peacebuilding at the local level. Intervention by international actors at the local level offers order and progress but risks superficiality and lack of sustainability because the actors are not rooted in the local context and culture. International actors have the capacity to design infrastructures for peace and facilitate their implementation at bureaucratic and structural levels, but they cannot ensure the quality of local commitment to the process. International actors are also not accountable to local communities. They determine local processes through the imposition of their agendas, ideas, and, most crucially, their funding. In so doing, they undermine, albeit unwittingly, local ownership—the one indispensable condition for successful local peacebuilding.

The most successful examples of local peacebuilding are those that are locally initiated, owned, and managed, such as the examples of Wajir (Kenya) and Mpumalanga (KwaZulu-Natal, South Africa). The Wajir LPC in Kenya was established after CSOs had left the area due to the violence that had occurred. Their departure, however, became "a blessing in disguise" as their absence gave the communities the opportunity to take charge and begin their own peace initiatives (Adan and Pkalya 2006:7). Following their success, the model was replicated in a number of neighboring districts, this time at the initiative of CSOs (who, by now, returned) and with their funding support. These LPCs were less rooted in and accountable to communities as they were more beholden to their initiators and funders. There is even evidence of competition between CSOs in this matter, resulting in more than one LPC established in some districts. Payment of sitting fees further intensified competition between LPCs—a behavior that Mohamud Adan and Ruto Pkalya correctly labeled as "uncouth" (2006:19).

The systemic dilemma, however, is not solely caused by international actors. Local ownership is a double-edged sword because it conveys power to local actors, some of whom operate with rather opportunistic and even criminal objectives. Local ownership is not to be viewed too romantically. Anton Harber (2011), for example, provided a description of the Diepsloot community, a postapartheid informal settlement in South Africa of approximately two hundred thousand people that has become known for violent protest activities (the so-called service delivery protests that have become endemic in South Africa as a response to poor service delivery at the local level) and xenophobic violence. The state has been largely absent since its establishment, and therefore none of the state's rules or regulations applied because no one implemented them. Social and political structures grew in organic manners, and the competition to control access to political and economic resources and opportunities was, at times, ruthless. While much has happened that was inspiring and symptomatic of the resilience, humanity, and creativity of people, some of the structures thus created were corrupted and crossed the line into protection rackets. More relevant to the issue of ownership, the so-called gatekeepers, those who control access to the community (including external aid), do not necessarily act in the interest of the whole community but often in the exclusive interest of a specific clique (see also Smith 2004; Paffenholz 2005; Schmelzle 2005).

Ownership, furthermore, is not a constant factor but is as fluid as the more general political situation. The level of commitment to peacebuilding invariably differs within a community and within a single party. But it also varies over time with parties losing or gaining interest in the process as the advantages or disadvantages of the peacebuilding process become clearer.

The dilemma between externally driven efficiency and local ownership is therefore not easily solved, and no recipe exists that would guarantee success. From the survey of peace infrastructures that informs this study, three types of relationships between the international community and LPCs can be distinguished. These are not three watertight categories, rather three different positions on a spectrum of possibilities.

The first example is from Nicaragua—more specifically, the southern and eastern parts of Nicaragua, where international faith-based organizations played a major role in supporting LPCs. What distinguished their approach was that the bulk of the engagement between local and international actors took place at the middle and local levels and not at the national or international levels.

The history of LPCs in Nicaragua dates back to the 1980s. At the peak of the civil war, religious leaders from the Catholic Church and Evangelical churches joined forces to negotiate conflict-free zones and to foster dialogue between the Sandinistas and the contras (Spalding 1999). They formed small, informal "peace commissions" whose tasks included documenting and investigating human rights violations, advocating on behalf of victims, and sharing credible information (Kauffman 1994). They created an "unprecedented space for dialogue" between Sandinistas and contras (Preston 1987) and were able to negotiate peace zones to allow peasants to plant crops during the war (Paul 1997).

With the thawing of the Cold War in the middle to late 1980s, Costa Rican president Oscar Arias initiated a series of negotiations and agreements between Central American governments that resulted in the Esquipulas Peace Accord of 1987. The objective was to stabilize the whole Central American region. The peace accord consisted of a series of steps leading to cease-fires and demobilization in all the wars in the region. It led to a cease-fire agreement in Nicaragua signed in 1988.

The Esquipulas process focused specifically on achieving cease-fires and demobilization and gave little attention to an articulation of the causes of the conflict or the grievances of opposing sides (Spalding 1999). It envisaged National Reconciliation Commissions, though, that would be tasked with internal reconciliation processes. In Nicaragua, President Daniel Ortega moved quickly to establish a National Reconciliation Commission composed of four prominent individuals representing different sides of the conflict. Its principal task was to monitor and verify the cease-fire. Going beyond the requirements of the accord, Ortega tasked the National Reconciliation Commission with establishing a more extensive internal structure that included region-specific commissions and an extensive network of local commissions to promote in-

ternal reconciliation. It led to the formation of region-specific peace commissions, such as the East Coast commission that focused specifically on the
conflict between the Sandinistas and an indigenous resistance movement
(Lederach 1997:50). It also led to the formation of numerous *comisiones de
paz* (peace commissions) at the local level. Thus, possibly the world's first
formal infrastructure for peace was established that included LPCs.

By 1987, twenty-eight LPCs were established in the area around Nueva
Guinea in the south, and by 1990, there were sixty (Paul 1997). Most LPCs
had five members: an evangelical pastor, a Catholic delegate, a representative
of the Nicaraguan Red Cross, the opposition party, and the government.
Zonal commissions oversaw and directed the work of the LPCs since the
creation of the National Reconciliation Commission. The demobilization
process, however, collapsed quickly. The majority of contra combatants had
rearmed by 1991. By 1997, over two thousand people had died because of
consequent violence involving the Sandinista government and the rearmed
combatants (or *rearmados*) (Paul 1997). The rearmados did not present a
unitary front anymore but were fractured, necessitating separate agreements
with each small component. The LPCs continued to mediate local agreements and facilitated the reintegration of combatants into society. In a context characterized by "the grand absence of the government" in many rural
communities, the LPCs mediated land and domestic conflicts and maintained a semblance of order in an otherwise government-less situation (Paul
1997:4). Their work required a level of commitment and service that was
impressive and even heroic. For example, a contra commander, Martin Za-
vala, had fled with 190 contra combatants to the mountains within months
of their disarmament. These fighters did not lay down their weapons until
1994 and only after LPC members had spent months in the mountains engaging them in dialogue and taking actions, at times risking their own lives,
to ensure the safety of the rearmados (Paul 1997).

These LPCs clearly demonstrated a high level of local ownership, which
did not mean, however, that there was no input by the international community. Under the auspices of the Evangelical Committee for Aid and Development (CEPAD), an ecumenical arm of the Protestant churches, and the
Catholic Church, a substantial amount of training in conflict transformation
took place, as well as institutional strengthening of the churches' capacity
to fulfill this role. External (i.e., non-Nicaraguan) individuals and churches
played a critical role in this respect. All the capacity-building initiatives
resulted in the development of expertise and some uniformity of practice
(Kumar 1999; Spalding 1999). The context of the peace commissions in
Nicaragua, in fact, enriched the conflict transformation literature with two

important concepts, insider-partials (as discussed earlier) and "elicitive training." Both were coined by John Paul Lederach, who was at the time a member of the zonal committee in the east—in spite of not being a Nicaraguan.

Elicitive training is an important concept that not only explains a specific training model but also points to a particular understanding of the relationship between international actors and local ownership. Lederach (1995, 1997) has coined this term in contrast to "prescriptive training"—the approach that assumes that the recipients of training know nothing or very little. In prescriptive training, the expert trainer (often someone from the West) has to transfer knowledge and skills to the recipients, whose main task is to understand and memorize. In the process, the cultural assumptions and values of the West are transferred in uncritical and arrogant manners.

In contrast to this approach, elicitive training makes two assumptions. The first is that it is indeed necessary to engage and challenge the cultural context. The "old" has in some ways become insufficient because of the challenges of violent conflict. There is need for new ideas and approaches. The second assumption is that local actors are not empty vessels but have a deep knowledge of their own context and culture. A productive transfer of ideas can take place only when there is substantial dialogue between trainer and participants that uncovers the true meaning and relevance of contextual understandings and responses to conflict on all sides and that communicates new insights in manners that link the new and the old. The new does not replace the old or declare it inferior. Rather, the quest of elicitive training is to forge a productive, creative fusion of the existing understanding of local actors and the possibilities that new ideas open up.

The distinctive characteristic of the engagement of international actors with the LPCs in the south of Nicaragua, therefore, was the fact that much elicitive training had taken place. The input of international actors was also not primarily at the national level but rather at the middle level (that of church leadership in the districts). The peace infrastructure could, as a result, be grafted onto existing structures and experiences. It resulted in a high level of local ownership.

The second example of the manner in which international actors supported LPCs is by far the dominant approach. The distinctive characteristic, in these cases, is that the international actors are deeply involved in promoting the concept of an infrastructure, the design of the infrastructure, setting up the structures and procedures of the infrastructure, providing training to key role players, and funding the enterprise. However, the explicit objective of these international actors is not to impose; the assumption is rather that productive collaboration takes place and that the political decisions are taken by national actors. This approach is therefore premised on the assumption that local ownership is an indispensable precondition to success. Outcomes, however, vary depending on success in managing the inherent "systemic dilemma."

The case of Sierra Leone provides an illustration of a relatively successful intervention. The UN Integrated Office in Sierra Leone (UNIOSIL), in collaboration with UNDP and the UN Department of Political Affairs (DPA), appointed a technical adviser in 2006 to support internal peacebuilding, especially in view of the looming elections of 2007. The adviser, Clever Nyathi, found a completely dysfunctional Political Parties Registration Commission (PPRC)—the statutory body tasked with regulating the behavior of political parties. As a result, the setting up of an infrastructure for peace entailed a hugely challenging list of tasks: developing the administrative capacity of the PPRC, orienting the PPRC toward the best approach to follow, supporting the PPRC to facilitate a code of conduct for political parties, establishing and supporting a National Code of Conduct Monitoring Committee, and establishing, introducing, and supporting district committees. UNIOSIL was ably supported in this tack by the IFES. The input by these service providers was indeed substantial. In fact, without their input very little would have happened. Yet the actual work of violence prevention was done admirably by Sierra Leonians, both at the local and national level.[39] They took ownership of the peace infrastructure and utilized it in pursuit of their own interest in peace. UNIOSIL and IFES have not defused a single local crisis—the LPCs have defused many.

In Ghana, UNDP/DPA played a similar role. The case study of Ghana will be discussed in detail in chapter 6, but of importance here is that when parliament, in 2011, accepted the bill to institutionalize a peace infrastructure, it was done with complete bipartisan support and much enthusiasm. It demonstrated a high level of national ownership of the peace infrastructure. This milestone was achieved seven years after UNDP/DPA appointed Ozonnia Ojielo as peace and development adviser in Ghana. Over seven years, Ojielo and his successor, Clever Nyathi, provided patient and skillful support toward the building of this infrastructure. It's noteworthy that possibly the most successful process to institutionalize a peace infrastructure took much patience and time and still is far from complete. It should serve as a warning against any notion of quick rollouts.

What these examples point to is that it is possible to deal successfully with the systemic dilemma when the international community acts in a manner that pays more than lip service to the principle of local ownership. It

---

39. For a more detailed description, see chapter 6.

requires, however, that key personnel act with considerable skill in building trust and promoting productive collaboration.

The third example of how international actors supported LPCs again comes from Nicaragua, but this time from the central and northern regions of the country. On August 7, 1989, at a meeting of Central American presidents in Tela, Honduras, the International Support and Verification Commission (La Comisión Internacional de Apoyo y Verificación, or CIAV) of the OAS was constituted. Its mandate was to support and oversee the demobilization, repatriation, and voluntary resettlement of contra fighters and their families and to ensure the full exercise of their fundamental rights. Central and northern Nicaragua experienced the bulk of violence during the war and produced the majority of refugees. The CIAV assumed primary responsibility for the care of the disarmed combatants, family members, and repatriated individuals (Lincoln and Sereseres 2000).

In the first years of operation, the CIAV helped fill an institutional vacuum and mitigate local conflicts in the most violent areas through mediation and human rights verification. By the end of 1990, when the contras began to rearm, the CIAV had negotiated thirty agreements between rearmados factions and the government and helped to demobilize twenty thousand rearmed combatants (Paz 2005). Most of this work, however, was done by CIAV staff members, consisting of professionals recruited throughout Latin America and a small number of Nicaraguans. In 1994, as the CIAV mandate neared its end, the mission sought to ensure that its peacebuilding and human rights work continued after it left the country through the development of LPCs, particularly in the most highly conflicted areas. The absence of state institutions or even CSOs that would have been able to assume conflict resolution meant a dearth of legitimate public mechanisms for arbitration of disputes and criminal punishment (Spehar 2000). The primary mission of the LPCs would be the defense of human rights and promotion of peace and assuming the responsibilities of verification, conflict resolution, and mediation upon the withdrawal of the CIAV. It was, therefore, by design a mixed and rather incompatible collection of tasks envisaged for the LPCs, but noteworthy for our purposes because it included community peacebuilding and conflict resolution.

By 1995, the CIAV supported the creation of ninety-six LPCs (Spehar 2000). However, the LPCs in the north did not achieve the same quality of impact as their counterparts in the south (Paul 1997). A number of reasons may explain this situation. The violence in the north was more intense than in the south, pointing to local dynamics that might have made the operation of LPCs in the north more problematic. Furthermore, the LPCs in the north were led by *campesinos* (farm workers), while those in the south were led by local church leaders. The latter suggest a higher level of leadership capacity. Of major importance, though, is the fact that the quality of local ownership that was achieved in the south was not matched in the north, and that the principal implementing agent of LPCs in the south, the churches, enjoyed much higher levels of legitimacy than CIAV in the north.

The CIAV mission had been criticized on a number of grounds. First, the mission was seen by some as an instrument of the US government. Ninety-seven percent of its total budget was funded by the US Agency for International Development (USAID). The mission was perceived, at best, as caught between the wishes of its funder and of the OAS bureaucracy, and at worst, not designed to be politically neutral. A perception, whether correct or not, developed that the mission was biased in favor of protecting the contras (Child 1992; Spalding 1999).

Second, the high profile of Argentine officials in the CIAV mission generated negative feelings in some circles. The Argentines were linked by association with the Argentine military and intelligence officers who had first trained and armed the contras in 1980–81. It created a lasting and negative perception, however unfair (Child 1992:86).

Third, the CIAV mission was too late in developing local capacity. The formation of LPCs was too much of an afterthought and not a central ingredient of its strategy (Paul 1997; Bendaña 1999). In the dilemma between efficiency and local ownership, CIAV chose efficiency and initially achieved good results—but at the cost of sustainability.

On the whole, therefore, the CIAV's attempt to establish LPCs was not highly successful because it smacked too much of an external intervention that was tainted by perceptions of political partiality and driven by the need to complete a task that was defined by international actors rather than by local decision and ownership.

* * *

In summary, from the examples highlighted in this chapter, it is clear that the systemic dilemma is not managed by precooked formulas but rather by the manner in which the relationship between international actors and all relevant stakeholders is managed. The development of perceptions of political bias is quite harmful, whereas an approach such as the one implicit in "elicitive training" is certainly healthy. The involvement of international actors is, in most contexts, necessary and potentially constructive, but only in so far as they succeed in galvanizing and enabling local ownership.

5

Gluing the Shattered Vase
Social Reconstruction at the Local Level

"Milošević did not kill—our neighbors were killing."

This comment, made to the research team of Eric Stover and Harvey Weinstein (2004:303) by a male Croat respondent of Vukovar, Croatia, captures the rationale for social reconstruction at the local level in a manner that few theoretical discussions can. Slobodan Milošević, the former president of Yugoslavia and leader of the nationalist Serbian campaign to "cleanse" Serbia of non-Serbian elements, is possibly one of the best examples of an "ethnic entrepreneur"—someone who deliberately manipulates ethnic identity in the pursuit of a political agenda. The mobilization of ethnicity for political purposes was in fact perpetrated by all the main actors in the drama of Yugoslavia's ethnic deconstruction and was deliberate and cynical. The violence, in other words, was designed at the top and implemented from above. Yet the actual killing and raping was done by neighbors, colleagues, and former classmates (Corkalo, Ajdukovic et al. 2004). As a consequence, the very fabric of the social cohesion of local communities was ruptured. What existed in terms of interethnic coexistence and civic collaboration lay shattered—like a beautiful, expensive but fragile vase broken into pieces. In the eyes of community members, neighbors were guiltier than anyone else of the atrocities that had been committed. Most of all, they were guilty of betrayal—either factually so or, at a minimum, because they had done nothing to warn their neighbors of what was to come (Ajdukovic and Corkalo 2004).

In all the research and planning done to address postviolent reconstruction, little attention has yet been paid to the fact that people who once were neighbors, who then had learned to see each other as the enemy, now have to learn to live together again. Most of the focus in international and national planning is on institution building and physical reconstruction. These tasks are clearly important, but, as Jodi Halpern and Harvey Weinstein (2004:304) argue, it is the interpersonal ruins, rather than the ruined buildings and institutions, that pose the greatest challenge for rebuilding society. Efforts to glue the vase of social cohesion together again have, to date, been made mostly by international and local CSOs. Their projects, in many instances, were innovative and inspiring (see Van Tongeren, Brenk et al. 2005). Yet these efforts suffered from the familiar dilemmas of CSO work: the piecemeal quality of many of their interventions, their lack of legitimacy in the eyes of important stakeholders, and their vulnerability to the whims of funders.

Therefore, there are two questions that have to be addressed: what is the potential contribution of LPCs in addressing the deficit in social cohesion at the local level in postviolence situations, and how should the interpersonal ruins be reconstructed?

Social Reconstruction

Social reconstruction is the term favored by Stover and Weinstein (2004) for all the collective "mechanisms of social repair" needed in war-torn societies.[40] It describes the process in a community, following its violent destruction, that normalizes individual and social functioning and reestablishes a sufficient level of social cohesion—namely, a level of social functioning where sufficient communication and collaboration takes place across the conflict divide to enable constructive, joint attention to matters of common concern.

The reestablishment of normality, however, does not imply that the past can or must be reconstructed faultlessly. It should rather refer to a transformed reality where a new sense of normality has been achieved, one with greater levels of inclusion, fairness, and accommodation. A return to normality without addressing some of the deeper causes of the conflict can only mean that the table is being set for a repeat of the violence.

Social reconstruction at the local level relies very much on local ownership and agency. The policies and acts of the national government and the international community may create an environment that is favorable to social reconstruction, but in the final analysis, the social reconstruction of a community can only reach a level of functioning that is acceptable to the majority of its members. "It is a level on which they recognize that some common inter-

---

40. They have suggested it as an alternative term for reconciliation because the latter was ambiguous and overworked. I do find "social reconstruction" a more precise and less sentimental description than reconciliation. Reconciliation is, however, still widely used and is, in some contexts, more appropriate. When, for example, referring specifically to the offering and receiving of forgiveness as an aspect of the process of restoring relationships, reconciliation has a more appropriate feel. In their edited volume, Stover and Weinstein continued to use reconciliation and social reconstruction more or less as synonyms, and I am happy to follow their example.

ests cannot be accomplished through individual efforts, or through separate interest groups, or by the state, but that the members of that community need to reach an agreement" (Ajdukovic in Corkalo, Ajdukovic et al. 2004:152). In other words, the pace of social reconstruction is set by members of the community themselves and driven by their own needs and interests.

It is possible, though, to stimulate and support the process of social reconstruction in communities in a manner that recognizes the importance of local interests and agency. In discussing the contribution of peace infrastructures in this respect, this chapter focuses on two key areas of the social reconstruction process—namely, the facilitation of dialogue and the complex interconnectedness of justice and reconciliation at the local level. Case studies of Northern Ireland, Kenya, Rwanda, and East Timor will inform the discussion.

Dialogue

Dialogue is at the heart of the consensus-building methodology. In fact, without dialogue no consensus building is possible. In the peacebuilding field, differences may exist about the appropriateness of specific strategies to facilitate dialogue, but not on the question of whether dialogue itself is necessary.[41] The objective with dialogue is to achieve a level of communication between parties in conflict that will uncover deeper fears, needs, interests, and concerns. Such communication produces a better mutual understanding, which enables processes of conflict transformation (Pruitt and Thomas 2007; UNDESA 2007). Dialogue is therefore the enabling catalyst of conflict transformation. The quality of dialogue determines the potential for moving away from violence toward an inclusive future.

There are three broad categories of dialogue—namely, dialogue to support the search for mutually acceptable outcomes to intractable problems, dialogue to overcome prejudice and misunderstanding and build trust, and dialogue to deconstruct violence-producing discourses and foster nonviolence discourses (Ramsbotham, Woodhouse et al. 2005). The latter two categories are particularly relevant for our current topic. Two interlinked questions must be considered. First, has dialogue as a strategy succeeded in enabling postviolence social repair at the local level? In other words, has concerted

---

41. The importance of dialogue is so central to the larger peacebuilding field that it almost has the status of an article of faith. Ramsbotham et al. (2005) have made the telling point that none of the standard approaches to dialogue take the phenomenon of radical political disagreement or deep-value conflicts—where the contradictions are indeed mutually exclusive—sufficiently serious. It is in fact characteristic of the approach that the limitations to the usefulness of dialogue are not recognized nor considered. This blind spot is not helpful. A better understanding of its limitations will certainly enhance the application of dialogue. For a detailed treatment of the topic, see Oliver Ramsbotham (2010).

efforts at facilitating dialogue contributed to greater social cohesion? Second, is it feasible to build a national infrastructure to support such local dialogue projects? The experiences of Northern Ireland and Kenya offer insights into these questions.

Two Cases of Dialogue: Northern Ireland and Kenya

Northern Ireland

In Northern Ireland, a peace infrastructure was established to facilitate dialogue on a very specific issue: policing. Policing was controversial in Northern Ireland from the moment of its birth in 1921 when it was partitioned off from the Republic of Ireland. The Unionists, who were mostly Protestant and loyal to Great Britain, felt threatened and took the necessary steps to ensure their security. Apart from their reliance on the security forces of Great Britain, the Royal Ulster Constabulary (RUC) was equipped with powers and resources to maintain stability and provide security. For example, the Ulster Special Constabulary (USC, or B-Specials) was a quasi-military force established in 1920 with a specific focus on countering insurgency. It was almost exclusively Protestant and Unionist. Whereas Unionists viewed the USC as a valiant bulwark against illegal insurgency and terrorism, the Republican minority in Northern Ireland saw it as a brutal instrument used to enforce their marginalization in society. The USC was disbanded in 1970.

These perceptions also spilled over onto the RUC in general. The RUC was on the whole staffed by Protestants (in 1998 88.1 percent of members were Protestant and 8 percent Catholic). They were seen by the Republicans as nothing less than "the armed wing of Unionism" and the key bulwark of "British occupation." They were the defenders of the state during a severe contestation over the legitimacy of the state. They became the visible and deeply resented "symbols of oppression." For the Unionists, however, they were heroes in the front-line against terrorism—the "custodians of nationhood" (Lloyd 1999; Patten Commission 1999).

The transformation of these deep-seated perceptions of the police was therefore a necessary peacebuilding objective. The Good Friday Agreement (1998) acknowledged the relevance and sensitivity of police reform by making provision for the establishment of a commission to advise on the best way to transform policing. One of the instructions given to the Patten Commission (as it became known after its chairperson, Lord Chris Patten) was to ensure that "there are clearly established arrangements enabling local people, and their political representatives, to articulate their views and concerns about policing and to establish publicly policing priorities and influence policing policies, subject to safeguards to ensure police impartiality and freedom from partisan political control" (1998:25).

The Patten Commission recognized that "the issue of policing is at the heart of many of the problems that politicians have been unable to resolve in Northern Ireland" (Patten Commission 1999:2). It recommended the establishment of a Policing Board that would hold the chief constable to account and that would have to approve annual policing plans to determine policing priorities. In addition, it recommended the formation of District Policing Partnership Boards in all the districts. All these bodies would consist of representatives of political parties across the spectrum, as well as independent members from civil society appointed for their stature or independent knowledge of policing issues. Elected representatives would always have the majority over civil society representatives. Patten's idea with these bodies was to ensure a constant dialogue at local levels between the police and the community—a mechanism to compel the more powerful actor, the police, to engage with the community (Ryan 2008). In this way, consensus would be built within a divided community on priorities for policing, and trust would be restored across the spectrum of the community in the police as a professional service.

The Patten Commission report was received with alarm in Unionist circles. David Trimble, leader of the Ulster Unionist Party (UUP), called it the "shoddiest report in 35 years" (*Guardian* 1999). Part of his concern was that the police force would "be dominated by politicians and district policing partnerships, again dominated by politicians—and constructed, particularly with the gerrymandering of Belfast, in such a way as to enable certain paramilitary-related politicians [*read: Sinn Féin*] to exercise undue influence over policing" (Hillyard and Tomlinson 2000; italicized note is author's).

The recommendations of the Patten Commission had to be enacted in law. The Police (Northern Ireland) Act of 2000 contained, in light of the controversy raised, some inevitable and substantial compromises. The bill was criticized for completely rejecting the Patten Commission report's core project. "The [Patten Commission report's] structure of a central Police Board and district partnerships is retained, but both levels are stripped of effective powers and many democratic elements are neutralized" (Hillyard and Tomlinson 2000). The complaints related specifically to the following: (1) District Policing Partnerships (DPPs; note how the word "Board" was dropped) would have only "consultative powers," leaving final decision making with the police; (2) persons convicted of terrorist offences would not be allowed to serve on the DPPs, thereby preventing Sinn Féin (who was mostly affected by this stipulation) from nominating some community leaders on the DPPs;

and (3) DPPs would not be allowed to deal with the "unfinished business" of the past. They were strictly confined to the present and future. By opting for this model, Barry Ryan (2008) stated, the potential of DPPs to facilitate the deliberations needed in such divided communities was curtailed.

While the Democratic Unionist Party (DUP), the UUP, and the Social Democratic and Labour Party accepted the bill, Sinn Féin rejected it. It refused to take up the two seats on the Policing Board that it was entitled to and encouraged all Republicans not to serve on DPPs, stating: "They have whittled down the powers of the partnerships in terms of accountability so you have a local community body to which the RUC Chief might speak but it has no actual accountability" (in Ryan 2008). It was only in late January 2007 that the general membership of Sinn Féin decided to support policing reforms. Subsequently it joined the Policing Board and DPPs. Almost ten years after the signing of the Good Friday Accord, therefore, the infrastructure put in place to facilitate police reform could claim to have the support of all the main actors.

Surveys of citizens' perceptions and attitudes of policing in general and the DPPs in particular have been conducted regularly (in 2003, 2004, 2006, and the latest one in February 2008). The findings support the view expressed in 2008 by Sir Hugh Orde, chief constable of the Police Service of Northern Ireland (PSNI)—as the police was now formally called. He said that policing has come through "massive changes" with positive results (Orde 2008).

According to the February 2008 survey, more Catholics (33 percent) than Protestants (30 percent) were generally satisfied with policing in their districts. The satisfaction of Protestants has in fact dropped by a significant 4 percent since 2006, mainly due to perceptions that the justice system was too lenient. The bulk of respondents had neutral attitudes toward the police (Catholics 40 percent and Protestants 38 percent), while those dissatisfied were 25 percent among Catholics and 27 percent among Protestants. What is striking is the extent to which attitudes toward the police have normalized. The negative perception regarding policing among Catholics has, to a large extent, been overcome. As another example, 83 percent of Protestants believe that people are willing to engage with the police, and 77 percent of Catholics believe the same. It is also noteworthy that public views regarding DPPs did not show significant sectarian variance. If anything, Catholics were more favorably disposed towards DPP than Protestants (Northern Ireland Statistics and Research Agency 2008).

The lingering impact of the "troubles" can still be seen, though, when respondents were asked to state why people would be unwilling to engage the police. In this respect, 60 percent of Protestants blamed the justice system that was too lenient, while 45 percent of Catholics had the same view. Dislike or fear of the police was mentioned as a factor by 20 precent of Protestants and 34 percent of Catholics. A person's political opinion mattered for 20 percent of Protestants and 33 percent of Catholics, while the history of the troubles was a factor for 12 percent of Protestants and 32 percent of Catholics. Only 8 percent of Protestants thought that the police were not representative of their community compared to 19 percent of Catholics.

However, these statistics do not capture the depth of the resentment amongst minorities who still distrust the police. The decision by Sinn Féin to support the PSNI has led to a number of defections from the party (Rusk 2008). More worrying was the threat to use violence. On December 9, 2007, for example, the Irish Republican Liberation Army, a dissident group, issued a statement vowing to kill Sinn Féin members who sit on DPPs (Breed 2007). Sinn Féin ignored the threat.

What have we learned from the experience in Northern Ireland? First, it is significant that the political elite of Northern Ireland have realized the need to decentralize the peacebuilding process to local levels. In this case, the peacebuilding infrastructure had a fairly narrow focus on policing, but policing was such a central issue that it was nonetheless hugely relevant and important.

Second, the distinctive feature of this infrastructure is its emphasis on dialogue. The manner in which dialogue became its only significant strategy was controversial. The Patten Commission clearly had bodies in mind that would have had "teeth" by holding the police accountable. In subsequent legislation, DPPs were confined to being consultative forums. I have argued the case for a peacebuilding approach that does not rely on coercion. From this perspective, the focus on dialogue was beneficial. The power to hold the police accountable would, arguably, have turned these bodies, composed as they were of a majority of politicians, into arenas of fierce political battle. The task of police transformation would have been politicized even more and right down to the local level.

Furthermore, the Good Friday Agreement has opted for a consociational dispensation. Consociational theory postulates that communal identities are irreconcilable and should be politically accommodated through systems of power sharing that are based on the explicit recognition of identities. The adoption of this model for Northern Ireland contributed to the persistence of deep communal divisions and increased political polarization (Farry 2006). Politicians had no incentive to moderate identity-based discourses, and the ongoing political debate was much more focused on meeting identity-based interests than on a larger nation-building project. "Peace has come at the price of reconciliation" (Farry 2006). As a counterpoint to this state of affairs, the DPPs were the only formal mechanism at the local level that included both political and civil society representatives and that, by design, facilitated constructive and inclusive dialogue.

However, the fact that the unfinished business of the past was not allowed on the agenda and that certain persons were prohibited from being members, diluted the quality of dialogue and limited its potential to reach a deeper level of empathy.

Third, the enabling legislation stipulated that the chairpersons of the DPPs had to be elected representatives, meaning local politicians. The chair was rotated regularly to prevent one party from capturing the position. It was an unfortunate decision because it hindered the achievement of an optimum level of dialogue. There were undoubtedly good chairpersons and facilitators of dialogue among the politicians, but DPPs were prevented in this way from electing chairpersons in whom they, as a collective body, would have the greatest trust. The facilitation of dialogue requires a specific aptitude and attitude that are not necessarily found in politicians. By disregarding this fact, DPPs were unnecessarily hampered. The style of meetings, as a consequence, favored politicians, thereby disempowering community representatives (Ryan 2008). It resulted in fairly high levels of petty political grandstanding—at least in some DPPs. Furthermore, police presentations at meetings were at times too stylistic and defensive to enable substantive discussions. Also, it seems as if much depended on the local police commander. If the latter was not well disposed to the DPP, it resulted in top-down communication and overly bureaucratic discussions (Farry 2009).

All of these concerns could have been addressed by competent and evenhanded facilitation.

Lastly, the establishment of this infrastructure has made, on the whole, a significant contribution to peacebuilding. The DPPs were clearly not the only actors and much of the credit for the progress in normalizing police-community relations should go to the internal steps that the police took to professionalize their behavior. However, the two most important actors in this process, the police and Sinn Féin, both credited the DPPs for playing a significant role (Northern Ireland Policing Board 2007; Adams 2008; Orde 2008). In offhand ways, the threat by dissidents to use violence against DPPs confirmed their relevance. If the DPPs were useless "talk shops," they would certainly not have attracted such serious attention. From the other end of the political spectrum, the new DUP chair of a certain DPP said in November 2009 that he thought the DPP was a waste of time. "There was a hidden agenda to DPPs when they were first set up," he said. "It was to get certain people to sit down with police. Now that Sinn Féin has come on board with policing, there's no real purpose to them. . . . I did agree with DPPs but they've run their course" (Newry Democrat 2009). Without necessarily intending it, the speaker confirmed the relevance of the DPP as a body that had legitimized police transformation at the local level. It was of course not only Sinn Féin's participation that was noteworthy but also the DUP's and the fact that the DUP and Sinn Féin, among others, were now publicly and by agreement working together.

The DPPs were instrumental in overcoming some of the deep distrust in the police through the manner in which they facilitated dialogue and built consensus on policing priorities. As quoted in this book's introduction, a Northern Ireland newspaper article described the first meeting of the DPP in West Belfast. The journalist called it a "pinch yourself moment"—the mere sight of people on both sides of an "ancient conflict" sitting down and talking constructively. Such moments were enabled by the infrastructure that was set up for this specific purpose.

Kenya

An intriguing example of the ability of LPCs to facilitate dialogue comes from Kenya—a completely different context than Northern Ireland. What is of particular interest is the fact that the dialogue took place at the level of those core values and worldviews that underpin—and divide—societies. In a series of articles, Tanja Chopra (2008a; 2008b; 2009) has drawn our attention to this development.

I have now, on more than one occasion, referred to the origin and development of the Wajir Peace and Development Committee in Kenya and mentioned the fact that its success led to the establishment of a number of such committees in the northeast of Kenya. The government took notice of this development, especially because local officials participated and, in some cases, chaired these LPCs. In 2001, the government established the National Steering Committee on Peace Building and Conflict Management with the objective to formulate a national policy on conflict management and to provide coordination to various peacebuilding initiatives, including the LPCs. Though the Steering Committee was an interim body, it effectively granted formal status to the LPCs. The supportive infrastructure, though, is still incomplete and a work in progress.

The conflict in the northeast of Kenya was caused by pastoralist groups engaged in a desperate struggle for survival in a context of water scarcity, competition for grazing resources, and severe government neglect. However, at a deeper level the conflict was exacerbated by a disconnection between two distinct paradigms of justice. For the pastoralist communities, justice was determined by rules that regulated their communal, nomadic lifestyle that centered on cattle ownership. For the Kenyan state, justice was derived from the constitution, much of it imported. At heart it protected the land ownership rights of individuals and settled communities. The same situation exists in the Karamoja region of Uganda and South Sudan (Muhereza, Ossiya et al. 2008). For the pastoralist clans, cattle rustling is a core activity to ensure the continuation of local sociopolitical orders (Chopra 2008a). It is, for example, an important means for a boy to prove his manhood and to increase his social status, which will eventually allow him to find a wife. In addition, culpability is always communal, not individual. The decision to conduct a raid on neighbors' cattle was always taken communally. No individual would assume such authority. To punish an individual by putting him in prison following a costly, lengthy, and incomprehensible process in court is, in the pastoralist view, not justice but a travesty of justice. The manner in which they understood justice therefore clashed at a fundamental level with the justice paradigm of the Kenyan state.

In addition to the philosophical disjunction between two worldviews, the situation was exacerbated by the weakness of the state's judicial institutions in that area. Mohamud Adan and Ruto Pkalya (2006: 3) stated that Kenyan LPCs had their roots in the failure of the state to provide security and justice. "The realization that community members themselves are better placed to manage their own conflicts was anchored on the inaccessibility of the formal judicial system and lack of trust in government led conflict prevention interventions."

In 2001, the Kenyan government entered into a negotiation process with the various pastoralist clans through the facilitation of five peace committees in the northeastern region. The negotiations resulted in the Modogashe Declaration. The declaration essentially laid down ground rules for dealing with ongoing conflict associated with cattle rustling. The declaration was revisited in May 2005, amended, and renamed the Garissa Declaration. The agreements contained elements from both legal paradigms. For example, it affirmed the customary rights of clans over certain grazing areas and water holes and required visiting herdsmen to seek permission from the elders of that clan first and to follow the customary practices of the hosting clan while in their area. Stipulations regarding procedures to recover stolen cattle and to compensate for any losses occurred also followed, to a large extent, the customary practices. Interestingly—and controversially—peace committees were involved in the recovery process to ensure that it was taking place according to the rules. On the other hand, the declaration affirmed that the possession of illegal firearms was against the laws of Kenya, and that no grazer was supposed to carry arms. The chiefs assumed responsibility for prohibiting illegally possessed firearms in their area. In case of the killing of any person, the perpetrator should be arrested and tried by the court in addition to paying customary compensation (Chopra 2008a).

The reference to firearms points to another reality that is having a major impact on the situation. The easy availability of small arms—in the context of weak state security—has in many ways perverted the traditional practice of cattle rustling. Battles that have been fought with spears are now fought with AK-47s. These guns imbue young warriors with a new form of power that is deeply destructive to the very traditional culture (see Mkutu 2008). The gun has become an economic asset because it contributes to the commercialization of cattle rustling. It is a new source of power that challenges the power of the elders. It guarantees security in the face of government neglect and has become a major cause of the excessive traumatization of communities and the deepening of intergroup polarizations (Mkutu 2008:83–115). The traditional pastoralist culture is therefore not only threatened by contrasting concepts of justice but also by its fatal contact with this aspect of the modern world. The Garissa Declaration was therefore also an attempt to address this situation by emphasizing the responsibility of the chiefs to prohibit the possession of illegal firearms.

The declarations have made a major contribution to relative stability in the northeastern part of Kenya. The agreed upon ground rules have proved relatively effective in managing ongoing tensions and conflict. Kennedy Mkutu (2008:152), without any reference to LPCs, mentioned Wajir as a success in an otherwise quite bleak description of the government's success in the disarmament of pastoralist communities. He ascribed the success in part to the established trust and good communication between the administration and the community. The major asset of the network of peace committees was their ability to engage all the actors in these conflicts at their own level. The different clans are not homogeneous. There are variations and nuances in their understanding of justice, and their culturally determined responses to violations also differed among each other. The methodology that peace committees followed enabled them to mediate between clans because they understood and respected these differences. At the same time, they were able to access and leverage the collaboration of officials at higher levels. The declarations acknowledged and worked with local concepts and local sociopolitical structures, and they defined common ground rules between different local systems. But they also acknowledged the formal legal system and the responsibilities of government. The declarations, as Chopra (2009:536) stated, are therefore "an interesting example of bottom-up lawmaking."

The peace committees in Kenya provide us with an example of the ability of LPCs to facilitate dialogue at the level of basic cultural values and understandings. More impressive is the fact that they were able to engage the state in this dialogue—a process that delivered the concrete results of a more efficient response to cattle rustling. As such, it is indeed an example of facilitating social cohesion because, for the first time, a bridge was established linking the justice paradigms of the communities with that of the state and making a constructive exchange possible.

Comparison of the Two Cases

In both examples, dialogue at the local level had some impact on strengthening the legitimacy of the state. In Northern Ireland, the matter of policing was closely linked to state legitimacy. In Kenya, the dialogue served to bridge contrasting views of justice and enabled a more functional system of conflict management, with state endorsement, than the police and courts were able to provide. The fact that the LPCs enjoyed formal status contributed to their ability in this respect.

In both cases, the dialogue also served to strengthen horizontal social cohesion. The fact that joint collaboration took place to deal with crises is perhaps the best indicator of such emerging cohesion. In Kenya, the impact was more visible because violence was dramatically reduced. It led to concrete benefits like the reopening of schools and the return of internally displaced persons (Gunja and Korir 2005). The rebuilding of trust in the police in Northern Ireland and joint collaboration on policing priorities, however, is also a significant indicator of increased social cohesion.

The most significant challenge has to do with the manner in which dialogue is facilitated and the need for competent and credible facilitators. It is a matter that needs attention in the design of peace infrastructures. It is not helpful to saddle LPCs with incompetent and biased facilitators. If the LPCs do not have suitable facilitators in their own midst, they should have access to specialist facilitators who can come in from outside. It is also not helpful to attempt to place limitations on the issues to be discussed and the persons with whom to discuss these issues. The principles of openness and inclusivity are important for the effective functioning of dialogue and not mere fads of political correctness.

Justice and Reconciliation

In the design of most of the peace infrastructures, reconciliation is stated as a priority outcome of the work of LPCs. Yet the nature of the reconciliation that ought to be achieved has in no case been clearly defined. If in Nepal, for example, reconciliation were to mean the complete eradication of all traces of the "feudal system" from public and private life, it is clearly not an objective that LPCs can achieve. Similarly, in South Africa, racial harmony in all its forms required such a fundamental restructuring of the total society that it would be naive to expect LPCs to deliver on that.

Reconciliation as a peacebuilding task in general suffers from the fact that it is "an undertheorized phenomenon in studies of civil and international conflict resolution" (Long and Brecke 2003:147). It is furthermore complicated by its intimate connectedness with justice. For many, the task of reconciliation is achieved best by prosecuting those responsible for atrocities. The reigning argument has been aptly summarized by Antonio Cassese, the first president of the International Criminal Tribunal for the former Yugoslavia: "Justice dissipates the call for revenge, because when the Court metes out to the perpetrator his just deserts, then the victims' calls for retribution are met; *by dint of dispensation of justice, victims are prepared to be reconciled with their erstwhile tormentors, because they know that the latter have now paid for their crimes*" (quoted by Stover and Weinstein 2004:3-4; italics added).

The problem is that the credibility of court trials is often determined by political perceptions. What counts as the dispensation of justice for some is seen as partiality and injustice by others. The assumption that reconciliation automatically follows a court trial is unfortunately not always supported by evidence. The point is not that the dispensation of justice is irrelevant. On the contrary, it is a necessary contribution toward breaking the cycle of violence and counterviolence and ending impunity. The question is rather whether it is a *sufficient* precondition for reconciliation, and here the answer seems to be more complicated. Bill Long and Peter Brecke (2003), in their study of truth and reconciliation processes, concluded that reconciliation required four elements: truth telling or acknowledgement of the harm by the perpetrators; a transformation of stereotypes, particularly the victim/wrongdoer stereotypes, toward an acknowledgement of mutual humanity; giving up on the option of full revenge and settling for limited justice in order to break the cycle of injury and counterinjury; and a public reconciliation event to confirm the offer of a new relationship. None of these elements are satisfied fully by criminal prosecution. The most difficult aspect of the equation, and the one where opinion is most divided, is rejecting full revenge and settling for limited justice. It entails a compromise on the demand for justice and for many such a compromise is unpalatable.

In addition, there are differences in the way reconciliation and justice are perceived at the international, national, and local levels. At the international level, the most pressing concern is to stop impunity and install respect for the rule of law. At the national level, political concerns dominate, in particular the need to manage and sustain a fragile peace. Issues of truth, justice, and reconciliation inevitably have huge political significance. In reality, processes of truth and reconciliation end up being fine balancing tricks between political and judicial solutions to the dilemma of accountability for past misdeeds. At the local level, however, the needs for justice and reconciliation are more personal and holistic.

The findings of Eric Stover and Harvey Weinstein (2004:323–25) are particularly relevant in this respect. Beginning in 1998, they led a multidisciplinary team of researchers over a four-year period in an investigation of social reconstruction in local communities. They studied communities in Bosnia and Herzegovina, Croatia, and Rwanda. They found, first, that there was no direct causal link between criminal trials and reconciliation. Criminal trials, especially those of local perpetrators, often divided small multiethnic communities by causing fear and suspicion. The way in which such trials are perceived plays a crucial role. If the trials take place in a context wherein one of the parties views the trials as "victor's justice," the value of such trials for reconciliation is limited. Second, justice meant much more than criminal trials. Justice included the return of stolen property; locating and identifying the bodies of the missing; capturing and trying *all* war criminals and not only high-profile ones; securing reparations and apologies; providing security, meaningful jobs, good schools, and teachers; and helping those traumatized by atrocities. Justice, therefore, had definite emotional and socioeconomic dimensions in addition to the judicial dimension. Interestingly, they found that claims that criminal trials have some "therapeutic value" and provide a sense of "closure" were questionable. Reconciliation is a slow and complex process that entails much more than the once-off event of a court of law.

Reconciliation at the community level is therefore the outcome of long-term, complex processes that operate at emotional, economic, educational, political, and judicial levels. Justice procedures are important, but as in all else, the manner in which such processes are perceived and experienced determine the value that is attached to them. Put differently, there has to be some prior consensus on the need for and credibility of court procedures for them to be effective instruments of reconciliation. Such consensus cannot be assumed.

The following sections address the preliminary nature of the reconciliation achieved by the formation of LPCs and discuss two examples of formal attempts to achieve both justice and reconciliation at the local level, namely

Rwanda and East Timor. In neither of these two cases were LPCs involved, but the experiences in these countries provide important insight into the challenges to achieve justice and reconciliation at the local level. As such, it has relevance for understanding the importance of local structures in facilitating social reconstruction.

Preliminary Reconciliation

A functioning LPC presupposes that some initial reconciliation has taken place, at least among the persons that serve on the LPC. By virtue of their consent to serve on the LPC, participants have agreed to take the first step toward reconciliation. One must be realistic about the nature of this reconciliation, though. It is often hesitant and conditional, which does not mean that it is unimportant. It is an important point to note because so much reconciliation work labors under the tyranny of absolute expectations. Another example from South Africa may illustrate the point.

In early 1993, I was involved in establishing an LPC in a specific town. I completed all the preliminary consultation work with the relevant parties, and all agreed to form an LPC. The parties then had to submit names to me of their representatives on the LPC, which I circulated among all the parties. Among the names were those of Captain Botha,[42] the police representative, and Reggie Oliphant, the ANC representative. Oliphant was a well-known and respected leader in the community and a person who was at the forefront of almost all protest actions in that region. Soon after sending out the list of names, I received a phone call from Captain Botha. He said that there might be a problem with the ANCs choice of Oliphant as its representative. Captain Botha would only say that he had "a history" with Oliphant and had to arrest and interrogate him on a number of occasions. I drove to Oliphant's house and asked him whether he would object to Captain Botha's presence on the LPC. Oliphant, who had clearly not yet read his mail, reacted with shock and anger. He told me that he had suffered greatly at the hands of Captain Botha and that the vendetta between them had become very personal. "Not only did he torture me, but I suspected him of trying to kill me. There have been a number of incidents where, for example, my car was tampered with. I felt his hatred for me as a very personal matter. It went beyond the call of duty."

I offered to ask the police to submit another name. Oliphant thought for a while, then he said: "This peace process is bigger than individuals. I'll set my personal feelings aside and work with Captain Botha for the sake of peace."

---

42. Not his real name.

On the day of the first meeting of the LPC, Captain Botha arrived early and stood alone in a far corner of the room while the others filtered in and filled the room. Oliphant was one of the last to arrive. As he entered, the two men immediately noticed and approached each other. Oliphant held out his hand and said: "Good afternoon, Captain Botha." The policeman took his hand and said: "Good afternoon, Mr. Oliphant." They said nothing more but took their respective seats, and the meeting started. Following that meeting the two had, on a number of occasions, to interact and work together to defuse difficult situations. Their relationship was nothing but professional and functional. No deeper personal reconciliation had taken place that I was aware of, but I believe that both had interpreted their handshake as an agreement to work together—in spite of the past. Their reconciliation was functional. It was preliminary and incomplete and aimed at cooperating in a larger project. That did not mean that it was insincere or insignificant. Reconciliation is rarely a once-off event. It is a long-term project. In this case, the LPC had enabled the first step in that process.

Of course this is but one individual example, and there are examples where LPCs achieved deeper levels of reconciliation between former enemies, as well as examples of complete failure in even establishing such a level of preliminary reconciliation. The example of Reggie Oliphant and Captain Botha, however, best captures, in my mind, the overall achievement of LPCs regarding reconciliation. The Institute for Justice and Reconciliation in Cape Town, South Africa, has invented a South African Reconciliation Barometer, which is a nationally representative public opinion survey that has taken place annually since 2003. Its findings demonstrate the ongoing and complex nature of reconciliation and the fact that, almost two decades after the watershed event of democratic elections in 1994, reconciliation is far from complete.[43] Neither is the reconciliation process progressing along linear and progressive lines. The title of its 2009 survey is telling: "Jangling Discords or a Beautiful Symphony?" (IJR 2009).

No LPC in South Africa can therefore claim to have finally and successfully achieved reconciliation. At most, they have, in many communities, established the first tentative and fragile links between representatives of antagonistic groups and facilitated collaboration on those early and necessary

---

43. Six variables are tested to assess the progress made in reconciliation: (1) human security that includes physical, economic, and cultural security; (2) political culture, testing citizens' views of the institutions, structures, and values of government; (3) cross-cutting political relationships, testing citizens' willingness to support multiracial political parties; (4) citizens' commitment to dialogue; (5) historical confrontation, referring to the willingness to acknowledge past actions, to ask and grant forgiveness, and to reduce levels of vengeance; and (6) race relations, testing the prevalence of racial stereotypes, citizens' interracial contact, and interracial social distance (IJR 2009).

peacemaking and peacebuilding tasks. But there should be no underestimation of the importance of these first steps. Fragile and tentative though they may be, they represent acts of extraordinary courage. Few human acts are so difficult as to take the first step to reach out to someone whom you have hated, feared, or despised.

Rwanda: Local Justice in the Aftermath of Genocide

Rwanda provides us with an example of a concerted, formal attempt to involve local communities in processes of justice and reconciliation.

Following the genocide of 1994, the Rwandan Patriotic Front (RPF)-led government, with strong international support, decided that judicial action against those who were responsible for and participated in the genocide should be an essential element of social reconstruction. More than 120,000 people were arrested by 1996, and soon the realization dawned that the courts would be unable to deal with such a caseload. The high-profile cases were handled by the International Criminal Tribune for Rwanda, with the country's own severely damaged courts (many of the judges and lawyers did not survive the genocide) shouldering the bulk of the task. Consequently the decision was made to devolve less serious cases to the local level. This decision was a fairly inclusive process—at least at the national level. Between May 1998 and March 1999, the then president, Pasteur Bizimungu, facilitated a number of meetings attended by leaders from government, business, and civil society. These meetings reflected on the country's future and concluded that citizen participation in the search for justice was critical. Not only should they participate in establishing the truth of what happened, but they should also collaborate in the creation of an environment conducive for the reconciliation of Rwandans (Karekezi, Nshimiyimana et al. 2004). The outcome of these talks was the decision to use local-level community courts, called *gacaca*, for the trials of less serious genocide crimes.

Gacaca courts drew considerable international attention because of their innovative character and their promise. In the past, the gacaca were informal mechanisms used to dispense justice in noncriminal local disputes through the offices of respected local leaders. In the traditional version, in other words, the state was not involved. They functioned as voluntary, interfamilial dispute resolution mechanisms, which enforced sanctions through social pressure to restore social harmony. In the new version, the gacaca were transformed into hybrid courts that fused the retributive logic of formal criminal courts with the restorative logic of the traditional mechanism. They were tasked to deal with all but the most serious genocidal crimes, ranging from participating in the killing under command of others to property crimes.

In the new version, the trials were no longer voluntary but coercive. The law that established gacaca courts stipulated that testifying was an obligation and that all inhabitants had to relate the facts of what happened in their district. They were obliged to disclose information about the guilty perpetrators. They were also expected to attend the weekly sittings of the gacaca. Most important, gacaca courts had the authority to condemn the guilty to lengthy prison sentences, particularly those who had refused to confess. On the other hand, the courts had a distinct local character with some aspects of restorative justice. The judges were community members elected by popular vote on the basis of their integrity, who then received a crash course in the judicial process to be followed. A total of 250,000 judges were thus appointed countrywide. The trials relied on public participation. The gacaca could commute prison sentences into community service if the confessions of the guilty were deemed to be truthful. In addition, the simplification of the procedures, the important role played by social pressure, and the absence of professional judicial participation added to the gacaca's local character and restorative image (Karekezi, Nshimiyimana et al. 2004:74).

At the time of its conceptualization, the gacaca were viewed very favorably by the majority of Rwandans. A survey done by Timothy Longman, Phuong Pham, and Harvey Weinstein (2004) in 2002, before the actual trials started, revealed that gacaca courts were viewed much more favorably than the international trials and than the national trials. Of those polled, 84.2 percent believed that the gacaca would make an important contribution to reconciliation. The positive view of the gacaca was to a large extent informed by the desire to demonstrate that Rwandans could solve problems using their own traditions.

The theoretical attraction that gacaca offered was, alas, not met with unqualified success (Zorbas 2004; Rettig 2008; Apuuli 2009; Lahiri 2009; Longman 2009; Human Rights Watch 2011, Brounéus 2010). An estimated 1.5 million people stood trial in gacaca courts by 2010. It is certainly too early to come to a final assessment on its impact on social reconstruction, but the signs have been mixed. On the one hand, in some communities, the gacaca enabled dialogue between victims and perpetrators. Timothy Longman reported attending sessions that included dramatic confrontations between witnesses and the people they accused, "with people showing extraordinary courage and forthrightness in ways that could only be positive" (2009:308). Some survivors received information about how family members died. In some cases, bodies could be disinterred and reburied properly, providing emotional relief. The fact that such a massive attempt at dealing with the past and holding people accountable was pulled off is certainly impressive.

On the other hand, though, there are grounds for serious concern.[44] Two factors stand out in this respect: the fairly cynical manipulation of the gacaca by the government and the unproductive mix of punitive and restorative methodologies employed by the gacaca.

The most critical element of the government's unhelpful manipulation of the process was its decision not to allow gacaca courts to handle any case of RPF violence. In the RPF's mind, the genocide was perpetrated by Hutu *genocidaires,* and thus the violence that the RPF caused was to stop the genocide and, therefore, was not criminal in nature. Regardless of the validity of this argument, the perception that it created on the ground was that the criminal processes, including the gacaca, were punitive and aimed at the community of "former Hutus."[45] The very unfortunate result was that the process actually reinforced ethnic identities (see Longman 2009). The one means of determining whether a crime was genocidal in nature was the ethnic identity of the victim. If the attacker was Tutsi, it was, according to the official view, not genocidal since the Tutsis were the victims of genocide, not its perpetrators. The 1.5 million people tried by gacaca courts represent over half of Hutu adult men at the time of the genocide, reinforcing the impression of the collective guilt of the Hutu. Further, conviction in gacaca courts excluded people from holding public office. "*Gacaca* has thus served effectively to place much of the Hutu population in a socially subservient and vulnerable position" (Longman 2009:310). Since the Hutu are the vast majority (84 percent of the total population of Rwanda), it also meant that Hutus, through the gacaca, were required to participate in the conviction of their fellow Hutus. It may explain the widespread lack of popular participation and reluctance to testify that was observed—in spite of the legal obligations in this respect.

The gacaca also brought charges against people who had criticized the postgenocide regime. This reinforced the perception that the gacaca had become a mechanism of political control. It resulted in many people being reluctant to testify in defense of the accused and judges being reluctant to find people innocent. A Human Rights Watch report (2011) stated: "Some defense witnesses were afraid to testify for fear of being accused of genocide

---

44. Karen Brounéus (2010) questioned the assumption that truth telling contributes to healing. She found that witnesses at the gacaca courts in fact showed higher levels of depression and posttraumatic stress syndrome than nonwitnesses, suggesting that truth-telling experiences in a once-off, highly pressurized context such as the gacaca courts were not conducive to psychological healing.

45. Ethnicity has been banned in Rwanda in an attempt to overcome the deep divisions of the past. In terms of the current reigning ideology, the ethnic labels of Hutu, Tutsi, and Twa were colonial inventions. Only one identity is currently recognized, that of being Rwandan.

themselves, and there were numerous allegations that gacaca courts sacrificed the truth to satisfy political interests." It also created opportunities for people to use the gacaca as a means of taking personal revenge on enemies and eliminating rivals (Longman 2009:310).

The second matter of concern is the fusion of two distinct methodologies. Punitive justice and restorative justice are two different paradigms that can coexist as two distinct options within a larger justice system but cannot easily be fused into one procedure. In spite of its intentions to be a restorative process, the gacaca ended up being "distinctly punitive" (Rettig 2008). The restorative element, in other words, lost out to the stronger punitive imperative. A precondition for effective restorative justice processes is the existence of sufficient bipartisan trust in the process itself and in the facilitators or guarantors of the process. The "court" should be a safe space where people feel free to open up and share their experiences—a space where forgiveness can be asked and given. It is emotionally a more difficult process to manage than adjudication. A problem arises when the very people trusted to be the facilitators of reconciliation turn out to be jail masters. Regarding the gacaca, Max Rettig has argued that the Rwandan state did not establish sufficient trust at the local level to enable the gacaca to operate as instruments of restorative justice. "Local justice that depends on the participation of the population can succeed if community trust is strong. But if community trust is weak, then local justice (particularly punitive justice) will fray the social fabric" (2008:46). To add to this, if the methodology that is followed is not focused on strengthening whatever little trust may exist, the result is invariably negative.

East Timor: The Community Reconciliation Project

The Democratic Republic of Timor-Leste, also known as East Timor, provides us with an interesting contrast to the experience in Rwanda. It is the only example of a truth and reconciliation commission that went beyond paying lip service to local reconciliation and actively implemented a program at the local level. Truth and reconciliation commissions are, by and large, instruments to deal with elite behavior during violent conflicts. Local actors come into play mainly for their stories to highlight atrocities that have taken place, but little is done to actively promote local reconciliation.[46] The Commission for Reception, Truth and Reconciliation in East Timor followed a different route (Stahn 2001; CAVR 2006).

---

46. For a fascinating account of the impact that testifying before South Africa's Truth and Reconciliation Commission had on a rural woman, see Antjie Krog, Nosisi Mpolweni, and Kopano Ratele (2009).

Since the annexation of East Timor in 1975 by the Indonesian military, the country suffered from repression in general and numerous human rights violations. In 1999, the United Nations successfully mediated an agreement to allow a referendum on the country's future, in which a majority (78.5 percent) opted for independence. The event was followed by widespread looting and burning, along with murder and rape, perpetrated by pro-Indonesia militias. After the violence ended, the decision was made to establish the aforementioned commission to assist in reconciliation.

The decision of the commission to implement what was called the Community Reconciliation Process was influenced by two main considerations. The first was the excessive workload of the court system and its inability to deal with all the cases related specifically to the political violence of 1999. A distinction was made between "serious crimes" and "less serious crimes." The former fell under the jurisdiction of a Serious Crimes Unit, which was largely administrated by the United Nations. The lesser crimes had to be dealt with by East Timor's nascent legal infrastructure, which was buckling under the process. Granting a general amnesty was not an option because of concerns regarding the negative impact impunity would have on establishing a political culture that respects the rule of law. In this context, the decision was made at an official level to engage in a *formal* process of community reconciliation in order to deal with the backlog of less serious crimes. The emphasis on the formality of this process is important. Reconciliation work had taken place in the informal sphere relying on local cultural and religious practices (Hohe 2002). Through the process facilitated by the commission, though, locally made agreements on reconciliation and its demands would enjoy legal status.

The second consideration for going this route was provided by the process of consultation that was followed in planning the establishment and functioning of the commission. The planning committee visited the districts. The feedback that they received highlighted the compelling imperative for local reconciliation. The report on these consultations (CAVR 2006 ch.9, par 26) stated, for example: "Any reconciliation process should take place at the village level. Participants expressed dissatisfaction that the reconciliation initiatives up to that point had focused on leaders." Although it was accepted that leaders should also reconcile, it was felt that there was need for a formal mechanism to resolve grassroots differences, whose origins lay in the conflicts of the past. Furthermore, "It was not realistic to imagine that national leaders could simply command the population to reconcile. A forum was needed where those who had harmed their communities could explain their actions and apologise for them."

The process worked in the following way: Perpetrators of harmful acts submitted a statement to the commission detailing all the relevant facts. The Office of the General Prosecutor then decided whether the offense qualified as a lesser crime and whether it was appropriate for the Community Reconciliation Process. If so, the commission had to organize a hearing in the relevant community. A regional commissioner of the commission had to set up the hearing and chair the procedure. Setting up the hearing included conducting prior consultation meetings in the district or village to determine what local customs or religious practices would be used and who should serve on the panel. Panel members were selected for their ability to act in a just and impartial manner, their influence and credibility in the community, and their demonstrated commitment to reconciliation (CAVR 2006 ch. 9, par 64). The panel therefore consisted of the regional commissioner and three to five local leaders. The hearings took place in public and, after the deponent had made his or her submission, members of the community could participate and question him or her. If the panel was satisfied that the deponent was truthful, they would determine what acts of reconciliation were needed. These mostly included an apology to the community and acts of community service. The latter were largely symbolic. The whole procedure was deeply reliant on cultural and religious practices. These practices mainly catered to the emotional dimensions of reconciliation through reliance on rituals of penance and forgiveness. After completion of the hearing, the deponent signed a community reconciliation agreement that stipulated the crime, the findings of the panel, and the deponent's apology. This document was forwarded to the district court where it was registered as an order of the court.

Two monitoring and evaluation surveys were conducted to assess the effectiveness of the procedure (CAVR 2006 9.5). It was found that 96 percent of persons interviewed felt that the process had achieved its objective of reconciliation. One particular limitation was the time limit for the commission's operation. Effectively, the community process had three months for hearings. It was not sufficient. Almost 1,400 hearings took place, but the commission estimated that a further 3,000 could have taken place if not for the time limit. In its recommendations, the commission underlined the need for an institution to continue after the demise of the commission with community reconciliation work, which would maintain the link between the formal justice system and community reconciliation. It is not clear whether this recommendation was implemented.

The example of East Timor is very important for our purposes. The link between formal judicial processes and community reconciliation is particularly noteworthy. It demonstrated that reconciliation need not be an alternative to justice and that the promotion of social cohesion need not undermine the rule of law. The process valued the cultural, religious, and emotional dimensions of reconciliation while at the same time safeguarded respect for the law and the country's emerging legal infrastructure. However, the community was, in cultural terms, fairly homogeneous. The task of appointing community judges would be exponentially more complex were different and deeply distrustful identity groups to share the same district, as would be the challenge to manage divergent perceptions regarding the process.

Social Reconstruction at the Local Level: A Few Pointers

The restoration of the interpersonal ruins in communities that have suffered violence is clearly a daunting task. No clear recipe or winning formula has emerged from this discussion, but there are a few pointers.

First, there is a compelling obligation to pay serious attention to the demand for social reconstruction at the local level. The designers of peace processes should not be allowed to ignore this dimension any more.

Second, it is the local community that determines its own readiness for reconciliation. One of the most important findings of Stover and Weinstein was that reconciliation would only begin to take hold in divided communities once the societal context allowed for and promoted social interaction between individuals from hostile groups (2004:324). In a context where social pressure prohibited meaningful interaction, little reconciliation was possible. The achievement of an LPC, when its establishment is truly the result of a local process of peacemaking, is that it legitimizes activities that seek to build peace and facilitate reconciliation. The fact that such legitimacy is supported at the national level is very important. In the final analysis, though, it is legitimacy in the eyes of the local community that matters—the fact that its members have made their own decision to repair their own community.

Third, the ability of LPCs to create spaces for dialogue is an important contribution to social reconstruction. The design of a peace process should recognize the advantages of locally facilitated dialogue and should put measures in place to ensure that the manner in which dialogue is facilitated is productive.

Fourth, the demand for justice at the local level is multifaceted and complex. Deeply divided communities should not be asked to punish perpetrators of atrocities in their midst as long as opposing perceptions of justice and victimhood exist in that community. Moreover, if punitive justice is to be pursued as an instrument of reconciliation, it has to take place in a dispassionate and professional manner and in a context wherein sufficient consensus on credible judicial processes exists.

Restorative justice processes are by their nature more attuned to the need for reconciliation and are therefore more appropriate in peacebuilding contexts. The example of East Timor is, in this respect, intriguing because of the manner in which formal justice was linked with restorative justice at the community level.

Perhaps the most appropriate conclusion to reach is that the design of each peace process should carefully consider the particular complexities, needs, and anxieties regarding justice and reconciliation at the local level. It should understand the multifaceted need for justice—that is, the fact that, at the local level, the need for justice encompasses more than court procedures. It should also understand the different perceptions that exist in a community. The potential role of LPCs in this respect is to contribute to a more thorough understanding of the nature of justice that is required at the local level.

A last comment is that the creation of an enabling national policy framework is a necessary but not sufficient condition for social reconstruction. Stover and Weinstein have developed "an ecological model for social reconstruction" (see 2004:325-339). It is an important model, backed up by intensive empirical research. Interestingly, though, the bulk of the tasks identified by them have to be performed by the national government,[47] though their specific concern was with community-level reconstruction. In terms of their model, the onus is squarely on the national government to establish a policy environment to facilitate the emergence of a new social cohesion at the community level.

The model therefore assumes that a functional government is in place. This is, of course, not the case during the initial postagreement phase and can only be a mid- to long-term development. Missing in the model is provision for structures or procedures to stimulate local agency in the social reconstruction process, particularly during the initial postagreement stage. The logic of LPCs is that the responsibility for social reconstruction is located at the local level, although in the context of a national agreement.

---

47. They have identified eight components of the task to support social reconstruction: (1) establishing security; (2) ensuring the freedom of movement, particularly the return of refugees; (3) institutionalizing the rule of law at every level of society, which includes the development of a fair system of justice, the intent to treat each individual in light of particular, demonstrated evidence, and a commitment to redress for past harms; (4) providing access to accurate and unbiased information; (5) facilitating "meaningful" justice; (6) educating for democracy; (7) pursuing economic development; and (8) facilitating cross-ethnic engagement.

The importance that LPCs have for social reconstruction lies in the fact that they legitimize dialogue and collaboration in the immediate aftermath of violence and facilitate local processes to reach consensus on joint peace-building priorities. In the process, they enable the beginnings of a better understanding between different groups and mediate a sufficient level of reconciliation between actors to enable cooperation. To the extent that they are successful in these respects, they build much-needed trust, which is an essential element of social cohesion.

6

Extinguishing the Small Fires
LPCs and Violence Prevention

L PCs cannot and do not enforce peace. They do not prevent violence through physical peacekeeping.[48] But they do make a significant contribution toward preventing violence primarily by defusing tense situations and seeking inclusive solutions to conflicts with violence potential. This chapter, following a brief justification for the attention to violence prevention at the local level, discusses—with examples from South Africa, Northern Ireland, Sierra Leone, Malawi, Kenya, and Ghana—the contribution of LPCs to violence prevention, including election-related violence and violence caused by unresolved community disputes.

Violence Prevention at the Local Level

The specter of a relapse into violence is one that haunts postviolence contexts. In fact, negotiated peace agreements do not seem to be automatically good for stability and democracy. In more than half of the cases, peace did not last for five years (see Suhrke and Samset 2007; Fortna 2008:50).[49] On the other hand, civil wars that end with a decisive victory for one side, in particular the rebel army, seem to produce greater stability and levels of democratization than those that do not (Weinstein 2005; Toft 2006). It is not surprising that, in light of these research findings, some niggling doubts have entered the

---

48. Violence is indeed a "conceptual minefield" (Kalyvas 2006:19). In this discussion, violence refers to acts of physical violence against persons and property.

49. The figure of 50 percent of postconflict countries relapsing into violence within five years was first mentioned by Paul Collier et al. in a 2002 paper in the *Journal for Conflict Resolution*. For ˙ ̇ ̇̇ ̇̇e of the figure, see Astri Suhrke and Ingrid Samset (2007). Virginia Fortna (2008) has, howev quently confirmed the correctness of the figure. She relied on the Polity IV Project data set and Jaggers 2002) and the Freedom House World Comparative rankings (2006).

peacemaking and peacekeeping debates. Should belligerents not therefore be allowed to fight it out until a clear winner has emerged? Does premature peacemaking and the presence of peacekeepers lead not to short-term decreases in violence but to long-term instability and, therefore, more persistent violence? Do such actions by the international community not cancel out the statebuilding effect of war as it functioned, for example, in Europe's history, by prematurely and haphazardly intervening in other peoples' wars?

These are intriguing but largely academic questions. In reality, more civil wars today end at the negotiation table than through military victory (Toft 2006; Jarstad and Sisk 2008). In addition, civil war is increasingly being viewed not through the lenses of realpolitik and assumptions about absolute state sovereignty but through the lenses of international law. The indictment by the International Criminal Court of rulers in power (President Omar al-Bashir of Sudan and Muammar Gaddafi of Libya), in addition to the prosecution of two former presidents (Slobodan Milošević of Yugoslavia and Charles Taylor of Liberia) by international tribunals, are early signs that the growing use of violence in pursuit of internal political objectives is viewed as a criminal and not a political matter. It is, at this stage, still a fairly new and therefore controversial development, one that is wide open to accusations of bias and inconsistency.[50] But it is a sign of the improbability that the world will, in the future, allow violent internal conflicts to play themselves out with no external attempts to intervene.

The real question is therefore not whether to allow civil wars to play themselves out but rather how to address the serious issue of the potential relapse into violence following a peace agreement. Much research has in fact been done on what makes peace agreements succeed or fail (see Hartzell, Hoddie et al. 2001; Stedman 2001; Walter 2004; Quinn, Mason et al. 2007),[51] and most of the work in this respect has to be done at the level of postagreement statebuilding and economic reconstruction (World Bank 2011). For the purposes of this discussion, the question is how to prevent violence at the

---

50. The argument that the International Criminal Court is a neocolonialist instrument wielded by the West to pursue its own interests has been eloquently made by Charles Taylor's attorney, Courtenay Griffiths, for example, during his interview with South Africa's eTV News Channel reporter, Chris Maroleng, on September 27, 2010.

51. Some of the risk factors that lead to a relapse into violence are economic underdevelopment, the lure of control over lucrative natural resources (oil is bad for peace), geographical factors (the absence of mountains is good for peace), weak state conditions or the relative weakness of democratic institutions, the length and intensity of the previous war, and the manner in which the war ended. Quinn et al. (2007) provided a useful summary of the research on this topic. In their own research, they identified "dual sovereignty" and agency as two key risk factors. Dual sovereignty refers to a situation where an opposition group has sufficient organization, support, and resources to pose an alternative to the incumbent government. Agency refers to the "decision calculus" whereby potential combatants determine the utility of returning to war or accepting peace.

local level, particularly at a time when state authority is weak. Dealing with violence at the local level when and where it occurs is an important strategy in preventing its escalation. By extinguishing a fire while it is still small, a raging bushfire can be prevented.

This book has already noted the types of violence that occur at the local level and stated the need for concerted action at the local level to prevent violence (chapter 1). Two factors are particularly important: The first is that postagreement violence takes place in a context wherein the state capacity and legitimacy to control violent behavior is weak. No new culture of responding to crises and violence has yet developed; no new institutions with fresh, legitimate mandates are in place to contain the violence. The police often suffer from a lack of credibility and are demoralized. Much uncertainty therefore exists with little automatic consensus on how to deal with all the manifestations of discontent and anxiety. The second factor is that the local violence is best dealt with by seeking inclusive, local solutions to conflicts. Inclusive local solutions are the best option under these circumstances because of the importance of local dynamics in the production of violence, but more particularly because inclusive local solutions strengthen social cohesion. The quest for security in a postagreement context cannot be isolated from the quest for peace and fairness. Ongoing violence cannot be dealt with in a manner that will lead to further polarization and hatred. A strategy, therefore, that strengthens social cohesion as it prevents violence is valuable. In fact, violence that occurs in postagreement settings serves to test the spirit and substance of the negotiated peace (Höglund 2008:100). The response to such violence has to be very careful not to undermine that spirit and substance.

The challenge for peacebuilders, therefore, is to design a strategy that will provide nonviolent, inclusive options to local communities to deal with the inherent complexities and tensions of the transition phase. The question is whether LPCs are a viable option in this respect.

Violence Prevention in Action

The one place where a peace infrastructure was established with the primary objective to prevent violence was South Africa. As mentioned in chapter 2, LPCs were not successful in stopping the violence altogether, only in containing it. But LPCs have, in many cases, prevented violence. The funeral of Chris Hani, secretary-general of the South African Communist Party, was the major test case in this respect. After his assassination by white right-wing elements on April 10, 1993, the country hovered on the edge of the abyss. Genuine anger and grief mixed with deep frustration at the slow pace of the negotiations. Most peace-loving South Africans felt it in their bones: If the period leading up to Hani's funeral, including the day of the funeral, could be relatively peaceful, there was hope for the country. But there were no guarantees, safeguards, or certain outcomes.

The response to the crisis was multifaceted and multilayered. At the highest level, it called for statesmanship from both the president (F. W. de Klerk) and the leader of the ANC (Nelson Mandela). Both responded admirably, with Mandela in particular playing a key role in calling for calm and, importantly, acceleration in the pace of negotiations—not the abandonment of negotiations. The ANC called for a week of "mass action"—protest marches and rallies across the country as a mechanism to channel the anger. In each place where mass action was planned, the LPCs were required to intervene and ensure that the events were violence free. On the day of the funeral, approximately eighty thousand people attended the memorial service at a soccer stadium with many more milling around on the outside, unable to enter the packed stadium. Many of these people made the journey to the graveyard, forty-five kilometers away. The event did not pass without violence. Six people were killed on the day of the funeral, and some property was destroyed, but compared to what might have happened, this figure was relatively small. More important, the country survived intact. The crisis was averted (Gastrow 1995; Ball 1998; Collin Marks 2000; Höglund 2004).

The strategy that the LPCs used on this and the numerous other occasions when they were called upon to intervene in order to prevent violence consisted of a number of steps. The first step was to be alert to, and analyze the potential for, violence. At a time when "early warning" was not yet a widely used phrase, the various networks that fed into the peace committees served as very effective early-warning mechanisms. LPCs anticipated the threats to peace and potential flashpoints. The second step was to bring all relevant actors to a strategic planning meeting prior to a scheduled event. These actors were, typically, the party organizing the event, the party that felt threatened by the event, local government officials, the police, and any other group or individual that could contribute to the process. The meeting was normally chaired by the peace committee chairperson or by a staff member of the RPC. The meeting served two important purposes—namely, to deal with rumors by developing reliable scenarios and to agree on a strategy to keep the peace. Such strategies normally included a reconfirmation of the shared commitment to nonviolence, agreement on the venue that would be used, the routes that would be followed, the arrangements that the organizers had made to ensure that the event was peaceful, the manner in which the event would be monitored, and the role that the police should play. Many of these meetings were difficult, complex matters that required skillful facilitation. On the one side were those who wanted to assert their right to express their anger and frustration; on the other side were those who experienced the dramatic developments with anxiety and a deep concern for security. The bigger events, such as Hani's funeral, were also served by joint operational centers staffed by police, the ANC, and LPC members. They were linked through handheld radios with monitors in the field.

The third step was to actually monitor the event and to intervene when necessary. Such interventions were on-the-spot affairs where quick thinking and calm action were required. It mostly took the form of on-the-spot mediations, but monitors were required to play a whole range of urgent roles (Collin Marks 2000). I remember a protest march in George, a town in the Southern Cape, which followed a route through a white suburb. At a very sensitive point in the middle of the suburb, the police stopped the march, came to me, and said that they have information that some of the marchers had petrol bombs with them. These were homemade devices but could easily set a house alight when thrown through a window. The possible scenario was frightening indeed because I knew that many of the homeowners had locked themselves in their homes for the duration of the march with their guns ready. The idea of the police intervening and dispersing the march in that setting, resulting in agitated marchers running uncontrolled through a very tense and armed white suburb, was nightmarish. I approached the leaders of the ANC at the front of the march and asked them to deal with the situation in light of assurances that they had given at the planning meeting. They came back to me after about fifteen long minutes and said that it was safe to continue. Without admitting that some individuals had petrol bombs, they gave their firm assurance that everything was under control. The march proceeded without any further incident.

The LPC monitors were therefore different from international monitors, whose role was largely restricted to observation. LPC monitors had a mandate to intervene. In this particular case, the ANC would most likely have been reluctant to respond to a direct police instruction. The fact that the request came from an LPC monitor made it legitimate, and the leaders responded positively.

In the areas of the country where violence took place mostly between supporters of the ANC and the IFP, extensive use was made of joint monitoring. It meant that both parties provided teams of monitors who were then paired up. Together, as a pair of ANC and Inkatha representatives but with an LPC mandate, they monitored events and intervened jointly when necessary. This type of monitoring was, of course, appropriate only in situations under threat of sporadic violence, namely in cases of planned protest marches, political rallies, or politically sensitive funerals.

The fourth step that peace committees took to prevent violence was to conduct a postevent review at the next LPC meeting. This was an important exercise, first, because of the need to learn lessons. There were no precedents or best practices to follow. The LPCs had to learn what worked best by reflecting on their own experience. Second, these were important confidence-building opportunities. The sense of having jointly managed a major threat to peace and having dealt successfully with the crisis built some much-needed trust.

The strategy therefore consisted of joint early analysis, joint planning, joint monitoring, and joint learning. It was particularly effective to prevent sporadic violence. However, it was also able, in some cases, to deal with violence by defusing tension, facilitating political consensus, and building trust. A colleague, Patrick Nyuka, had to intervene in a potentially violent situation created by the murder of a man over the price of a packet of cigarettes. The problem was that the deceased and the shopkeeper were linked to different factions of the ANC in that specific township at a time of strong antagonism between the factions. There were great concerns that the funeral would be violent and that a spiral of revenge and retaliation would develop. Patrick facilitated a number of meetings under the auspices of the LPC. These meetings were not easy as the resentment and anger ran deep, but two days before the funeral, all the organizations in that community, whether political, religious, business, or cultural, committed themselves at a public meeting to a peaceful funeral. On the day of the funeral, all went well until after the grave was covered up. A group of young men suddenly broke into a war dance, singing a song indicating that they were going to attack the house of the person responsible for the murder. Patrick also noticed that some were armed with handguns. They proceeded as a group down a narrow street toward the house of the accused person. Patrick jumped into his car and blocked the narrow street with his car. He then stood in the door of his car and addressed them, telling them that the whole community had agreed to a peaceful event and called on them to respect the expressed wish of the community. It worked.

There are two noteworthy aspects to this intervention. First, the funeral was peaceful primarily because the LPC under Patrick's facilitation managed to defuse much of the political tension through the various discussions and negotiations. All actors eventually agreed to a nonviolent strategy (in this case allowing the law to take its course), thereby removing the option of violence from the table. Second, it was possible to stop the attempt to use violence by relying on the authority of the consensus within the community—a soft authority compared to the anger and guns of the young men, but on the day of the funeral, it was sufficient. Building consensus or agreement on alternative, nonviolent options to deal with a crisis is therefore a key strategy in defusing tension and preventing violence.

Let me conclude this section with a final and somewhat different example from Northern Ireland. It concerns the extrajudicial punishments that paramilitary groups regularly meted out on offenders. Over the six years after the Good Friday Agreement, more than 1,800 paramilitary-style shootings and assaults were recorded in Northern Ireland. Those punished were people who were guilty—in the eyes of the paramilitary forces—of antisocial or criminal behavior. Civil society groups, such as the Community Safety Partnerships and other restorative justice projects like Community Restorative Justice Ireland and Northern Ireland Alternatives, worked at addressing the situation (McEvoy and Eriksson 2006; Mika 2006). In an independent assessment of these projects, Harry Mika (2006) has found that they had "measurable and significant impact" with a demonstrable reduction in paramilitary punishments. The projects were undertaken in communities where "a perceived absence of legitimate policing" existed and where statutory bodies appear to be indifferent to victims who resided in working class areas (Mika 2006:3). The projects relied on former paramilitary leaders to enhance confidence in their work and promote reconciliation and restitution between offenders and victims rather than punishment. Even though these examples do not reflect the work of LPCs, they similarly demonstrate the role of trust building and reliance on the soft power of communication in preventing violence in contexts where formal authority is weak.[52]

Preventing Election-Related Violence

The conduct of elections is often prescribed as the best solution to end civil war. Elections are supposed to produce legitimate governments, thereby resolving the underlying contest for power. Elections in postwar societies are, however, fundamentally different from "normal" ones (Kumar, quoted by Höglund 2008:85). In fact, while democracy is seen as a precondition to stable peace, the process of democratization is often dangerous and violent (Reilly 2008).

---

52. There is no evidence of any linkage between these projects and the District Policing Partnerships discussed in the previous chapter, though. It is a consequence of the specific mandate given to DPPs and the manner in which the composition of the DPPs was regulated.

In conditions of a fragile peace, political mobilization for the election is bound to take place along conflict faultlines. In reality, therefore, a highly competitive, polarizing process is inserted into a fragile postviolence environment, often under pressure of the international community. It is no wonder that election processes have emerged as particularly violence prone (see Sisk 2008).

Against this background the question whether LPCs have a contribution to make to the prevention of election-related violence is important. The cases of Sierra Leone, Malawi, and Kenya offer some insight into this question.

Sierra Leone

The Report of the Truth and Reconciliation Commission (TRC) of Sierra Leone (2004) described preconflict Sierra Leone as a "fragmented, exploited and deeply insecure country." By the end of the 1980s, the failure of the state was such that notions of citizenship and patriotism had become meaningless concepts. For communities and individuals alike, the struggle to survive depended on their success in accessing the patronage system. The civil war started in 1991. It was finally brought under control through an intervention of the British Army in 2000. A characteristic of the war was its particularly brutal nature. The violence had a devastating affect on the social fabric of communities. Social taboos were deliberately undermined through the forced rape of mothers and sisters, the violation of children, and the abuse of elders. Old scores were settled in vicious manners, with each district and village experiencing violence aimed at the very values and customs that had held those communities together. This violence was not only perpetrated by outsiders but also, more devastatingly, by neighbors and even by members of the same family.

A peace settlement in 2000 was followed by UN managed elections in 2002. The country passed additional hurdles by conducting presidential and parliamentary elections in 2007—this time successfully managed by its own institutions—and local elections in 2008. The successful elections of 2007–08 were a remarkable achievement, more particularly because the opposition won the election and a peaceful transfer of power took place. This positive outcome was never a foregone conclusion, though. An early warning report by the West Africa Network for Peacebuilding (WANEP) in July 2007 sounded a pessimistic note (WARN 2007), seeing a return to anarchy as a possible, though not unavoidable, scenario. The election period was tense and complicated by various splits and tensions in the main political parties.

Several factors contributed to the success of the elections. The critical success factor was the professional management of the elections by the National Electoral Commission—for which it received well-deserved credit (ACE Project 2007; Commonwealth Expert Team 2008; Wyrod 2008). The District Code of Conduct Monitoring Committees (DMCs), however, also made a positive contribution that was recognized by the European Union Election Observation Mission (2007), among others. The DMCs are examples of LPCs since they were inclusive local bodies with a peacebuilding mandate that derived from a national consensus.

The DMCs were established by the Political Parties Registration Commission (PPRC)—a statutory body whose tasks included the regulation of the behavior of political parties. The PPRC initially wanted to perform its task by using the law and the courts but soon realized that it was totally unrealistic for two reasons: First, the court system was almost nonexistent in the districts, and even at the national level, it was quite dysfunctional; and second, the justice system was implicated in the corruption and mismanagement of the past. The TRC specifically referred to this fact (2004 par. 420, 441). The courts therefore suffered from a credibility problem. The opposition was, at the time, accusing the ruling party of mismanaging the peace again and reverting to old ways. The imposition of legal punitive sanctions on political parties that breached the electoral law would have been highly problematic and possibly provocative. In reality, therefore, the court system was unable to dispense credible justice during the election period, especially in a highly charged political environment.

That left the PPRC with only one option—to adopt a strategy of peer monitoring. It consequently facilitated negotiations between all the political parties to formulate a code of conduct. Following an intense period of negotiations, the code of conduct was publicly signed at an impressive ceremony at Parliament on November 23, 2006 (Nyathi 2006). In addition to the parties' voluntary and public commitment to the code of conduct, a National Code of Conduct Monitoring Committee was established, consisting of a representative from each of the registered political parties, a representative of the National Electoral Commission, two representatives from civil society, and a representative from the police, the Inter-Religious Council, and the National Commission for Democracy and Human Rights (ReliefWeb 2007). The committee selected its chairperson from its nonpolitical members and became an effective platform for dialogue and problem solving between political parties during the election period. One of its first decisions was to replicate the structure at the regional level and in each of the fourteen districts.

The DMCs had the same composition as the national body. A number of the DMC's features are important to note. First, their national mandate was rooted in an implicit acknowledgement of consensus as the primary source of authority. The authority of DMCs did not rely on the coercive nature of the state but on the consensus that was achieved and on the principle of peer monitoring. Second, they were chaired by a nonpolitician—a critical step in ensuring evenhandedness. Third, the task of peer monitoring was strengthened by the inclusion of civil society, statutory bodies, the religious sector, and the police on the DMCs. Effectively, the DMCs were platforms for local political parties to jointly deal with their tensions, as facilitated and supported by the presence of local peacebuilders. Fourth, the DMCs had direct access to two national bodies: the parent National Code of Conduct Monitoring Committee as well as the PPRC. This access was a critical element of their success because, on a number of occasions, DMCs had to call on national actors to provide support in defusing local tensions (Nyathi 2009). Lastly, the DMCs received specialist support in the form of training and ongoing advice from experts located at the country's UN office and the IFES.

The DMCs served three functions during the election period (Ohman 2010). First, the DMCs demonstrated to the electorate that representatives from different political parties could work together for peaceful elections. They symbolized the only form of social cohesion that existed at the time. This helped to reduce tensions. The important collaboration between DMCs and district radio stations belonging to the Independent Radio Network strengthened this perception. DMC members participated in biweekly radio programs. Second, their local knowledge allowed them to identify potential areas of conflict and act to avoid these from developing further. Third, where conflicts did occur, the DMCs were well placed to mediate between the different actors. Magnus Ohman (2010) listed forty-six incidents during the August 2007–August 2008 period (covering both the national and local elections of 2007 and 2008, respectively) where DMCs mediated or intervened in situations of conflict and potential violence.

Malawi

Turning now to Malawi, the difference between Malawi and Sierra Leone is that Malawi never knew the type and extent of violence as experienced by Sierra Leone. Malawi is a relatively peaceful country. Yet its political landscape is characterized by deep regional, ethnic, and religious fault lines. At several times in its recent history, the political temperature has reached a boiling point. The outcomes of all the elections since the introduction of a multiparty system in 1994 have been contested. A particular feature of the political culture has been the use of party youth structures to destabilize the political opposition, and their use has contributed to local incidents of violence, particularly in the 1999 and 2004 elections. On the whole, however, Malawi is a country that has been successful thus far in preventing large-scale violence in spite of very tense experiences with elections.

The expectation at the time of the first multiparty elections in 1994 was that the elections would be troublesome but thereafter things would improve. This expectation was wrong. The performance of the Malawi Electoral Commission (MEC) and, with it, the quality of elections, steadily declined mainly because of two reasons: the government's lack of will to allow the MEC independence and sufficient resources to perform its task and, largely as a consequence of the first reason, the lack of legitimacy that the MEC enjoyed in the eyes of political parties, civil society, and the donor community (Rakner and Svasand 2005:11). In 2002, the German development agency, GTZ, agreed to fund the establishment of a multiparty forum called the National Elections Consultative Forum (NECOF). The forum operated under the auspices of the MEC. It was envisaged as a forum where political parties, civil society, and the MEC could meet to discuss electoral issues and manage conflict. However, it was largely ineffectual and rarely met. When it met, parties sent low-profile representatives and did not feel themselves bound by its decisions (Rakner and Svasand 2005).

At the same time, however, Multi-Party Liaison Committees (MPLCs) were established in the districts as part of the same infrastructure. They had more or less the same composition and objectives as the NECOF. The MPLCs qualify as LPCs because of their national mandate (located in both NECOF and, more important, MEC) and their inclusive local composition. These LPCs have been widely credited for their effective impact (Gloppen, Kanyangolo et al. 2006; Patel 2006; Kazembe and Engel 2009; Patel 2009, Mwale and Etter 2011). During both the 2004 and the 2009 elections, the MPLCs were instrumental in dealing with local conflicts and defusing potential violence. Incidents of violence have in fact declined over this period, with the 2009 elections being "virtually" free of violence, according to the MEC chairperson (Patel 2009). There was only one incident. This was a significant achievement since the 2009 elections had greater violence potential than previous elections due to the specific nature of the political scene at the time.[53] The MPLCs have received substantial training and support from the Forum for Dialogue and Peace, a GTZ-supported CSO.

As in the case of Sierra Leone, the LPCs therefore demonstrated their ability to deal with local tensions during electoral periods by providing an inclusive platform for communication, consensus building, and problem solving. The LPCs were able to play this role despite being linked to weak national bodies. The sustained support and training from a reputable CSO undoubtedly contributed to their impact.

Kenya

As a last example, consider the case of Kenya. Kenya shocked the world in early 2008 with the extent and venom of its postelection violence. More than 1,300 people lost their lives, more than half of these during the first two weeks of the violence. More than 500,000 were displaced (Wachira 2010). The underlying instability of Kenya was, however, not a surprise for more informed observers (see Klopp 2001). Election violence regularly occurred since 1991—at the time, to oppose the introduction of multipartyism and subsequently to achieve electoral dominance. It frequently coincided with the displacement of people along ethnic lines. Disturbingly, the election of December 2007 was preceded by a substantial effort by the international community and Kenyan civil society to ensure fair and peaceful elections. Local peace committees were part of this process. The failure of all these efforts is a stark reminder of the fragility of violence prevention efforts in the face of a deliberate commitment to the use of violence.[54]

Jacqueline Klopp and her colleagues (2010) described the situation in one of the most affected districts, Kuresoi. The district experienced ethnic violence and displacement as far back as the early 1990s that was partly driven

---

53. The president, Bingu wa Mutharika, had established his own political party while president. He was the presidential candidate in 2004 for the then ruling party, the United Democratic Front (UDF). He was handpicked by his predecessor, Bakili Muluzi, who was not eligible after two terms in office but stayed on as leader of the UDF. Mutharika, once elected, soon fell out with Muluzi, left the UDF, and established his own party, the Democratic Progressive Party. A number of MPs from all parties in Parliament joined his party, but he did not have a parliamentary majority, thus creating various constitutional dilemmas and legislative logjams. The election of 2009 was the first opportunity for Mutharika and his new party to test their strength, and they won handsomely. But with all the bad blood and bitterness, a real concern existed that the election process might be violent.

54. In his indictment of six prominent Kenyan politicians, the prosecutor of the International Criminal Court, Luis Moreno Ocampo, provided detailed information regarding the planning that went into the attacks. As early as December 2006, he alleged that preparations for a "criminal plan to attack supporters of the PNU in the Rift Valley" began, establishing a network of perpetrators and an "organisational policy to commit crimes." A chain of command was allegedly set up, coordinating transport, logistics, meetings, fund-raising, paying off perpetrators, rewards, the identification of target areas, and the provision of guns and ammunition (Africa Confidential 2010).

by local memories of injustice and partly by political party competition. The trauma and bitterness, therefore, ran deep. Several local peacebuilding initiatives were undertaken, including the formation of a fifty-member LPC. In spite of having achieved some significant results, such as engaging elders and the youth in reconciliation work and resettling displaced persons, these efforts were not sufficient to prevent what was to come. In October 2007, for example, two people were killed, including an LPC member, and seven injured in a night of violence that, ironically, followed directly after a three-day training workshop for the LPC. The postelection violence saw more than fifty people killed and tens of thousands displaced in the district. The LPC was defenseless against political opportunists and violence specialists. Their failure was their inability to engage two critical actors in their peacebuilding processes: the police and those politicians, local and national, who were willing to exploit local tensions for political gain.

However, not all of Kenya exploded. Some districts, particularly the northeast and the coastal region, remained calm. The northeast was the region where Dekha Ibrahim Abdi and her colleagues built a peace infrastructure of LPCs. In the absence of more comparative information, it is premature to draw easy comparisons between the calmness of the northeast, where LPCs played a dominant role over the past years, and the regions where violence raged in 2008, particularly the Rift Valley. According to Jacqueline Klopp et al. (2010), however, the peacefulness in these regions was not coincidental. Violence started in the coastal region, but it was contained by a successful mobilization involving elders, mosques, local government, civil society, and prominent individuals that provided the collective moral authority to turn against violence. The operating words here are "successful mobilization." Whoever was responsible for the successful mobilization of the collective potential for peace in those communities had done what LPCs ideally should do.

LPCs and the Police

The police are supposed to be the primary security providers at the local level. In most peacebuilding contexts, though, the police are weak. Either they suffer from a lack of legitimacy because of perceptions that they have been used as tools of oppression by previous regimes, or because they lack capacity and resources. The area where the weakness of central authority during peacebuilding phases is often most painfully visible is, in fact, in the area of policing. The substantial challenge regarding policing in postagreement contexts is that the reform of police has to take place in a context where violence (and crime) escalates. At the same time when the police should ideally focus internally on their own reform, they are required to deal with high demands on their service. Conversely, at a time when there is dire need for security at the local level, the police are often not trusted to provide, or capable of providing, that security.

LPCs have a direct relevance for policing. We have seen how, in Northern Ireland, LPCs have facilitated dialogue and contributed to rebuilding trust between communities and the police. In the various anecdotes relayed herein regarding the work of LPCs in South Africa, the interaction between LPCs and the police has been a central theme. The police should be an active member of LPCs, particularly when LPCs are involved in efforts to contain or prevent violence. The advantages of police participation in LPCs are, first, that LPCs offer a platform where misunderstanding and rumors can be cleared up and reliable information communicated. This aspect is as important for the police as it is for other actors. Second, through engaging in dialogue with the community, the process of restoring trust between the police and the community may begin. Third, by building consensus on the most appropriate strategy to deal with violence, the problem of the police's low morale and lack of legitimacy is addressed in a manner that supports the long-term ideal of "community policing"—that is, sound interactions and collaboration between local communities and the police. Fourth, by achieving consensus on violence prevention strategies, the police's capacity problem is addressed. Community collaboration in this area means a substantial lessening of the police's burden.

Some concern has been expressed that the police's participation in LPCs potentially compromises their legal mandate.[55] Should the police therefore take their orders from community members instead of their legal authorities? If the police, for example, were to refrain from stopping a protest action under instruction from an LPC, who should account if the protest action leads to mayhem? The police can certainly not be legally accountable to a community forum that enjoys no statutory status. In this respect, it is necessary to reemphasize that an LPC is nothing more than a forum with no mandate to exercise executive authority. The police's participation in, and collaboration with, LPCs is in their own and the community's best interest, but under all circumstances, they remain bound by their legal mandate and authority structures.

---

55. The concern was expressed by the United Nations Mission in Nepal (UNMIN) in its comments on early drafts of the terms of reference of LPCs. In Northern Ireland, initial concerns about the Patten proposals were partly motivated by the reluctance to subject police to the machinations of community actors.

The Mediation of Local Disputes

The last aspect of the LPCs' contribution toward violence prevention is their role in mediating local disputes. Not all local disputes necessarily qualify for attention by LPCs. Local disputes, however, that feed on or contribute to the production of violence and that hinder the achievement of a sufficient level of social cohesion need attention. If left unattended, they block the larger peacebuilding project. The potential of such disputes to become violent, destabilizing not only the local situation but also the national peace process, makes attention to their resolution an urgent matter.

It is not possible to state the overall success rate of LPCs in mediating local disputes because of the lack of quantitative data, but there is a steady stream of evidence of LPCs mediating successfully in local disputes coming from countries such as Ethiopia (Teklemariam 2010), Kenya (Adan and Pkalya 2006; Chopra 2008a), Nicaragua (Lederach 1997:50), Sierra Leone (Ohman 2010), South Africa (Odendaal and Spies 1997), and, to a lesser extent, Nepal (NTTP 2008).

Ghana's experience is quite instructive in this respect. The decision to institutionalize a peace infrastructure in Ghana has been based on the success achieved in mediating local disputes.

Ghana

Ghana is not a country that is emerging from civil war. It is, on the contrary, a relatively stable, democratic country. There is, however, a marked difference in prosperity between the southern and northern parts of the country. For example, the proportion of Ghanaians living in poverty fell from 52 percent in 1991–92 to 29 percent in 2005–06. In the Northern Region, however, it declined only slightly over the same period, from 63 percent to 52 percent. In the Upper West Region, it remained static at 88 percent, while in the Upper East Region, it actually increased from 67 percent to 70 percent (Harsch 2008:4). The sense of relative deprivation in the north is not a new phenomenon. It has its roots in colonial experiences and has been a source of political tension in Ghana since independence (Bawumia 2005).

The northern region of Ghana had, possibly as a consequence of its relative neglect by the government, been the scene of a number of violent conflicts. Between 1980 and 2002, no less than twenty-three violent conflicts took place, mainly over succession and chieftaincy issues, inter- and intra-political-party tensions, land rights, identity conflicts (religion and ethnicity), and access to mineral and economic resources (Ojielo 2007). One of these, the Konkomba-Nanumba conflict in 1994–95, led to almost 5,000 deaths (Bombande 2007) with 423 villages burned or destroyed (Assefa 2001:165–66). The Dagbon conflict—a conflict over succession to the Dagbon kingship—which began in 2002, was deemed so serious that the government declared a state of emergency in the northern region of Ghana in 2003. The conflict was deeply politicized with the two main political parties taking opposite sides. The general elections of 2004 were threatened by the possibility of the conflict escalating into full-blown political violence (Bombande 2007; Ojielo 2007). The fact, therefore, is that national stability was threatened by unsolved local disputes.

The government's response to these conflicts was a typical law-and-order response (Ojielo 2007). The Konkomba-Nanumba conflict was a case in point. The conflict was also called the "guinea fowl war" because it erupted after a Nanumba man was killed following a quarrel with a Konkomba over the price of a guinea fowl. The dispute between the two societies related to their different social structures, with one being acephalous and the other ruled by hereditary chiefs.[56] The chiefs were seen, by their group, as the legitimate owners of the land, which reduced the acephalous group to a minority, landless status. The conflict was further exacerbated by religious differences (Assefa 2001).

The government's response to the violence produced by the conflict was to send in the military, which temporarily restored calm. It then appointed a high-level government commission, the Permanent Peace Negotiation Team, which managed to negotiate a cease-fire agreement in June 1994. In March 1995, violence broke out again, leading to 150 people killed, 14 villages burned down, and 21,000 people displaced (Assefa 2001). Temporary success in peace enforcement, therefore, did not lead to sustainable peacebuilding. "Political leaders often operated under the assumption that once violence was suppressed, the conflict was dealt with or that at least it will gradually fizzle out and a return to peace will ensue" (Bombande 2007:47). According to Ozonnia Ojielo (2007:3), "Efforts at resolution mostly focused on the triggers . . . with outcomes imposed by the government authority. The peace in the communities was not sustainable." In addition, these efforts were very costly. The Dagbon conflict, for example, had cost the government 72 billion cedis (almost US$8 million) between 2002 and 2005 (Ojielo 2007).

The conflict was eventually resolved by the signing of the Kumasi Accord on Peace and Reconciliation on March 28, 1996. The accord was the outcome of a patient mediation process that had the following characteristics (Assefa 2001; Bombande 2007):

---

56. An acephalous society does not have a social hierarchy and hereditary chieftainship system. They are therefore small-scale egalitarian or nonstratified societies, such as hunter-gatherer groups.

- The mediation was initiated and driven by CSOs but with tacit government support. The government did not officially support the initiative from the outset but allowed it sufficient leeway and provided limited logistical support. When the agreement was signed, however, the regional minister presented the accord to top government officials and the president, who pledged their commitment toward greater rehabilitation efforts.
- The process was guided by specialists from the Nairobi Peace Initiative, a Kenyan CSO.[57]
- A group of sixteen potential insider mediators representing all sides of the conflict had been identified early on in the process. They constituted the Peace and Reconciliation Follow-Up Committee. This committee played a crucial role by contributing to the ongoing analysis of the conflict and identification of stakeholders. Moreover, they made a substantial contribution to the legitimacy of the mediation process by continuously interacting with the communities, keeping them informed, and eliciting their views.
- Much time was spent on joint analyses of the conflict and the identification of all the stakeholders. Specific care was also taken to ensure that the mediation process was seen as legitimate by all the stakeholders. When a preliminary agreement was reached, the draft was taken back to the communities. Delegates had one month to explain the agreement to their constituencies and to come back with their endorsement of the agreement. It meant that a second round of negotiation was necessary because of community inputs. The second round of negotiation was much more difficult because the delegates now had less flexibility—they were under direct instruction of their constituencies. But it also meant that the eventual accord enjoyed a high level of support and buy-in.

The success achieved with the above approach informed a new strategy regarding such conflicts in Ghana (Bombande 2007:48–49). The Dagbon conflict that erupted in 2002 provided a testing ground for the new approach. The conflict was over succession rights to the Dagbon chieftaincy, one of the most important chieftaincies in West Africa. Traditionally, two sections of the same royal family rotated the "skin" (or throne), but for more than a century, the inherent competition led to outbursts of violence. In

---

57. They were Hizkias Assefa, then executive director of the Nairobi Peace Initiative, and his Ghanaian colleague, Emmanuel Bombande, who is currently the executive director of the West Africa Network for Peacebuilding (WANEP).

2002, the incumbent king and forty of his elders were killed. The government's response to the crisis was twofold. On the one hand, it responded in its usual way by declaring a state of emergency, sending in troops, and appointing a commission of inquiry. On the other hand, though, it sought support from civil society "to provide facilitated dialogue amongst the key stakeholders in the conflict." Assistance was also requested from the UN Country Office. UNDP/DPA subsequently sent an assessment team to Ghana, which found that one of the factions had little trust in government or its institutions. This faction had in fact boycotted the government's commission of inquiry and rejected its final report. The United Nations then appointed a peace and development adviser who, in collaboration with civil society and government, proceeded to deal with the conflict using, in essence, the strategy that had worked in the Konkomba-Nanumba conflict. The difference was that the regional government had by then established the Northern Region Peace Advocacy Council, composed of representatives chosen by the stakeholders themselves that included chiefs, women, and youth groups. The state security agencies were also represented. The objective of the council was to be a "mediation and conflict resolution mechanism to deal with the issues of trust among the factions" (Ojielo 2007). The council, therefore, was effectively the LPC that legitimized the process and facilitated important linkages.

According to Ozonnia Ojielo (2007), who was the UN peace and development adviser at the time, the process that developed under the auspices of the Peace Advocacy Council had a number of objectives. The first was to transform the perceptions and attitudes of specific target groups regarding the dynamics of violence and conflict. A series of conflict transformation workshops were conducted with an extraordinary range of actors—many of whom had been excluded from previous processes. These included youth chiefs (that led in battle), butchers and blacksmiths (key business people deeply affected by and implicated in the violence), women's groups (which, through songs, celebrated those who died fighting and derided those who canvassed for peace), politicians (who were driving the conflict to reap electoral benefits), and chiefs (the principal belligerents, fighting for ascendancy of their faction to the "skin").

The second objective was to establish a relationship of greater trust between some factions and institutions of the state. The security forces in particular suffered from perceptions that they were selective in the way that they had operated—for example, when performing raids on alleged gun traffickers. Much work was therefore done helping security agencies to develop a more evenhanded and constructive approach to the conflict. The third objective was to address the serious lack of trust between the two factions vying for the chieftaincy. In this respect, the government appointed a committee of eminent chiefs—that is, neighboring paramount chiefs in Ghana—who engaged in a series of facilitated dialogues with the factions and who are still involved in mediating a final peace agreement. The final objective was to correct the manner in which the government had chosen participants in the peace process and the limited consultation on the nature and intended outcomes of the peace process. The process itself, therefore, had to be legitimized in light of the fact that one of the factions had previously rejected the government-led process.

The process that was followed was essentially the same as in the Konkomba-Nanumba conflict, but what distinguished it from the previous one was its formal nature. The Peace Advocacy Council was an official body with government actively participating in it. The government's participation was in fact critical because of the threat to national stability and the declaration of a state of emergency, the high profile and importance of the chieftaincy issue in Ghanaian politics, and the need to transform the approach of security agencies. Achieving results without the substantial involvement of government and state institutions would have been extremely difficult.

It is also important to stress that the legal system was incapable of dealing with these conflicts. Ghana had 147 magistrate courts at the time—only 53 of these courts had sitting magistrates. Lawyers were, in general, unwilling to serve in the rural areas as magistrates. Consequently, lay magistrates had been appointed, untrained in law. The subsequent congestion in the courts was causing substantial delays (Ojielo 2007). The quality of justice delivery, therefore, was such that it was just not an option in dealing with such complex intercommunity conflicts.

The mediation process produced a number of positive outcomes. The elections of 2004 proceeded peacefully. There were two cases of violence during the elections in the region, but these occurred well outside the intervention areas. Subsequently there have been two minor incidents of violence in Dagbon. Ongoing consultations have produced a "road map to peace" that was signed by the chiefs in Kumasi in March 2006. The progress made it possible to bury the late king and install his son as regent (Ojielo 2007).[58] The violence potential of the conflict was largely defused, but the

---

58. The fact that the murdered chief, Ya Na Yakubu Andani, could not be buried was a major destabilizing factor. A number of ritual and customary requirements could not be met until the "skin" had been occupied by his successor. It therefore took four years to achieve closure on his death.

negotiation of a final agreement was still in process at the time of writing—an indication of the complexity of the conflict.

A further positive outcome of the intervention was its impact on the decision to institutionalize peace structures (Kan-Dapaah 2006; Bombande 2007; Ojielo 2007). The National Peace Council Bill of 2011 authorized the first peace infrastructure in a country that is not emerging from widespread violent conflict. National, regional, and district peace advisory councils will be established with the primary objective to facilitate intra- and intercommunity conflict transformation processes. The National Peace Council has in fact operated informally since 2006 pending the approval of legislation. It has been involved in a number of conflicts and played a key role in defusing tensions between the two dominant political parties during the 2008 national elections (Bombande 2010).[59]

The most striking characteristic of the above approach was the manner in which the conflicts were dealt with in terms of their real dynamics and not with a "view-from-the-top" approach. This was demonstrated by the way in which actors and parties were identified, the selection of issues that had to be dealt with, and the process that was followed. The key determining aspect regarding the process was its legitimacy in the eyes of all parties because their needs and concerns were being taken seriously. A further characteristic was the manner in which specialist expertise combined with the role of local peacebuilders. The specialists provided key inputs in terms of the design of the process and expertise in dealing with some of the difficult moments. Local peacebuilders, however, were mandated and empowered to make a substantial contribution. They took ownership of the process at an early stage and worked with the experts every step of the way.

It is, however, also important to note that a bottom-up approach on its own, devoid of any engagement with government, would not have progressed far. This was particularly true of the Dagbon conflict, where the government-appointed committee of eminent chiefs played a crucial role. Building peace from below, the process included active interaction with the regional and national levels of government and the involvement of political parties and other national personalities. It is a good example of joint peacebuilding.

The demonstrable benefits of this approach led to the institutionalization of a peace infrastructure. The principle that community violence is best prevented by dealing with the drivers of conflict in a participative and inclusive

---

59. The National Peace Council has also been involved with overseeing processes regarding other local conflicts, such as the Bawku conflict where, on May 9, 2010, a peace agreement was signed to bring an end to a cycle of violence related to chieftaincy issues. The agreement included a commitment to collaborate in the "interethnic peace committee" to find lasting solutions.

manner, rather than by the exclusive resort to a law-and-order approach, was formally accepted.

Beyond Violence Prevention

LPCs are not able to have an equal amount of success with all the types of violence experienced at the local level. They are, in particular, defenseless in the face of the deliberate use of violence by external actors, violence specialists, and opportunists. There should be no delusion in this respect. LPCs cannot enforce the peace. But they can support the social reconstruction of a society as discussed in the previous chapter—and thereby prevent violence. They can also facilitate local negotiations to arrive at local resolutions for potentially threatening situations, and they can mediate local pacts to prevent the resort to violence. One of the main causes of public violence is the disappearance of stabilizing third parties (Tilly 2003:230), which leads to extreme polarization and confrontational strategies. An LPC is a deliberate attempt at strengthening the stabilizing core of a community. Its inclusive composition ensures that moderate voices are empowered and heard and a more tolerant approach adopted.

The success of LPCs in preventing violence depends largely on their capacity to facilitate agreement, build trust, and mediate disputes. In a context where the coercive power of the state is weak and social cohesion fragile, LPCs offer something that goes beyond the mere prevention of violence. They strengthen social cohesion as they prevent violence. When a community has been able to avert violence through deliberate collaborative action, it has an immeasurable impact on trust building and social cohesion. If only for this reason, the strategy of seeking local consensus and agreement on nonviolent options is worth pursuing.

7

Conclusions

The Argument for Local Peacebuilding

Local peacebuilding should be a necessary aspect of a national peacebuilding strategy. Local peacebuilding matters because local conflicts, if left unresolved, have the potential to destabilize a fragile peace forged at the national level. Conversely, local peacebuilding has the ability to anchor peace at the local level, thereby strengthening the resilience of a peace agreement.

In pursuing this argument, I have made a deliberate distinction between local peacebuilding efforts that take place in the absence of a national peace agreement and initiatives that follow such an agreement. My focus was on the latter situation. A peace agreement has an important effect on the prospects of local peacebuilding. Peace agreements are rarely complete watershed events. They do not solve all problems and do not necessarily put a stop to violence. They are fragile and frequently transgressed. Yet at the local level, they open up opportunities for peacebuilding that did not exist before. When Nelson Mandela and F. W. de Klerk (in South Africa) or Gerry Adams and David Trimble (in Northern Ireland) or Mwai Kibaki and Raila Odinga (in Kenya) publicly shook hands in agreement, it certainly meant that, in all the towns and villages of their respective countries, it had become politically acceptable to engage former protagonists in peacebuilding. However fragile and tentative, a national peace agreement validates the search for peace at the local level.

While a peace agreement opens new opportunities for local peacebuilding, it does not automatically translate into peace at the local level. The main reason is that people at the local level have their own interests and needs. They may have bought into the dominant narrative that justified war and violence, but they have done so with their own interests at heart. Local actors, in other words, support national elites not because they are necessarily motivated by the grand justifications for war but rather because they believe that their own interests will be met by an alliance with one of the parties in conflict. The end of the fighting does not necessarily translate into a situation where these local expectations have been met. When local actors are in a life-and-death struggle over the use of land or water, for example, or in a desperate battle for dignity and recognition, the existence of a national peace accord will have little meaning unless it is appropriated at the local level. In fact, a peace agreement may spell deep disappointment and anger for some local actors. Rather than peace, it may incite more violence.

In addition, conditions at the local level in the aftermath of violent conflict are of a nature that often encourages rather than discourages ongoing violence. The weakness or dysfunctionality of conflict management institutions at the local level, which is often a feature of postviolence situations, is partly responsible for this situation. Whether in pursuit of interests that are shared by substantial sections of a community or for more opportunistic reasons, local actors may exploit the absence of authority and resort to violence. Furthermore, the occurrence of violence has a devastating impact on local communities; it ruptures the social fabric of a community. Extensive violence has the ability not only to deepen polarizations to the point where collaboration is almost impossible but also to alter long-held customs and practices. Social reconstruction at the local level in the aftermath of violence therefore poses particularly complex and difficult challenges. An aspect of this challenge is the deeply emotional and personal nature of conflict in close-knit communities. On the whole, because of the extensive damage done to social and political institutions and personal relationships, the task of peacebuilding at the local level cannot be achieved by barking instructions from the top. It requires specific and focused interventions. Peacebuilding at the local level is therefore necessary not only for its relevance for national stability but also because of the particular conditions that require specialized attention.

There is, at least in some circles, a growing appreciation of this perspective. Local peacebuilding, consequently, is seen as a necessary ingredient of a larger peacebuilding strategy. In fact, as Séverine Autesserre (2010) has argued, the reigning peacebuilding narrative has to be challenged because its neglect of local peacebuilding is a cause of general peacebuilding failure. The difficulty, however, is to know what approach to follow to support and facilitate local peacebuilding. To date, most of the international support for local peacebuilding has been channeled through CSOs. The specific problem associated with peacebuilding through CSOs, however, is their weakness in linking their projects with other processes taking place in the same context. They often fail to link effectively with other CSOs, with the broad spectrum of political actors, with local and national government, and with processes happening at provincial or national levels. The piecemeal quality of their interventions, combined with their lack of implementing power, result in their limited impact on the deeper causes of conflict.

Infrastructures for peace find their rationale against this analysis. The objective with an infrastructure for peace is to optimize linkage between local and national levels and between all former protagonists and those institutions or actors that seek peace, including CSOs. For this reason, it is important that the infrastructure receive formal or official recognition, meaning that the state and its institutions are active participants in its activities.

Three main assumptions underpin the concept. First, peacebuilding is the joint responsibility of a whole society and not the sole domain of the political elite. At all levels of society and in all its sectors, the responsibility for peace has to be shared and pursued jointly. Second, the main resources needed for peacebuilding are located in a society and not externally, but conscious efforts are needed to galvanize them. It does not mean that no external support is necessary, but in order for peace to be sustainable, a society has to depend mainly on its own human and other resources. Third, because local actors have agency and each local conflict is caused by a unique combination of local and national factors, the process of local peacebuilding has to engage with the specific dynamics of that situation. Local conflicts are not mere carbon copies of the national conflict and cannot be dealt with by the imposition of nationally designed solutions. Local conflicts have to be assessed and dealt with in terms of their own dynamics but in interaction with the national level.

This is the core argument for LPCs. The question is whether it has more than theoretical attraction. Is there any evidence that LPCs work in practice?

Do LPCs Work?

The study has set out to explore and compare our collective practical experience with this specific local peacebuilding formula: a national mandate for local peacebuilding plus local mechanisms (LPCs) to facilitate implementation in a manner that values local agency. By relying on case studies, experiences in a number of contexts have been analyzed and compared. This methodology, of course, does not allow us to reach definitive conclusions in all respects. I have also been selective in the evidence that I have presented because of my primary objective to demonstrate that it is a feasible option that deserves attention and to point to the main benefits and challenges associated with this strategy.

There is indeed significant evidence that this approach to peacebuilding is viable and has considerable potential. In countries such as Ghana, Kenya, Nicaragua, Northern Ireland, Sierra Leone, and South Africa, it has contributed toward meeting the two main peacebuilding objectives, namely preventing violence—though not all forms of violence—and promoting peaceful coexistence. It has achieved these results mainly by virtue of its ability to facilitate dialogue and mediate the resolution of local conflicts. This is the overall conclusion, but it has to be tempered by realism. Peacebuilding contexts are by nature deeply traumatized and unstable contexts with no preexistent recipe to guarantee success. Furthermore, LPCs' success relies on a volatile political environment that tolerates local peacebuilding and on local agency for peace. Results will therefore be patchy, varying between parallel local contexts because of local dynamics and changing over time as the volatile political environment changes. While this is the case, infrastructures for peace that support local peacebuilding were, in the cases examined in this book, relatively effective. More specific conclusions can be reached regarding the way in which a formal infrastructure for peace supports local peacebuilding. They relate to legitimacy, ownership, expertise, and linkage.

Legitimacy

The mere fact that a formal peace infrastructure has been established sends a strong message regarding the legitimacy of peacebuilding. It is a matter that should not be underestimated. It means a complete reversal of the discourses at the time of war and violence, when hatred and suspicion reigned and any sign of engagement with the enemy was seen as treason. Now a peace infrastructure exists, endorsed by all the relevant national leaders, with the objective to support local communities in building their own peace. If, furthermore, the local collective leadership have the freedom to decide for themselves whether to establish an LPC or not, a decision in favor of an LPC adds significant *local* legitimacy to the LPC. It implies that the local leadership has agreed to accept joint responsibility for the task of peacebuilding. The LPC, therefore, is indeed a platform with significant legitimacy for the launching of local peacebuilding processes. In countries like Nicaragua, South Africa, Northern Ireland, Macedonia, and Sierra Leone, this fact has enabled former enemies at the local level to meet and engage in dialogue and joint problem solving. However, the risk of "political capture" is real; when the ruling party or another actor seeks to exercise exclusive control of the peace infrastructure, it undermines the infrastructure's legitimacy—and thereby its raison d'être. The relationship between the peace committees, state institutions, and the government has, in fact, emerged as one of the most complex aspects of the functioning of a peace infrastructure and will be discussed in more detail below.

What is noteworthy is the way in which LPCs not only benefit from the political legitimacy they enjoy but also contribute to the legitimacy of state institutions. In cases such as Northern Ireland and South Africa, LPCs have contributed to the legitimacy of the police, while in Kenya and Ghana they have facilitated improved government responsiveness to local issues and conflicts. In Macedonia and Serbia, they facilitate greater sensitivity in municipal councils to ethnic relationships. The legitimacy enjoyed by the LPCs therefore begat a measure of legitimacy for those institutions with which they interacted.

Ownership

LPCs rely on local resources for their success. By allocating the responsibility for local peacebuilding to a widely representative local forum, the message is clear: The peacefulness of a community will be determined by its own people. A key resource in this respect is the insider-partials or local peacebuilders—people with the aptitude and credibility to take the lead in peacebuilding processes. This reliance on local agency, in fact, has been a key theoretical assumption of this book. There is, undoubtedly, a strong correlation between the quality of local ownership and the success of LPCs. It is also clear that the formation of an LPC provides local peacebuilders with a strong mandate, thus galvanizing their potential role.

An important benefit of local ownership is that local conflicts are respected and addressed in terms of their real dynamics. In contrast to a law-and-order approach that is top-down and, as demonstrated in the cases of Ghana and Kenya, insensitive to the actual causes and conditions of the conflict, an approach that is locally owned and managed does better in terms of engaging all the relevant actors and stakeholders and addressing the issues that really matter. It also strengthens the social cohesion within that community while addressing the conflict. In addition, with reference to the experience in Ghana, when an LPC has been successful in solving conflict, the success has an important affect on the confidence of a community in its collective ability to address its own deep polarizations, thus enabling a culture of constructive conflict resolution to develop.

The main unanswered question is what to do when local agency does not support peace—when the polarization is such that no local peacebuilders step forward to accept responsibility for a peace process. Séverine Autesserre (2010:264–69), for one, has argued in favor of direct international intervention in local conflicts in the absence of local capacity or will—a strategy

I am hesitant to propagate. I rather prefer intensified efforts by mediators mandated by the national peace committee. It is, however, an area of concern that is in need of clearer answers and further research.

Expertise

A peace infrastructure ensures administrative and technical support to LPCs. The latter is particularly important and refers to expertise in peacebuilding, including the facilitation of complex dialogue and negotiation processes. LPCs, with some notable exceptions, are not able to go it alone. Conflict transformation processes are, by their nature, extraordinarily complex, especially given the particular conditions that characterize postviolence contexts at the local level: the ongoing vulnerability to violence, the damage done by violence to social cohesion, and the deeply emotional and personal nature of conflict. These conditions require that the facilitation of peacebuilding processes takes place with the utmost skill and care. LPCs need support in this respect, and it is a function of the peace infrastructure to ensure sufficient access for LPCs to such expertise. The case studies strongly suggest a correlation between the success of LPCs and the quality of technical support that they have received.

The obvious conclusion is that a serious investment is necessary in building the knowledge and skills base of these practitioners. At the moment, most of this work is done by those international organizations that support peace infrastructures. The substance and methodology of their training programs have not been subjects of this study, but both are certainly worthwhile topics of research. As mentioned, success is actually determined by the quality of dialogue that takes place between trainer and trainees, between their worldviews and contextual experiences. The important question is to what extent capacity building is informed by this approach.

Linkage

The real advantage that the peace infrastructure offers is effective linkage, both horizontally at the local level and vertically to the national and international levels. Where LPCs have been effective, they have succeeded in facilitating collaboration between actors that would normally not interact, both horizontally within a community and vertically within the different levels of a society. Of particular importance is the linkage between the government and civil society. This is, as mentioned earlier, often the missing link in local peacebuilding as performed by international or national CSOs. A formal peace infrastructure, on the other hand, enables interaction and collaboration between state institutions, political actors, and other social or cultural organizations at all the levels of society. It increases communication between the state and its citizens and enhances the responsiveness of the state to societal concerns.

A formal infrastructure for peace therefore contributes substantially to the potential of local peacebuilding. The major risk associated with such a formal structure, however, is excessive political manipulation—the undermining of the collaborative potential of the infrastructure for sectional political gain.

The Importance of Role Clarity

Peacebuilding is a political matter. There is no such thing as a peace that is politically neutral. Peacebuilding regards the future of a nation and requires that fundamental political decisions be taken on matters such as the constitutional order, fair access to material and other resources, and restitution in respect of past wrongs. While it is true that the major political decisions regarding the transformation of a nation will be made at the national level, local peacebuilding is similarly political in nature because it has to address the contest of local interest groups for fair access to political and economic resources. It would therefore be naive to consider an LPC as an apolitical body.

Yet LPCs have to fulfill a role that, while not apolitical, paves the way for "normal" political contestation without being a platform for actual political contests. This assumption has underpinned this book's analysis of the role of LPCs and description of an appropriate methodology for LPCs. LPCs should have no teeth. The core functions of LPCs are to facilitate dialogue, thereby promoting better mutual understanding and reconciliation, and to address local conflicts that have the potential for violence or that have a debilitating effect on reconstruction or development efforts by mandating and supporting mediated negotiations between the conflict parties. LPCs, consequently, should facilitate dialogue rather than debate; should mediate rather than arbitrate; should advise rather than decide; and should mobilize a community's resources in support of reconciliation, repairing broken relationships and restoring confidence rather than pursuing sectional political agendas.

There are a number of practices that help LPCs to perform this specific role. The first is that the infrastructure as a whole should fall under multistakeholder control and not the sole control of the ruling party. Second, LPCs should be as inclusive as possible, not only of the main protagonists but also of those institutions and actors that have the potential to support constructive peacebuilding. By including the latter, the assumption is that the middle ground will be strengthened, that centrifugal forces will be counteracted by centripetal social forces. Third, the LPC should operate on the principle of consensus. This arrangement implies that the LPC should focus more on forging a local social contract than on policy details. In case of highly divisive issues, the focus should be on reaching consensus regarding the most appropriate process to deal with such issues rather than on focusing on the issues themselves. In short, LPCs should build consensus on the best local strategies to achieve the peacebuilding objectives that have been jointly decided. Lastly, LPCs should preferably not be chaired by a politician but by an insider-partial—someone trusted within the community for her or his integrity and fairness. The LPC chairperson should be an able facilitator who understands the nature of dialogue and is skilled in its facilitation. The leadership of the LPC, therefore, does not dictate but enables constructive talking and listening.

In the cases that have been examined, there is evidence of the appropriateness of this approach. It is particularly significant that in those countries where the role of LPCs has been institutionalized, the enabling legislation has been quite clear in circumscribing their role as above. Yet it is also evident that there are areas where these role distinctions have an academic and inappropriate ring. In contexts where local government is either dysfunctional or absent, LPCs have performed services that belonged to government. It is a situation that peacebuilders are as uncomfortable with as statebuilders. It may well be, as Ken Menkhaus suggested, that such a hybrid arrangement is a necessary step on the longer road to indigenous statebuilding. It is certainly a development that deserves ongoing scrutiny.

A particularly sensitive aspect of the role of LPCs is their potential to take part in the administration of justice. In line with the argument that LPCs do not exercise executive authority, it is not advised that they administer any form of punitive justice. They do, however, have a potential role in facilitating restorative justice. This, again, is an area that deserves further attention, particularly the question regarding to what extent processes of community-based restorative justice deserve official or legal recognition and how such recognition should be arranged.

In summary, the role of LPCs vis-à-vis local government and state institutions is distinguished by the LPCs' emphasis on dialogue, consensus building, and mediation. As such, they are least likely to fall foul of undue political manipulation and interference, but there is of course no watertight guarantee against political capture. There are also aspects of the potential role of LPCs that have not been considered in this study primarily because of a lack of evidence. These include the link between peacebuilding and development, and thus the potential role of LPCs as a facilitator of consensus regarding development objectives.[60] They also include the more difficult issue of human rights monitoring and whether such a body is an appropriate platform for this role. These issues could open up additional areas of overlap or contradiction to government, thus complicating the LPCs' role.

LPCs and International Support

There is an increasing appetite among international organizations, particularly the United Nations, to support the establishment and functioning of infrastructures for peace (Kumar 2011, Van Tongeren 2011). It is a welcome development since, as noted, international support has been indispensible in the majority of cases. Such support has ranged from propagation of the concept to capacity building to funding. However, the success of international support hinges on the manner in which the "systemic dilemma" (the tension between local ownership and efficiency) is managed.

The most important conclusion to reach regarding the role that international actors have played in support of LPCs is that success has been determined by the skill of key personnel. Their respect for local ownership, skill in building trust, and ability to transfer knowledge and skills in a way that is truly empowering has made the difference. Put differently, it is not possible to export the concept of an infrastructure for peace from international headquarters somewhere in a global city to a nation in peacebuilding mode in a mechanical, perfunctory way. Local ownership is the key success factor, and it is not a quality that can be artificially or mechanically induced. International support is successful when its personnel have the sensitivity to assess the quality of local ownership correctly and to respond in appropriate ways.

This raises a question regarding the investment made in preparing such key personnel for their task. It does not make sense to spend substantial amounts of money in support of a peace infrastructure without attention to this matter. An academic understanding of issues is not sufficient. Having the relevant personal and professional qualities—such as empathy, respect, good listening skills, insight into one's own cultural and ideological assumptions, and skill in "elicitive training"—matters.

---

60. The only example of a conscious link between LPCs and development was in South Africa, where LPCs were required to form socioeconomic reconstruction and development subcommittees to address the link between development (or rather the lack thereof) and conflict. The experiment was unsuccessful largely because the task of socioeconomic restructuring required fundamental constitutional and political change at the national level—a task that had to be addressed by the national negotiation process (see Ball 1998:22).

Unanswered Questions

At the end of this road, there are more unanswered questions than answered ones. Given the methodology used for this study and the relatively small sample, every conclusion calls for further inquiry and research.

Possibly the most important unanswered question is what makes LPCs fail. LPCs do fail, and political manipulation or bureaucratic bungle is not the only cause. Very little documentation, however, exists on the failure of LPCs. It is just not a matter that is being written about. However, to sharpen this local peacebuilding tool, it is absolutely necessary to have a deeper understanding of the reasons for failure.

A question that begs further attention is to what extent the volunteerism of LPCs is sustainable. This matter is specifically pertinent in cases where LPCs have been institutionalized. During times of transition or in the immediate aftermath of a crisis, it is important that LPC members give freely of their time. It is, after all, in their direct interest to secure peace, and giving their time is an expression of the quality of their ownership of the process. However, LPC activities, particularly mediation processes, can absorb an extraordinary amount of time and energy, and it is unrealistic to expect that it can be sustained on a voluntary basis.

Another unanswered question is to what extent the approach is culturally determined. LPCs have been implemented in quite diverse contexts, suggesting that they are appropriate to all or most cultural settings. But is this a correct assumption? LPCs also seem to be particularly successful in Africa. Is it because they are well suited to African culture and conditions, or does the high incidence of peace infrastructures in Africa merely reflect the continent's unfortunate status as being conflict prone?

I have deliberately refrained from paying too much attention to the details of financial, bureaucratic, and other structural matters primarily because the manner in which an infrastructure is set up and organized has to be contextually determined. There should not be a model or recipe that can be applied to all contexts in a rather mindless manner. My focus has been on clarifying what I thought were the key principles and considerations that should go into the design of such an infrastructure. There are, in other words, many practical questions that remain unanswered because they can only be answered once the demands of the context have been understood.

* * *

The concept of a formal infrastructure for peace that enables or facilitates the functioning of local peace committees has many attractive characteristics. It acknowledges the importance of local peacebuilding and the need for effective linkage between local processes and national or even international agendas to promote stability and peace in conflict-affected areas. It creates the political space for local peacebuilding and leverages the collective resources of a society in the pursuit of the stated peace objectives. Furthermore, it provides coordination between the formal and informal sectors of a community, as well as the local and national levels of society. Most important, it goes about its task in a manner that strengthens the legitimacy of the peacebuilding agenda, that builds the confidence of a society in its collective ability to address its own deep polarizations, and that lays the foundation for the social cohesion that is a necessary precondition for effective governance.

Inevitably, the way in which this concept has thus far been applied to reality has not been without its imperfections and shortcomings. Yet enough has been achieved to earn it the serious attention of the peacebuilding community.

Appendix
Formal Infrastructures for Local Peacebuilding

Two criteria have been used to identify formal peace infrastructures:

1. The peace infrastructure has been established through a national agreement that has involved the most important stakeholders of a peace process
2. The peace infrastructure must provide for structures at the local level to achieve the objectives that have been agreed to.

The following list consists of two categories: the first category contains examples of contexts that meet the two criteria for formal peace infrastructures, and the second category contains contexts where there have been noteworthy developments but that do not quite meet the stated criteria. These lists do not pretend to be exhaustive.

Category 1

The first attempt at establishing a peace infrastructure, to my knowledge, is **Nicaragua.** A National Reconciliation Commission consisting of four individuals representing different sides of the conflict was established in the terms of the 1987 Esquipulas Peace Accord (Lederach 1997:50; Prendergast and Plumb 2002:341). The latter was actually an agreement between five Central American leaders to bring the number of Cold War–fueled civil wars in the region to an end. The main objective with the commission was to monitor cease-fire agreements but also to coordinate the activities of regional and local peace commissions, which became involved in the mediation of local agreements between the belligerents and a wider array of local disputes.

In **South Africa,** the National Peace Accord was agreed to by the government and political parties (with the exclusion of smaller fringe parties) in 1991 with the main objective to contain violence. The infrastructure that it mandated included peace committees at national, regional, and local levels and a secretariat under multiparty control that was responsible for its implementation. Eleven regional and approximately 260 local peace committees were established. The committees were composed of representatives of the signatories of the accord and all relevant regional or local CSOs. Following the democratic elections of 1994, the peace infrastructure was dismantled.

The Good Friday Peace Agreement of 1998 in **Northern Ireland** identified the normalization of policing as a critical peacebuilding task. The Patten Commission subsequently recommended a peacebuilding infrastructure to assist in this task that, with amendments, was formalized by the Police (Northern Ireland) Act of 2000. In the terms of this Act, a Policing Board was established composed of nineteen members, ten parliamentarians, and nine independent civil society members. The main task of the board was to be a platform where policing priorities would be determined. In addition, in each district, a District Policing Partnership (DPP) was established, following the same pattern of political and civil society representation, as a platform where local politicians, civil society representatives, and the police could meet and build consensus on matters concerning the police.

In **Nepal,** a peace infrastructure was established as early as 2003 in the form of a Peace Negotiation Coordination Secretariat to support peace negotiations with the Maoist insurgency. Control of this structure was one sided as the Maoists had no role whatsoever in its operation. The structure went through various mutations until, in 2006, as an outcome of the Comprehensive Peace Agreement with the Maoists, it became a full-blown Ministry of Peace and Reconstruction. One of the key tasks of the ministry is to implement local peace committees.

The peace process in **Côte d'Ivoire** encompassed a number of national peace agreements. In the terms of the Accra Peace Agreement II of 2003, a Ministère de la Réconciliation (Reconciliation Ministry) was established. The ministry subsequently underwent a number of structural changes, but its fundamental objectives remained the same until the renewed outbreak of civil war in 2010. One of its tasks was to establish and coordinate "local peace and reconciliation committees." Seventy-one such bodies were established with the objectives to prevent violence and strengthen social cohesion.

FYR Macedonia provides an example of LPCs institutionalized particularly for the purpose of normalizing ethnic relations. As an outcome of the

Ohrid Framework Agreement of 2001, Committees on Intercommunity Relations were established in districts with sizeable ethnic minorities. All ethnic minorities are equally represented in these committees. They have the task to advise the municipal council on issues of ethnic coexistence. The municipal council has the legal obligation to consider their opinions and recommendations and supply reasons for not implementing them—if that be the case. Essentially, therefore, the committees have the legal function to ensure that the municipal council is aware of how decisions that they are considering will affect the *relationship between* ethnic communities. As such they institutionalize local interethnic dialogue and ensure that the voices of minority communities are taken seriously by the council (Koceski 2008).

A similar arrangement exists in **Serbia**, where the Law on Local Self-Government, 2002, established Committees on Intercommunity Relations with much the same mandate.

In **Kenya,** following the peace agreement mediated by Kofi Annan to address the electoral violence of 2008, the National Accord and Reconciliation Act of 2008 recommended the establishment of District Peace Committees in all of Kenya's districts. The decision was influenced by the positive contribution of LPCs in the country's pastoralist areas. The latter operated under the auspices of the National Steering Committee on Peace Building and Conflict Management. The infrastructure is still in the process of construction.

In **Ghana,** a comparable process unfolded. Though at peace, with no major national-level violent conflict since the transition to democratic rule in 1993, a number of violent intercommunity conflicts occurred over the past two decades—particularly in the generally more deprived northern region. Following positive experiences with the use of regional and local peace committees in the north, Ghana, with multiparty support, adopted legislation in 2011 to institutionalize peace councils at the national, regional, and district level.

Sierra Leone provides an example of an infrastructure established to prevent violence during elections in 2007 and 2008 in the context of a very fragile peace. Under the auspices of the Political Parties Registration Commission (PPRC), a statutory body, the political parties negotiated a code of conduct and established a joint monitoring body, consisting of all political parties, the electoral commission, the human rights commission, the police, and civil society representatives. This body replicated itself in the regions and districts. The bodies in the districts were called District Code of Conduct Monitoring Committees and had the mandate to ensure peaceful elections.

A similar structure exists in **Malawi.** The Multiparty Liaison Committees were established in 2004 under the auspices of the Malawi Election Commission and composed of local representatives of registered political parties, the electoral commission, and civil society. They facilitated dialogue between political parties at the district level and jointly determined the strategy to ensure peaceful elections.

Category 2

In the eastern, violence-ridden part of the **Democratic Republic of the Congo,** a tripartite agreement was signed in February 2010 between the governments of the Democratic Republic of the Congo, Rwanda, and UNHCR. This agreement sets the stage for the facilitated return of over fifty thousand Congolese refugees from official camps in Rwanda. The agreement envisaged the establishment of LPCs, called Comité Locaux Permanents de Conciliation (CLPC), to facilitate the return and reintegration of refugees. The CLPCs will be set up in areas of return and are composed of local authorities, customary chiefs, civil society actors, representatives of the displaced and various ethnic and religious groups, and UN agencies. They will plan and prioritize reintegration projects, mediate in case of conflicts over land and resources, and ensure community participation in the overall return and reintegration process (UNHCR 2009; Hege 2010; Olson and Hege 2010). These LPCs are currently in the process of being established. It is therefore too soon to consider their experiences.

The Karamoja region of **Uganda** is distinctively different from the rest of the country in environmental and cultural terms. The Karimojong have resisted integration into mainstream society over the years and maintained a pastoralist lifestyle, resulting in their economic and political marginalization. The past decades have seen a drastic escalation of violence associated with cattle rustling, resulting in a concerted disarmament drive by the government since 2004. The government has now adopted an integrated development plan for Karamoja (Republic of Uganda 2007), which includes the establishment of District Peace and Development Committees. These committees, by virtue of their composition and objectives, have the potential to be forums for dialogue between the Karimojong and government on basic governance and development issues that have been sources of conflict. In particular, the administration of law and order has created multiple misunderstandings and conflict (Muhereza, Ossiya et al. 2008). However, lack of role clarity on the specific roles and mandates of these committees vis-à-vis other governance structures is delaying their implementation.

In **Ethiopia,** the Ministry of Federal Affairs had set up an infrastructure of peace committees from the national to the local level, including the level of the *kabele*, the smallest administrative unit, which consists of approximately five thousand people. More than seven hundred such peace committees have been established since 2009 (Teklemariam 2010). The reason for going this route was, primarily, growing dissatisfaction with the reactive response to violent community conflicts of the past. Despite the fact that, in the past, the ministry had deployed considerable resources and energies in conflict prevention and resolution, it had tended to react only after full-blown conflicts had erupted, with their attendant tragic consequences (Ministry of Federal Affairs 2010).

There are a number of significant features of the peace committees. First, the infrastructure encourages joint peace committees between neighboring communities that have a conflict. Second, representatives on the committees have the obligation first to report back to their constituencies and secure their buy-in before an agreement is finalized. Third, the committees clearly operate under oversight of the government. The president is the chairperson of the national peace committee, and the local committees are chaired by civil servants, the presidents, or administrators of the local administrative units. There is reason to be concerned that the hand of government rests too heavily on the infrastructure. Also, Ethiopia is still subject to rebel activity. The rebels have not been included in the agreement to establish the peace infrastructure. For these reasons Ethiopia is not included in the category 1 list. However, the minister of federal affairs stated in an interview that there is consensus between political parties in Parliament on this approach (Teklemariam 2010). Furthermore, initial results have been very impressive. More than 95 percent of local conflicts are dealt with at this level and do not require intervention from the ministry. In the Somali region of Ethiopia, development projects were, in the past, hampered in twenty-four of fifty-two districts because of debilitating local conflicts, which have now been resolved because of the new approach.

Aceh presents a study in infrastructure collapse. In 2002, local "zones of peace" were established as part of the Cessation of Hostilities Agreement (COHA). It was mainly a cease-fire agreement—not a detailed and final peace agreement. Its main goals were demilitarization and demobilization. The zones of peace were meant to be a confidence-building measure to help ensure the success of the ongoing peace process (Hancock and Iyer 2007:36). In other words, they were seen as a means to move the process forward, as a prelude to disarming, demilitarization, and the provision of humanitarian aid (Iyer and Mitchell 2007). Seven peace zones were established, and violence there dramatically decreased, but when disarmament was supposed to begin, violence erupted on a large scale, and COHA collapsed. Neither side showed any commitment to the COHA.

One factor that has contributed to the collapse was the fact that the local community was not involved in any discussions regarding the establishment and function of the zones of peace. "There seems to have been no sustained attempt to involve the local people—to give them space to express their own needs or suggest appropriate arrangements. From mute spectators of war they were asked to remain mute spectators of peace" (Iyer and Mitchell 2007).

The peace process in **Bougainville** presents a classic case study of the agency of local level communities in the production of both violence and peace (see Reilly 2008; Braithwaite, Charlesworth et al. 2010). At the national level, an impressive "contextually attuned architecture of linkages" existed, whereby various international actors played specific constructive roles at particular moments (Braithwaite, Charlesworth et al. 2010:60). Of importance, though, is that processes at the local level made a vital contribution to the overall success of the national peace process. Relying heavily on traditional and religious symbolism, local actors pursued reconciliation with passion and commitment. There is certainly much to learn from Bougainville, but the fact that the local processes were not formally linked to a peace infrastructure disqualifies it from inclusion in the category 1 list.

East Timor is of interest because it is the only example of a Truth and Reconciliation Commission that deliberately pursued reconciliation at the local level, albeit only for a brief period. Important lessons can be learned from this experience (see chapter 5), but the absence of structures at the local level similarly disqualifies it from inclusion in category 1.

Rwanda has drawn much international attention for its attempt to pursue justice and reconciliation through local gacaca courts. The concern with Rwanda, however, is not only the absence of LPC-like structures but also the lack of multistakeholder ownership of the process. Much can be learned from Rwanda about the pursuit of justice at the local level in the aftermath of genocide, though. See chapter 5 for a more detailed discussion.

References

ACCORD. *See* African Centre for the Constructive Resolution of Disputes.

ACE Project. 2007. "Sierra Leone's 2007 elections." *Elections Today*. http://ace project.org.

Adams, Gerry. 2008. "The Defining Moment." *Morning Star*, April 18.

Adan, Mohamud, and Ruto Pkalya. 2006. *The Concept Peace Committee:. A Snap-shot Analysis of the Concept Peace Committee in Relation to Peacebuilding Initiatives in Kenya*. Practical Action.

Adebajo, Adekeye. 2010. "The Seven Horsemen of Nigeria's Apocalypse." *Mail & Guardian Online* (Johannesburg), October 4.

The Advocacy Project. 2009. "Community Justice Thrives in the Villages of Eastern Congo." News Bulletin 192.

Africa Confidential. 2010. "Ocampo Names Six Subjects." *Africa Confidential* 51:25:1–2.

African Centre for the Constructive Resolution of Disputes. 2009. "ACCORD Re-presents APA to Mpumalanga Community." www.accord.org.za/

Ajdukovic, Dean, and Dinka Corkalo. 2004. "Trust and Betrayal in War." In *My Neighbor, My Enemy: Justice and Community in the Aftermath of Mass Atrocity*, eds. Eric Stover and Harvey M. Weinstein, 287–302. Cambridge: Cambridge University Press.

Akinteye, Akin, James M. Wuye, and Muhammad N. Ashafa. 1999. "Zangon-Kataf Crisis: A Case Study." In *Community Conflicts in Nigeria. Management, Resolution and Transformation*, eds. Onigu Otite and Isaac O. Albert. Ibadan: Spectrum Books.

Anderson, Mary B. 2004. "Experiences with Impact Assessment: Can We Know What Good We Do?" In *Berghof Handbook for Conflict Transformation*, eds. Martina Fischer and Norbert Ropers. Berlin: Berghof Research Centre.

Apuuli, Kasaija P. 2009. "Procedural Due Process and the Prosecution of Genocide Suspects in Rwanda." *Journal of Genocide Research* 11(1):11–30.

Arnson, Cynthia, ed. 1999. *Comparative Peace Processes in Latin America*. Washington, DC: Woodrow Wilson Center Press.

Assefa, Hizkias. 2001. "Coexistence and Reconciliation in the Northern Region of Ghana." In *Reconciliation, Justice, and Coexistence*, edited by Mohammed Abu-Nimer, 165–186. Lanham, MD: Lexington Books.

Autessere, Séverine. 2010. *The Trouble with the Congo: Local Violence and the Failure of International Peacebuilding.* Cambridge, Cambridge University Press.

Ball, Nicole. 1998. "Managing Conflict: Lessons from the South African Peace Committees." In *USAID Evaluation Special Study Report.* Center for Development Information and Evaluation.

Bawumia, Mumuni. 2005. *A Life in the Political History of Ghana.* Accra: Ghana University Press.

Bendaña, Alejandro. 1999. "Reflections." In *Comparative Peace Processes in Latin America*, edited by Cynthia Arnson. Washington, DC: Woodrow Wilson Center Press.

Berkeley, Bill. 2001. *The Graves Are Not Yet Full: Race, Tribe, and Power in the Heart of Africa.* New York: Basic Books.

Bloch, Corrine. 2005. "Listen to Understand: The Listening Project in Croatia." In *People Building Peace II: Successful Stories of Civil Society*, eds. Paul van Tongeren, Malin Brenk, Marte Hellema, and Juliette Verhoeven, 654–60. Boulder, CO: Lynne Rienner.

Bloomfield, David. 1995. "Towards Complementarity in Conflict Management: Resolution and Settlement in Northern Ireland." *Journal of Peace Research* 32(2):151–64.

Bombande, Emmanuel. 2007. "Ghana: Developing an Institutional Framework for Sustainable Peace—UN, Government and Civil Society Collaboration for Conflict Prevention." In *Joint Action for Prevention: Civil Society and Government Cooperation on Conflict Prevention and Peacebuilding*, Issue Paper 4, eds. Paul van Tongeren and Christene van Empel, 47–55. Den Haag: European Centre for Conflict Prevention.

———. 2010. "A Peace Infrastructure for Ghana." Paper presented at Infrastructures for Peace Seminar, United Nations Development Programme (UNDP), Naivasha, Kenya.

Boutros-Ghali, Boutros. 1992. *An Agenda for Peace: Preventive Diplomacy, Peacemaking and Peace-keeping.* New York: United Nations.

Braithwaite, John, Hilary Charlesworth, Peter Reddy, and Leah Dunn. 2010. *Reconciliation and Architectures of Commitment: Sequencing Peace in Bougainville.* Canberra: Australian National University Press.

Branch, Adam. 2008. "Gulu Town in War. . . and Peace? Displacement, Humanitarianism and Post-war Crisis." Cities and Fragile States Working Paper 36, London, Crisis States Research Centre.

Breed, M. 2007. "Sinn Fein Beware! 'IRLA' Warning on PSNI Support." *News of the World* (UK), December 9.

Bremner, Davin. 1994. "Development's Catch-22: No Development without Peace, No Peace without Development." *Track Two* 3(1).

Brounéus, Karen. 2010. "The Trauma of Truth Telling: Effects of Witnessing in the Rwandan Gacaca Courts on Psychological Health." *Journal of Conflict Resolution* 54(3):408–37.

Bruton, Bronwyn. 2009. "In the Quicksands of Somalia." *Foreign Affairs* 88(6): 79–94.

Burton, John. 1988. *Conflict Resolution as a Political System*. Fairfax, VA: Center for Conflict Analysis and Resolution, George Mason University.

Bush, Kenneth. 2004. "Commodification, Compartmentalization, and Militarization of Peacebuilding." In *Building Sustainable Peace*, eds. Thomas Keating and W. Andy Knight, 23–45. Tokyo: United Nations University Press.

———. 2005. "Field Notes: Fighting Commodification and Disempowerment in the Development Industry: Things I Learned about PCIA in Habarana and Mindanao." In *Berghof Handbook for Conflict Transformation*, Dialogue Series 4, eds. David Bloomfield, Martina Fischer, and Beatrix Schmelzle. Berlin: Berghof Research Centre.

Butt, Bridget. 2004. "Feasibility of Doing Peace Work in Situations of Violent Conflict in the Context of the Current Situation in the DRC," Quaker Service Norway.

Carmichael, Elizabeth. 2010. "Communicating Peace through the National Peace Accord, South Africa 1991–1994." IPRA Conflict Resolution and Peace Building Commission, Sydney.

CAVR. *See* Commission for Reception, Truth and Reconciliation of East Timor.

CCR. *See* Centre for Conflict Resolution.

Centre for Conflict Resolution. 1998. *Final Narrative Report on Project Saamspan Submitted to the Royal Netherlands Embassy*. Cape Town: Centre for Conflict Resolution.

Chalmers, Rhoderick. 2010. "Nepal: From Conflict to Consolidating a Fragile Peace." In *Civil Society and Peacebuilding: A Critical Assessment*, edited by Thania Paffenholz, 259–95. Boulder, CO: Lynne Rienner.

Chang, Kevin. 2009. E-mail communication with author, November 8. Kathmandu.

Chigas, Diana, and Peter Woodrow. 2009. "Envisioning and Pursuing Peace Writ Large." In *Berghof Handbook for Conflict Transformation*, eds. Martina Fischer and Norbert Ropers. Berlin: Berghof Research Center.

Child, Jack. 1992. *The Central American Peace Process, 1983–1991: Sheathing Swords, Building Confidence*. Boulder, CO: Lynne Rienner.

Chopra, Tanja. 2008a. *Building Informal Justice in Northern Kenya*. Nairobi: Legal Resources Foundation Trust.

———. 2008b. *Reconciling Society and the Judiciary in Northern Kenya*. Nairobi: Legal Resources Foundation Trust.

———. 2009. "When Peacebuilding Contradicts Statebuilding: Notes from the Arid Lands of Kenya." *International Peacekeeping* 16(4):531–45.

Cilliers, Jaco. 2001. "Local Reactions to Post-conflict Peacebuilding Efforts in Bosnia-Herzegovina and South Africa." PhD diss., Institute for Conflict Analysis and Resolution. George Mason University.

Clarke, Phil. 2008. "Ethnicity, Leadership and Conflict Mediation in Eastern Democratic Republic of Congo: The Case of the *Barza Inter-Communautaire.*" *Journal of Eastern African Studies* 2(1):1–17.

Collaborative Learning Projects. 2006. "Creating a River between Two Fires: Impact Assessment of the Locally Initiated Networks for Community Strengthening Program (LINCS), Lofa County, Liberia." Cambridge, MA. www.cdainc.com.

Collin Marks, Susan. 2000. *Watching the Wind: Conflict Resolution during South Africa's Transition to Democracy.* Washington, DC: United States Institute of Peace Press.

Commission for Reception, Truth and Reconciliation of East Timor. 2006. "Final Report: Commission for Reception, Truth and Reconciliation in East Timor."

Commonwealth Expert Team. 2008. "Report of the Commonwealth Expert Team, Sierra Leone Local Government Elections." Joint Commonwealth Secretariat and Commonwealth Local Government Forum Team. July 5. http://aceproject.org.

Corkalo, Dinka, Dean Ajdukovic, Harvey M. Weinstein, Eric Stover, Dino Djipa, and Miklos Biro. 2004. "Neighbors Again? Intercommunity Relations after Ethnic Cleansing." In *My Neighbor, My Enemy: Justice and Community in the Aftermath of Mass Atrocity*, eds. Eric Stover and Harvey M. Weinstein, 143–61. Cambridge: Cambridge University Press.

Danfulani, Umar H. D. 2006. "The Jos Peace Conference and the Indigene/Settler Question in Nigerian Politics." Unpublished.

Danfulani, Umar H. D., and Sati U. Fwatshak. 2002. "Briefing: The September 2001 Events in Jos, Nigeria." *African Affairs* 101(403):243–55.

Danida/HUGOU. 2005. "Reflections on Danida/HUGOU-supported 'Peace-Building' Initiatives, Danida/HUGOU." Unpublished.

Darby, John. 2001. *The Effects of Violence on Peace Processes.* Washington, DC: United States Institute of Peace Press.

Dressel, Denis, and Jochen Neumann. 2001. *The Long Road to Peace: Constructive Conflict Transformation in South Africa.* Munster: LIT Verlag.

Du Toit, André. 1993. "Understanding South African Political Violence. A new problematic?" Discussion Paper 43. United Nations Research Institute for Social Development.

Elgström, Ole, Jacob Bercovitch, and Carl Skau. 2003. "Regional Organizations and International Mediation: The Effectiveness of Insider Mediators." *African Journal on Conflict Resolution* 3(1):111–27.

European Stability Initiative. 2002. "Ahmeti's Village. The Political Economy of Interethnic Relations in Macedonia." Skopje and Berlin: ESI Macedonia Security Project.

European Union Election Observation Mission. 2007. "Republic of Sierra Leone Presidential and Parliamentary Elections: Statement of Preliminary Findings and Conclusions." August 11.

Farry, Stephen. 2006. *Northern Ireland: Prospects for Progress in 2006?* Special Report no. 173. Washington, DC: United States Institute of Peace Press.

———. 2009. Interview with author, October 27. Washington, DC.

Fisher, Roger, and William Ury. 1991. *Getting to Yes: Negotiating without Giving In.* Boston: Houghton Mifflin.

Fisher, Simon, and Lada Zimina. 2009. "Just Wasting Our Time? Provocative Thoughts for Peacebuilders." In *Berghof Handbook on Conflict Transformation,* eds. Martina Fischer and Norbert Ropers. Berlin: Berghof Research Center.

Fortna, Virginia P. 2008. "Peacekeeping and Democratization." In *From War to Democracy: Dilemmas of Peacebuilding,* eds. Anna K. Jarstad and Timothy D. Sisk, 39–79. Cambridge: Cambridge University Press.

Galtung, Johan. 1975. "Three Approaches to Peace: Peacekeeping, Peacemaking, and Peacebuilding." In *Peace, War, and Defense—Essays in Peace Research,* edited by Johan Galtung, 282–304. Copenhagen: Christian Ejlers.

———. 1996. *Peace by Peaceful Means: Peace and Conflict, Development and Civilization.* Oslo: Peace Research Institute Oslo.

Gastrow, Peter. 1995. *Bargaining for Peace: South Africa and the National Peace Accord.* Washington, DC: United States Institute of Peace Press.

Gellaw, Abebe. 2010. "Ethiopia's Embarrassing Elections: Stage-Managed Elections in the East African Country Deliver a Fourth Term for Meles Zenawi." *Wall Street Journal,* June 1.

George, Alexander L. 1993. *Bridging the Gap: Theory and Practice in Foreign Policy.* Washington, DC: United States Institute of Peace Press.

Gettleman, Jeffrey. 2007. "Rape Epidemic Raises Trauma of Congo War." *New York Times,* October 7.

Gibney, Jim. 2007. "Clear Progress Being Made on Policing Issue." *Irish News,* December 7.

Gloppen, Siri, Edge Kanyangolo, Nixon Khembo, Nandini Patel, Lise Rakner, Lars Svåsand, Arne Tostensen, and Mette Bakken. 2006. *The Institutional Context of the 2004 General Elections in Malawi.* CMI Report R 2006:21. Bergen: Chr. Michelsen Institute.

Government of Nepal. 2006. "Local Peace Council Related Work Process." Kathmandu.

Guardian. 1999. "A Service Not a Force: Patten Bridges Ulster's Religious Divide." *Guardian,* September 9.

Gunja, Peter J., and Selline O. Korir. 2005. "Working with the Local Wisdom: The National Council of Churches of Kenya Peace Program." In *People Building Peace II: Successful Stories of Civil Society,* eds. Paul van Tongeren, Malin Brenk, Marte Hellema, and Juliette Verhoeven, 441–47. Boulder, CO: Lynne Rienner.

Halpern, Jodi, and Harvey M. Weinstein. 2004. "Empathy and Rehumanization after Mass Violence." In *My Neighbor, My Enemy: Justice and Community in the*

Aftermath of Mass Atrocity, eds. Eric Stover and Harvey M. Weinstein. Cambridge: Cambridge University Press.

Hancock, Landon E. 2007. "El Salvador's Post-Conflict Peace Zone." In *Zones of Peace*, eds. Landon E. Hancock and Christopher Mitchell, 105–22. Bloomfield, CT: Kumarian Press.

Hancock, Landon E., and Pushpa Iyer. 2007. "The Nature, Structure, and Variety of Peace Zones." In *Zones of Peace*, edited by Landon E. Hancock and Christopher Mitchell, 29–50. Bloomfield, CT: Kumarian Press.

Hancock, Landon E., and Christopher Mitchell. 2007. *Zones of Peace*. Bloomfield, CT: Kumarian Press.

Harber, Anton. 2011. *Diepsloot*. Johannesburg: Jonathan Ball Publishers.

Harsch, Ernest. 2008. "Closing Ghana's National Poverty Gap: North-South Disparities Challenge Attainment of Millennium Development Goals." *Africa Renewal* 22(3):4–5, 21.

Hartzell, Caroline, Matthew Hoddie, and Donald Rothchild. 2001. "Stabilizing the Peace after Civil War: An Investigation of Some Key Variables." *International Organization* 55(1):183–208.

Hege, Steve. 2010. "Of Tripartites, Peace and Returns." *Forced Migration Review* (36):51–53.

Hillyard, Paddy, and Mike Tomlinson. 2000. "Patterns of Policing and Policing Patten." *Journal of Law and Society* 27(3):394–415.

Höglund, Kristine. 2004. "Violence in the Midst of Peace Negotiations." PhD diss., Department of Peace and Conflict Research, Uppsala University.

———. 2008. "Violence in War-to-Democracy Transitions." In *From War to Democracy: Dilemmas of Peacebuilding*, eds. Anna K. Jarstad and Timothy D. Sisk, 80–101. Cambridge: Cambridge University Press.

Hohe, Tanja. 2002. "The Clash of Paradigms: International Administration and Local Political Legitimacy in East Timor." *Contemporary Southeast Asia* 24(3):569–89.

Human Rights Watch. 2011. *World Report 2011*. Rwanda. www.hrw.org/.

Hutt, Michael. 2004. *Himalayan People's War: Nepal's Maoist Rebellion*. London: Hurst & Co.

Ibrahim, Dekha, and Janice Jenner. 1998. "Breaking the Cycle of Violence in Wajir." In *Transforming Violence. Linking Local and Global Peacemaking*, eds. Robert Herr and Judy Zimmerman Herr, 133–48. Scottdale, PA: Herald Press.

ICG. *See* International Crisis Group.

IJR. *See* Institute for Justice and Reconciliation.

INCAF. *See* International Network on Conflict and Fragility.

Institute for Justice and Reconciliation. 2009. *SA Reconciliation Barometer 2009*. Cape Town: Institute for Justice and Reconciliation.

International Alert. 1993. *Mission to Evaluate the National Peace Accord and Its Peace Structures*. Report. London: International Alert.

International Crisis Group. 2010a. *Northern Nigeria: Background to Conflict*. Africa Report No. 168. Dakar/Brussels: International Crisis Group.

———. 2010b. *Nepal's Political Rites of Passage*. Asia Report No. 194. Kathmandu/Brussels: International Crisis Group.

International Network on Conflict and Fragility. 2010. *The State's Legitimacy in Fragile Situations: Unpacking Complexity*. Paris: Organisation for Economic Co-Operation and Development (OECD).

Iyer, Pushpa, and Christopher Mitchell. 2007. "The Collapse of Peace Zones in Aceh." In *Zones of Peace*, eds. Landon E. Hancock and Christopher Mitchell, 137–65. Bloomfield, CT: Kumarian Press.

Jarstad, Anna K. 2008. "Dilemmas of War-to-Democracy Transitions: Theories and Concepts." In *From War to Democracy: Dilemmas of Peacebuilding*, eds. Anna K. Jarstad and Timothy D. Sisk, 17–36. Cambridge: Cambridge University Press.

Jarstad, Anna K., and Timothy D. Sisk. 2008. *From War to Democracy: Dilemmas of Peacebuilding*. Cambridge: Cambridge University Press.

Jeffrey, Paul. 1997. "Risky Business: Peace Commissions in Nicaragua." *Christian Century* 114(27):860–63.

Kalyvas, Stathis. N. 2006. *The Logic of Violence in Civil War*. Cambridge: Cambridge University Press.

Kan-Dapaah, Albert. 2006. "A National Architecture for Peace in Ghana." Concept Paper, Accra, Ministry of the Interior. Unpublished.

Karekezi, Urusaro A., Alphonse Nshimiyimana, and Beth Mutamba. 2004. "Localizing Justice: Gacaca Post-Genocide Rwanda." In *My Neighbor, My Enemy: Justice and Community in the Aftermath of Mass Atrocity*, eds. Eric Stover and Harvey M. Weinstein, 69–84. Cambridge: Cambridge University Press.

Kauffman, Craig. 1994. "Reflecting on Nicaragua." *Institute for Conflict Analysis and Resolution Newsletter* 6(2):9–10.

Kazembe, Willard, and Ulf Engel. 2009. *Final Evaluation of GTZ Project "Forum for Dialogue and Peace," 2002–2009*. Lilongwe: GTZ.

Kleiboer, Marieke. 1996. "Understanding Success and Failure of International Mediation." *Journal of Conflict Resolution* 40(2):360–89.

Klopp, Jacqueline M. 2001. "'Ethnic Clashes' and Winning Elections: The Case of Kenya's Electoral Despotism." *Canadian Journal of African Studies* 35(3):473–517.

Klopp, Jacqueline M., Patrick Githinji, and Keffa Karuoya. 2010. "Internal Displacement and Local Peacebuilding in Kenya: Challenges and Innovations." Special Report no. 251. Washington, DC: United States Institute of Peace Press.

Klopp, Jacqueline M. and Elke Zuern. 2007. "The Politics of Violence in Democratization: Lessons from Kenya and South Africa." *Comparative Politics* 39(2):127–46.

Koceski, Sreten, ed. 2008. *Committees for Inter Community Relations—CICR: Establishment, Mandate and Existing Experiences.* Tetovo, Macedonia: Community Development Institute.

Krog, Antjie. 2009. *Begging to Be Black.* Cape Town: Random House Struik.

Krog, Antjie, Nosisi Mpolweni, and Kopano Ratele. 2009. *There Was This Goat: Investigating the Truth Commission Testimony of Notrose Nobomvu Konile.* Scotsville: University of Lincoln KwaZulu-Natal Press.

Kumar, Chetan. 2011. "Building National 'Infrastructures for Peace': UN Assistance for Internally Negotiated Solutions to Violent Conflict." In *Peacemaking: From Practice to Theory*, eds. Susan A. Nan, Zachariah C. Mampilly, and Andrea Bartoli, 384–99. Santa Barbara, CA: Praeger.

Kumar, Krishna. 1999. *Promoting Social Reconciliation in Postconflict Societies.* Washington DC: United States Agency for International Development.

Lahiri, Karan. 2009. "Rwanda's 'Gacaca' Courts a Possible Model for Local Justice in International Crime?" *International Criminal Law Review* 9(2):321–32.

Lederach, John Paul. 1995. *Preparing for Peace: Conflict Transformation across Cultures.* New York: Syracuse.

———. 1997. *Building Peace: Sustainable Reconciliation in Divided Societies.* Washington, DC: United States Institute of Peace Press.

———. 2002. "Building Mediative Capacity in Deep-Rooted Conflict." *Fletcher Forum of World Affairs* 26(1).

———. 2005. *The Moral Imagination: The Art and Soul of Building Peace.* Oxford: Oxford University Press.

Lincoln, Jennie, and César Sereseres. 2000. "Resettling the Contras: The OAS Verification Mission in Nicaragua." In *Peacemaking and Democratization in the Western Hemisphere*, edited by Tommie S. Montgomery. Miami, FL: North-South Center Press.

Lloyd, John. 1999. "Patten Meets Flint on the Falls Road; the Former Hong Kong Governor Has to Decide the Future of Ulster's Police Force." *New Statesman* 129(4429).

Long, William J. and Peter Brecke. 2003. *War and Reconciliation: Reason and Emotion in Conflict Resolution.* Cambridge, MA: MIT Press.

Longman, Timothy. 2009. "An Assessment of Rwanda's *Gacaca* Courts." *Peace Review: A Journal of Social Justice* 21(3):304–12.

Longman, Timothy, Phuong Pham, and Harvey M. Weinstein. 2004. "Connecting Justice to Human Experience: Attitudes towards Accountability and Reconciliation in Rwanda." In *My neighbor, My Enemy: Justice and Community in the Aftermath of Mass Atrocity*, eds. Eric Stover and Harvey M. Weinstein, 206–25. Cambridge: Cambridge University Press.

Mason, Simon. 2009. *Insider Mediators: Exploring Their Role in Informal Peace Processes.* Berlin: Berghof Foundation for Peace Support.

M'banda, Martin. 2010. Interview with author, February 3. Naivasha, Kenya.

McCall, George J., and Miranda Duncan. 2000. "South Africa's National Peace Accord and Laue's Developmental Vision for Community Conflict Intervention." In *Reconcilable Differences: Turning Points in Ethnopolitical Conflict*, eds. Sean Byrne and Cynthia L. Irvin, 154–73. West Harford: Kumarian Press.

McEvoy, Kieran, and Anna Eriksson. 2006. "Restorative Justice in Transition: Ownership, Leadership and 'Bottom Up' Human Rights." In *A Handbook of Restorative Justice*, eds. Dennis Sullivan and Larry Tift, 321–37. New York, Routledge.

Menkhaus, Ken. 2008. "The Rise of a Mediated State in Northern Kenya: The Wajir Story and Its Implications for State-Building." *Afrika Focus* 21(2):23–38.

Miall, Hugh. 2004. "Conflict Transformation: A Multi-Dimensional Task." In *Berghof Handbook for Conflict Transformation*, eds. Martina Fischer and Norbert Ropers. Berlin: Berghof Research Centre.

Mika, Harry. 2006. *Community-Based Restorative Justice in Northern Ireland*. Belfast: Institute of Criminology and Criminal Justice, Queen's University of Belfast.

Ministry of Federal Affairs. 2010. "Conflict Prevention and Resolution Directorate: A Culture of Peace Director." Addis Ababa.

Ministry of Peace and Reconstruction. 2007. "Functions of the Ministry of Peace and Reconstruction of Nepal." www.peace.gov.np/.

———. 2009. "Terms of Reference of Local Peace Committees." www.peace.gov.np/

Mkutu, Kennedy A. 2008. *Guns and Governance in the Rift Valley: Pastoralist Conflict and Small Arms*. Kampala: Fountain.

MoPR. *See* Ministry of Peace and Reconstruction.

Muhereza, Frank. E., D. Ossiya, and I. Ovonji-Odida. 2008. *A Study on Options for Enhancing Access to Justice, and Improving Administration of Law and Order in Karamoja*. Kampala: DANIDA-HUGGOU (Human Rights and Good Governance Programme) and LABF (Legal Aid Basket Fund).

Mwale, Doc, and Rachel M. Etter. 2011. "Impact Survey of Multiparty Liaison Committees." Lilongwe: German Development Cooperation (GIZ).

Nathan, Laurie. 1993. "An Imperfect Bridge: Crossing to Democracy on the Peace Accord." *Track Two* 2(2).

———. 1999. "'When Push Comes to Shove': The Failure of International Mediation in Africa Civil Wars." *Track Two* 8(2):1–27.

———. 2007. *No Ownership, No Commitment: A Guide to Local Ownership of Security Sector Reform*. Birmingham: University of Birmingham.

———. 2009. "The Challenges Facing Mediation in Africa." Africa Mediators' Retreat, Oslo Forum Network of Mediators, Zanzibar.

Nepal Transition to Peace Initiative. 2008. "An Assessment of Local Peace Committees in Nepal." Kathmandu.

Newry Democrat. 2009. "New Chair Attacks DPP," *Newry Democrat*.

News24. 2010. "IFP Won't Attend Reconciliation Event." *News24*, www.news24.com/

Ningbabira, Aloyse. n.d. "Kibimba Peace Committee: Project Proposal."

Northern Ireland Peace Agreement. 1998. Belfast.

Northern Ireland Policing Board. 2007. *Reflections on District Policing Partnerships.* Belfast: Northern Ireland Policing Board.

Northern Ireland Statistics and Research Agency. 2008. "District Policing Partnership (DPP) Public Consultation Survey." Belfast.

NTTP. *See* Nepal Transition to Peace Initiative.

Nyathi, Clever. 2006. "Personal Mission Notes." Freetown. Unpublished.

Nyathi, Clever. 2008. Interview with author, February 12. Cape Town.

Nyathi, Clever. 2009. Interview with author, May 25. Cape Town.

Odendaal, Andries, and Retief Olivier. 2008. "Local Peace Committees: Some Reflections and Lessons Learned." Academy for Educational Development, Kathmandu. Unpublished.

Odendaal, Andries, and Chris Spies. 1996. "Local Peace Committees in the Rural Areas of the Western Cape: Their Significance for South Africa's Transition to Democracy," *Track Two*, Occasional Paper. Cape Town: Centre for Conflict Resolution.

———. 1997. "'You Have Opened the Wound, but Not Healed It': The Local Peace Committees of the Western Cape, South Africa." *Peace and Conflict: Journal of Peace Psychology* 3(3):261–73.

———. 1998. "Building Community Peace in South Africa." In *Transforming Violence. Linking Local and Global Peacemaking*, eds. Robert Herr and Judy Z. Herr, 119–32. Scottdale, PA: Herald Press.

OECD. *See* Organisation for Economic Co-operation and Development.

OECD-DAC. *See* Organisation for Economic Co-operation and Development–Development Assistance Committee.

Ohman, Magnus. 2010. E-mail communication with author, January 13.

Ohrid Framework Agreement. 2001. FYR Macedonia.

Ojielo, Ozzonia. 2007. "Designing an Architecture for Peace: A Framework of Conflict Transformation in Ghana." Unpublished.

Olson, Camilla, and Steve Hege. 2010. *DR Congo: Unstable Areas Endanger Returns.* Refugees International Field Report. Washington, DC: Refugees International.

Orde, Hugh. 2008. "Prosperity, People and Place: Policing Divided Communities." *Guardian* (Public Special).

Organisation for Economic Co-operation and Development. 2011. *Supporting Statebuilding in Situations of Conflict and Fragility: Policy Guidance.* Paris: OECD.

Organisation for Economic Co-operation and Development–Development Assistance Committee. 2001. *The DAC Guidelines. Helping Prevent Violent Conflict.* Paris: OECD.

———. 2008. *Guidance on Evaluating Conflict Prevention and Peacebuilding Activities: Working Draft for Application Period.* Paris: OECD.

———. 2010. "Dili Declaration: A New Vision for Peacebuilding and Statebuilding." www.oecd.org/

Ostien, Philip. 2009. "Jonah Jang and the Jasawa: Ethno-Religious Conflict in Jos, Nigeria." *Muslim-Christian Relations in Africa*. www.sharia-in-africa.net/.

Otite, Onigu, and Isaac O. Albert. 1999. *Community Conflicts in Nigeria: Management, Resolution, and Transformation*. Ibadan: Spectrum Books.

Paffenholz, Thania. 2003. *Community-Based Bottom-Up Peacebuilding: The Development of the Life and Peace Institute's Approach to Peacebuilding and Lessons Learned from the Somalia Experience (1990–2000)*. Kijabe: Life and Peace Institute.

———. 2005. "More Field Notes: Critical Issues When Implementing PCIA." In *Berghof Handbook for Conflict Transformation*, Dialogue Series 4, eds. Beatrix Schmelzle, David Bloomfield, and Martina Fischer. Berlin: Berghof Research Centre.

———. 2010. "Civil Society and Peacebuilding." In *Civil Society and Peacebuilding: A Critical Assessment*, edited by Thania Paffenholz, 43–64. Boulder, CO: Lynne Rienner.

Patel, Nandini. 2006. "Troublemakers and Bridge Builders: Conflict Management and Conflict Resolution." In *The Power of the Vote. Malawi's 2004 Parliamentary and Presidential Elections*, edited by Martin Ott and Bodo Immink, 217–41. Blantyre: Kachere.

———. 2009. *Malawi: Support to Conflict Prevention around the 2009 Elections: Project Evaluation Report*. Lilongwe: GTZ Forum for Dialogue and Peace.

Patten Commission. 1999. *A New Beginning: Policing in Northern Ireland*. Belfast: Independent Commission on Policing for Northern Ireland.

Paz, V. M. 2005. "La OEA y la prevención y resolución de conflicto: la última decada." *Futuros: Revista Trimestral Lationamericana y Caribeña de Desarrollo Sustentable*.

Prendergast, John, and Emily Plumb. 2002. "Building Local Capacity: From Implementation to Peacebuilding." In *Ending Civil Wars: The Implementation of Peace Agreements*, eds. Stephen J. Stedman, Donald Rothchild, and Elizabeth M. Cousens, 327–49. Boulder, CO: Lynne Rienner.

Preston, Julia. 1987. "Truce Plan Stirs Doubts in Nicaragua; Commissions Hear Complaints from Peasants with Contra Ties." *Washington Post*, October 11.

Pruitt, Bettye, and Philip Thomas. 2007. *Democratic Dialogue: A Handbook for Practitioners*. Stockholm: International IDEA.

Quinn, J. Michael, T. David Mason, and Mehmet Gurses. 2007. "Sustaining the Peace: Determinants of Civil War Recurrence." *International Interactions* 33(2):167–93.

Rakner, Lise, and Lars Svasand. 2005. *Maybe Free but Not Fair: Electoral Administration in Malawi, 1994–2004*. CMI Working Paper WP 2005:5. Bergen: Chr. Michelson Institute.

Ramsbotham, Oliver, Tom Woodhouse, Hugh Miall. 2005. *Contemporary Conflict Resolution: The Prevention, Management and Transformation of Deadly Conflicts.* Cambridge: Polity.

Ramsbotham, Oliver. 2010. *Transforming Violent Conflict: Radical Disagreement, Dialogue and Survival.* London: Routledge.

Reilly, Benjamin. 2008. "Post-War Elections: Uncertain Turning Points of Transition." In *From War to Democracy: Dilemmas of Peacebuilding*, eds. Anna K. Jarstad and Timothy D. Sisk, 157–81. Cambridge: Cambridge University Press.

ReliefWeb. 2007. "Sierra Leone Political Parties Registration Commission with UN Assistance Striving to Enhance Culture of Political Debate for Credible and Transparent Post-Confict Elections." www.reliefweb.int/

Republic of Uganda. 2007. *Karamoja Integrated Disarmament and Development Programme: Creating Conditions for Promoting Human Security and Recovery in Karamoja, 2007/2008–2009/2010.* OPM: Kampala.

Rettig, Max. 2008. "Gacaca: Truth, Justice, and Reconciliation in Postconflict Rwanda?" *African Studies Review* 51(3):25–50.

Richmond, Oliver. 2011. *A Post-Liberal Peace.* London: Routledge.

Risley, Paul, and Timothy D. Sisk. 2005. *Democracy and United Nations Peacebuilding at the Local Level: Lessons Learned.* Policy Options on Democratic Reform. Stockholm: International IDEA.

Ropers, Norbert. 2008. "Systemic Conflict Transformation: Reflections on the Conflict and Peace Process in Sri Lanka." In *Berghof Handbook on Conflict Transformation*, eds. Martina Fischer and Norbert Ropers. Berlin: Berghof Research Center.

Rusk, Diana. 2008. "Policing Decision Key Factor in Departure of Many Reps." *Irish News.*

Ryan, Barry J. 2008. "The Logic of a Justified Hope: The Dialectic of Police Reform in Northern Ireland." *Capital and Class* 32(2):83–107.

Salem, Paul. 1993. "A Critique of Western Conflict Resolution from a Non-Western Perspective." *Negotiation Journal* 9(4):361–69.

Sapkota, Bishnu. 2009. E-mail communication with author. Cape Town.

Schmelzle, Beatrix. 2005. "New Trends in Peace and Conflict Impact Assessment: Introduction." In *Berghof Handbook for Conflict Transformation*, eds. Beatrix Schmelzle, David Bloomfield and Martina Fischer. Berlin: Berghof Research Centre.

Secretary-General. 2009. "Report of the Secretary-General on Peacebuilding in the Immediate Aftermath of Conflict." United Nations.

Sharma, Kishor. 2006. "The Political Economy of Civil War in Nepal." *World Development* 34(7):1237–53.

Shaw, Mark. 1993. *Crying Peace Where There Is None?: The Functioning of Local Peace Committees of the National Peace Accord.* Johannesburg: Centre for Policy Studies.

Sisk, Timothy D. 1994. "South Africa's National Peace Accord." *Peace and Change* 19(1):50–71.

————. 1995. *Democratization in South Africa: The Elusive Social Contract*. Princeton, NJ: Princeton University Press.

————. 2008. "Elections in Fragile States: Between Voice and Violence." Paper presented at the International Studies Association Annual Meeting, San Francisco, California, March 24–28.

————. 2008. "Peacebuilding as Democratization: Findings and Recommendations." In *From War to Democracy: Dilemmas of Peacebuilding*, eds. Anna K. Jarstad and Timothy D. Sisk, 239–59. Cambridge: Cambridge University Press.

Smith, Dan. 2004. "Towards a Strategic Framework for Peacebuilding: Getting Their Act Together." Overview Report of the Joint Utstein Study of Peacebuilding, 1/2004, Royal Norwegian Ministry of Foreign Affairs.

Spalding, Rose. 1999. "From Low-Intensity War to Low-Intensity Peace." In *Comparative Peace Processes in Latin America*, edited by Cynthia J. Arnson. Washington, DC: Woodrow Wilson Center Press.

Spehar, Elizabeth. 2000. "Las Comisiones de Paz en Nicaragua." In *Conviciencia y Seguridad: un Reto a la Gobernabilidad*, edited by J. Salazar. Washington, DC: Inter-American Development Bank.

Spies, Chris. 2006. "Resolutionary Change: The Art of Awakening Dormant Faculties in Others." In *Berghof Handbook for Conflict Transformation: Social Change and Conflict Transformation*, eds. David Bloomfield, Martina Fischer, and Beatrix Schmeltze. Berlin: Berghof Conflict Research

————. 2010. Interview with author, November 9. Stellenbosch.

Stahn, Carsten. 2001. "Accommodating Individual Criminal Responsibility and National Reconciliation: The UN Truth Commission for East Timor." *American Journal of International Law* 95(4):952–66.

Stedman, Stephen J. 2001. "International Implementation of Peace Agreements in Civil Wars: Findings from a Study of Sixteen Cases." In *Turbulent Peace: The Challenges of Managing International Conflict*, eds. Chester. A. Crocker, Fen O. Hampson, and Pamela Aall, 737–52. Washington, DC: United States Institute of Peace Press.

Steenkamp, Chrissie. 2005. "The Legacy of War: Conceptualizing a 'Culture of Violence' to Explain Violence after Peace Accords." *Round Table* 94(379):253–67.

Stover, Eric, and Harvey M. Weinstein, eds. 2004. *My Neighbor, My Enemy: Justice and Community in the Aftermath of Mass Atrocity*. Cambridge: Cambridge University Press.

Suhrke, Astri, and Ingrid Samset. 2007. "What's in a Figure? Estimating Recurrence of Civil War." *International Peacekeeping* 14(2):195–204.

Svensson, Isak. 2007. "Mediation with Muscles or Minds? Exploring Power Mediators and Pure Mediators in Civil Wars." *International Negotiation* 12(2):229–48.

Teklemariam, Shiferaw. 2010. Interview with author, March 24. Addis Ababa.

Tilly, Charles. 2003. *The Politics of Collective Violence*. Cambridge: Cambridge University Press.

Toft, Monica. 2006. *Peace through Security: Making Negotiated Settlements Stick. Globalization and the National Security State.* Cambridge, MA: JF Kennedy School of Government, Harvard University.

TRC. *See* Truth and Reconciliation Commission.

Truth and Reconciliation Commission. 2004. "Witness to Truth: Report of the Truth and Reconciliation Commission of Sierra Leone."

UNDESA. *See* United Nations Department of Economic and Social Affairs.

UNDP. *See* United Nations Development Programme.

UNHCR. *See* United Nations Refugee Agency.

United Nations Department of Economic and Social Affairs. 2007. *Participatory Dialogue: Towards a Stable, Safe and Just Society for All.* New York: United Nations.

United Nations Development Programme. 2004. *Support for Peace and Development Initiatives (SPDI).* Annual report. Kathmandu: UNDP.

———. 2010. "Report of the Experience Sharing Seminar on Building Infrastructures for Peace Naivasha, Kenya 2–4 February 2010."

United Nations Refugee Agency. 2009. "Return, Reconciliation and Reintegration of IDP's and Refugees in the Eastern Democratic Republic of the Congo as Part of the United Nations Security and Stabilization Support Strategy."

Ury, William L., Jeanne M. Brett, and Stephen B. Goldberg. 1988. *Getting Disputes Resolved: Designing Systems to Cut the Costs of Conflict.* San Francisco: Jossey-Bass.

United States Agency for International Development. 2009. "Conflict Mitigation and Reconciliation Programs in Northern Uganda, Pader Peace Program, Final Report."

USAID. *See* United States Agency for International Development.

Van der Merwe, Hugo. 2001. "Reconciliation and Justice in South Africa: Lessons from the TRC's Community Interventions." In *Reconciliation, Justice, and Coexistence,* edited by Mohammed Abu-Nimer, 187–208. Lanham, MD: Lexington Books.

Van Tongeren, Paul. 2011. "Increasing Interest in Infrastructures for Peace." *Journal of Conflictology* 2(2):16–26.

Van Tongeren, Paul, Malin Brenk, Marte Hellema, and Juliette Verhoeven, eds. 2005. *People Building Peace II: Successful Stories of Civil Society.* Boulder, CO: Lynne Rienner.

Wachira, George. 2010. *Citizens in Action: Making Peace in the Post-Election Crisis in Kenya, 2008.* Nairobi: NPI-Africa.

Walter, Barbara F. 2004. "Does Conflict Beget Conflict? Explaining Recurrent Civil War." *Journal of Peace Research* 41(3):371–88.

WARN. 2007. "Sierra Leone: August 11, 2007 Elections: Challenges of a Transition and Beyond." WARN Policy Brief. West Africa Network for Peacebuilding (WANEP).

Wehr, Paul, and John Paul Lederach. 1991. "Mediating Conflict in Central America." *Journal of Peace Research* 28(1):85–98.

Weinstein, Jeremy M. 2005. "Autonomous Recovery and International Intervention in Comparative Perspective." Working Paper 57, Center for Global Development Working Papers.

Wood, Elisabeth J. 2003. *Insurgent Collective Action and Civil War in El Salvador.* Cambridge: Cambridge University Press.

World Bank. 2011. "Conflict, Security, and Development." In *World Development Report 2011.* Washington, DC: World Bank.

Wyrod, Christopher. 2008. "Sierra Leone: A Vote for Better Governance." *Journal of Democracy* 19(1):70–83.

Zorbas, Eugenia. 2004. "Reconciliation in Post-Genocide Rwanda." *African Journal of Legal Studies* 1(1):29–52.

Index

About the Author

Andries Odendaal is a senior associate at the Centre for Mediation at the University of Pretoria, South Africa. He also serves on the panel of experts for the United Nations Development Programme's Bureau for Crisis Prevention and Recovery and the mediation roster of the UN Department of Political Affair's Mediation Support Unit. He was a regional coordinator of the Western Cape Peace Committee (1993–94) during South Africa's transition to democracy and a senior trainer and project coordinator at the Centre for Conflict Resolution at the University of Cape Town (1995–2004). In 2009–10, Odendaal was a Jennings Randolph Senior Fellow at the US Institute of Peace. He has extensive experience in local level peacebuilding in South Africa and in providing consultation and training services to peacebuilding processes in Africa and elsewhere.

U.S. Institute of Peace Jennings Randolph Fellowship Program

This book is a fine example of the work produced by Senior Fellows in the Jennings Randolph fellowship program of the United States Institute of Peace. As part of the statute establishing the Institute, Congress envisioned a program that would appoint "scholars and leaders of peace from the United States and abroad to pursue scholarly inquiry and other appropriate forms of communication on international peace and conflict resolution." The program was named after Senator Jennings-Randolph of West Virginia, whose efforts over four decades helped establish the Institute.

Since 1987, the Jennings Randolph Program has played a key role in the Institute's effort to build a national center of research, dialogue, and education on critical problems of conflict and peace. Fellows come from a wide variety of academic and other professional backgrounds. They conduct research at the Institute and participate in USIP's outreach activities to policymakers, the academic community, and the American public.

Fellowship recipients are selected after a rigorous, multistage review that includes consideration by independent experts and professional staff at the Institute. The final authority for decisions regarding Senior Fellowship awards rests with USIP's board of directors. The Jennings Randolph Program also awards Peace Scholar Dissertation Fellowships to students at U.S. universities who are researching and writing doctoral dissertations on conflict and international peace and security issues.

United States Institute of Peace Press

Since its inception in 1991, the United States Institute of Peace Press has published more than 175 books on the prevention, management, and peaceful resolution of international conflicts—among them such venerable titles as Raymond Cohen's *Negotiating Across Cultures*; John Paul Lederach's *Building Peace*; *Leashing the Dogs of War* by Chester A. Crocker, Fen Osler Hampson, and Pamela Aall; and *The Iran Primer*, edited by Robin Wright. All our books arise from research and fieldwork sponsored by the Institute's many programs, and the Press is committed to extending the reach of the Institute's work by continuing to publish significant and sustainable works for practitioners, scholars, diplomats, and students. In keeping with the best traditions of scholarly publishing, each volume undergoes thorough internal review and blind peer review by external subject experts to ensure that the research and conclusions are balanced, relevant, and sound.

Valerie Norville
Director

About the
United States Institute of Peace

The United States Institute of Peace is an independent, nonpartisan institution established and funded by Congress. The Institute provides analysis, training, and tools to help prevent, manage, and end violent international conflicts, promote stability, and professionalize the field of peacebuilding.

Board of Directors

J. Robinson West (Chair), Chairman, PFC Energy
George E. Moose (Vice Chair), Adjunct Professor of Practice,
    The George Washington University
Judy Ansley, Former Assistant to the President and Deputy Security
    National Advisor under President George W. Bush
Eric Edelman, Hertog Distinguished Practitioner in Residence,
    Johns Hopkins University School of Advanced International Studies
Joseph Eldridge, University Chaplain and Senior Adjunct Professorial
    Lecturer, School of International Service, American **University**
Kerry Kennedy, President, Robert F. Kennedy Center for
    Justice and Human Rights
Ikram U. Khan, President, Quality Care Consultants, LLC
Stephen D. Krasner, Graham H. Stuart Professor of International
    Relations, Stanford University
John A. Lancaster, Former Executive Director, International Council on
    Independent Living
Jeremy A. Rabkin, Professor, George Mason School of Law
Judy Van Rest, Executive Vice President, International Republican Institute
Nancy Zirkin, Executive Vice President, Leadership
    Conference on Civil and Human Rights

Members ex officio

John Kerry, Secretary of State
Kathleen Hicks, Principal Deputy Under Secretary of Defense for Policy
Gregg F. Martin, Major General, U.S. Army; President,
    National Defense University
Jim Marshall, President, United States Institute of Peace (nonvoting)

Also Available from the United States Institute of Peace Press

Of Related Interest

Building Peace
Sustainable Reconciliation in Divided Societies
John Paul Lederach

208 pp. • 6 × 9
Paper: 978-1-87837-973-3
Ebook: 978-1-60127-092-4

Conflict Analysis
Understanding Causes, Unlocking Solutions
Matthew Levinger

280 pp. • 6 × 9
Paper: 978-1-60127-143-3
Ebook: 978-1-60127-166-2

Getting In
Mediators' Entry into the Settlement of African Conflicts
Mohammed O. Maundi, I. William Zartman, Gilbert M. Khadiagala, Kwaku Nuamah

229 pp. • 6 × 9
Paper: 978-1-92922-362-5

Peacemaking in International Conflict
Methods and Techniques, Revised Edition
I. William Zartman, editor

510 pp. • 6 × 9
Paper: 978-1-929223-66-4
Cloth: 978-1-929223-65-7

Power Sharing and International Mediation in Ethnic Conflicts
Timothy D. Sisk

170 pp. • 6 × 9
Paper: 978-1-87837-956-6

Watching the Wind
Conflict Resolution During South Africa's Transition to Democracy
Susan Collin Marks

256 pp. • 6 × 9
Paper: 978-1-878379-99-3

 United States Institute of Peace Press
http://bookstore.usip.org

A WOMAN'S GUIDE TO FORGIVING INFIDELITY

...and dealing with her past demons

CHRISTINA YOUNG

bookshaker

First Published in Great Britain 2011
by Bookshaker.com

© Copyright Christina Young

*This book is dedicated to my amazing Doug
and my three wonderful children, Nicky,
Rob and Mike, who have all stood by me,
and supported and encouraged me
through the writing of the book.*

*I am so proud of them all for
their honesty and love.*

Life is for Living

Life is a gift we're given each and every day.

Dream about tomorrow, but live for today.

To live a little, you've got to love a whole lot.

Love turns the ordinary into the extraordinary.

Life's a journey,

Always worth taking.

Take time to smell the roses, and tulips,

and daffodils, and lilacs, and sunflowers.

Count blessings like children count stars.

The secret of a happy life isn't buried

in a treasure chest, it lies within your heart.

It's the little moments that make life big.

Don't wait, make memories today.

Celebrate your life!

(Author unknown)

Acknowledgements

There are so many people I would like to thank for believing in me and supporting me in writing this book; those who believed it would be such a waste not to share my story because it could help so many people. In fact, so many people have helped me through my journey of healing over the last 10 years that if I mentioned them all, you might never get into the book!

I would like to say a huge thank you to Doug and my children for being so supportive and being there for me in the times of doubt. I love you all very much.

One special person I would like to thank is Andy Harrington. He not only helped me deal with some of my past challenges, but also believed in me enough to employ me on his sales team. During the time I worked for Andy, I learnt so much and grew immensely as a person.

I want to say a big thank you to Tony and Nicki who were there for Doug and me through our huge challenge. With their teachings, we are living as our true selves. You are an inspirational couple.

Another person I would like to thank is Mindy, my coach, who assisted me through the writing of this book. Without her plan and encouragement, it might never have happened.

I would like to thank Marsha Jordan for allowing me to share her story with you and for her loving contribution to others.

Also, my deepest gratitude to all my friends and family who have believed, encouraged and supported me on my journey of finding my true self!

And finally, I would like to say thank you to my readers – You amazing people who are willing to find out who you truly are and not simply settle for a life that is just okay!

Contents

Introduction

Sitting on a bench in Austria looking out at what had become a very special mountain, as the sun was just starting to rise over the peak, I looked back on what had led me to this amazing place in my life. Like the mountain, it had been a hard climb, but the view from the top was beautiful. I was determined to share the lessons I had learnt along the way, so that others could forge their own healing path. I know that many people want to write a book and for whatever reason do not follow through. Until I went through the toughest challenge of my life, I was one of them.

You could say that I had a very challenging up-bringing. My father was quick to lose his temper and was constantly critical, both verbally and physically abusive. He had multiple extramarital affairs and would make sexual innuendos to female family friends, including to my friends and me. The only exception was my younger sister, who, while on some occasions on the receiving end of his anger, seemed to be able to wrap him around her finger.

He had affairs throughout his marriage to my Mum, and I could not understand at the time why she stayed with him. I know that her reasons for staying were not right, but I admired her for her constant loyalty. On occasions when I asked her about leaving Dad, her answer was always the same: where would I go with two young children? Things were very different in those days.

My mother did all the things that were required of a mother. She kept a clean house; there was always food on the table; and she made sure we were comfortable, clean and clothed. She was very much a loner, enjoying her own company, happy with her sewing and knitting. We got on well, but as I got into my teens, we tended to argue more. My father's constant criticising and put-downs made her very hard and she would not allow her feelings to show. Nor was she happy to talk about her upbringing, but from the little she said, I am sure that it had not been easy. I realise now that she had shut down her emotions to keep herself from being hurt.

When my father passed away she found companionship with a man who treated her like a princess and I saw my Mum finally let go and find contentment and happiness. Unfortunately she died very suddenly four years later, at the time she was her happiest. Losing my Mum was very hard for me to come to terms with and even today I still miss her greatly.

I was a very unhappy child. At school I was a

loner and never seemed to fit in. During my early years at school there were times I was picked on and bullied, and things seemed to only get worse in senior school. I seemed to be forever in trouble, even when it was not my fault. I could not wait to leave and ended up leaving school after only a couple of exams. For many years I used this as an excuse for not being able do anything academic. Instead, I spent as much time as I could in my bedroom reading fantasy and romance novels, leading me to believe that this was what life was truly about.

We had an older couple living upstairs in our house to whom we used to relate as grandparents. I became close to the man because, unlike my parents, he always seemed to have time for me. After school I would go and see him and we would sit and play board games together. I felt that he really loved me, but once he had gained my trust and affections, he took advantage of them. He sexually abused me and told me not to tell, saying that it was our secret. Because I was just a child and he was an adult, I believed him, but I did stop going to see him as often as I had.

Once I reached my teenage years I was constantly looking for connection, which led to even more unhealthy situations. I soon met a man who I thought I loved and who I thought loved me. I was engaged at eighteen, married at nineteen and a mother at twenty. I remember the day after my beautiful daughter was born, crying uncontrollably, thinking to myself, "What the hell have I done?"

I soon learned that marriage was not what I thought. After five years with a man who gambled and drank too much, I knew I had to get out of the relationship, not only for my sanity, but also for my daughter. It was not an easy time. Through the divorce, and for 6 months afterward, while we still lived in the same home, he would verbally abuse me and make snide comments. All I had done was to replace one father with another.

Three years later I met my current husband, Doug. He seemed like a gentleman, was willing to become a stepdad to my daughter, and we got on well together; but looking back, I know that it was not love that brought us together. We had what seemed to others a good marriage: we did lots of things together, had similar interests, went away for weekends and had some great holidays. What we didn't have was an intimate connection and we had many arguments over this area of our marriage.

With all of the events of my childhood and youth, I was still looking for attention and connection and not always going about it in the right way. I had also not yet dealt with what had happened to me as a child. When my next child, my oldest son, was born I had everything I could have asked for, a good husband, lovely home and the boy I had always wanted. Yet, six months later, I began to self-destruct, suffering from bulimia.

After 6 long years, during which I had my second son, I finally admitted to the bulimia and agreed to get some help. At last, I recognised my self-destructive tendencies. When things started to go well for me, I felt that I was not worthy to have good things in my life because I had grown up being told I was stupid and would never amount to anything, so I would act in ways that destroyed the good things in my life and 'prove' what I had believed all along. I knew I needed to do something, so I started to look down the path of healing myself.

Over the next few years I saw many different kinds of therapists, healers and counselors. The turning point was a weekend course I attended in 2005 called *Fire Your Desire* (now *Power to Achieve*) with Doug and my youngest son. At the end of the weekend, I knew that I wanted to help others by training to be a personal coach. I signed up to do my Neuro-Linguistic Programming (NLP) Practitioner and Master Practitioner Certificate which, as well as teaching me how to help others, also helped me come to terms with all that had happened in my life.

In terms of my marriage to Doug, while we had always felt that at some level our souls were connected, our relationship had never been strong on physical intimacy. Because of our problems with intimacy and our inability to communicate our feelings about them, we were drifting further apart. A friend recommended that Doug and I attend a Relationship Weekend in Austria, because she and her husband had found their relationship had blossomed since they had attended the course. I discussed this with Doug and, reluctantly, he agreed to go.

Initially Doug was not that involved, but by the end of the weekend we had enjoyed ourselves and learnt a lot about how to be in a great intimate relationship. The trainers, Tony and Nicki, then told us about the other courses they run including a Relationship Coaching Course and an Advanced Intimacy Week. I decided to attend the Relationship Coaching Course to enhance my coaching skills and Doug and I both agreed to come back to do the Advanced Intimacy week later that year.

After the Relationship Coaching Course in the August, for the first time in my life, I felt that I knew exactly where I was going and had finally come to terms with my past. I was also really looking forward to the Advanced Intimacy week with Doug in October. I felt that we would finally be able to put the icing on the cake in our relationship.

A few days before we were due to go, Doug surprised me by throwing up every excuse possible not to go. I felt this was fear on his part, going into an area which we had both found challenging. He finally agreed to go, but for the first couple of days he was in a terrible space, such as I had never before seen. Three days into the course he announced that he had not been faithful to me from the day we met. As he was the one person I thought I could trust, his announcement shattered my world.

After I learned the truth, I went through many emotions and wondered, "How am I going to get through this?" It was most certainly the toughest challenge of my life. Having trained as a coach I knew that if I had a client in front of me, I would know exactly what to say and how to advise them to get through this challenge, but it wasn't as clear now that it was happening to me. After spending time away from Doug, and with the support of coaches and my children through what was a very difficult time, I started to learn what had been going on, not only in my life, but also my husband's life, in relation to intimacy. I learned valuable lessons that helped us to be true to ourselves and each other and to build the relationship we have today. It is these lessons that I would like to share with you through my story and this book. Through these pages, I want to share with you a greater understanding of how you can overcome pain, abuse, fear or infidelity in your life. I want you to know that if you are ready to deal with your issues, then there is a light at the end of the tunnel.

It was not always easy writing this book, especially reliving all of the emotions it brought up. At the time I was devastated, feeling as if my whole world had fallen apart. I thought my life was never going to be the same.

Looking back, I can say that I was right about life never being the same, but it was not in the doom and gloom way I had thought. In the end, my toughest challenge turned out to be my greatest strength. I am able to draw from all of my experiences in my work as a Relationship Coach helping others come to terms with pain they have experienced in their lives. I love what I do and nothing gives me more pleasure than to know that I am helping others on their journey through life. After many years of looking for the answers, I am finally living in my truth and a good relationship with Doug.

To help you follow me on this journey, I have divided the book into seven parts. In part one, *Exploring Your Feelings*, I share each emotion as I went through it, both as a result of Doug's infidelity, and also as a result of other challenges I faced in my life that led me to where I am today.

In the second part, *Looking At Yourself*, I provide further examples from my life, along with exercises that you can do on your own, to help you to understand your role in your own past challenges.

In the third part, *Taking Action*, along with further examples from my own life I provide specific actions that you can take to heal and move forward in your life.

In the fourth section, *Keeping It All Going*, I describe how I maintain the life I have built for myself. Throughout these sections I have included some exercises which I hope you will find useful. Rather than putting them at the back, I wanted you to have them as I talk about how they were beneficial to me, at the time I describe the challenge I experienced.

After these main sections, in the next chapters, Doug shares his thoughts on our journey together and I share with you my vision, which led to you holding this book in your hands today.

The book concludes with a section of further resources which I have included to help you in your own journey.

Through the book, you will find that I talk about different Neuro-Linguistic Processing (NLP) techniques that I use in my coaching sessions. Those unfamiliar with NLP may find this part hard to understand, so I have given an explanation of NLP in the appendix and urge you to persevere with the exercises I have included. Feel free to contact me if you have any difficulties, as I am here to help you.

You do have a choice how you want to live your life! I have learned that my life can be the romantic fairy tale I'd always imagined. If that is truly what you want, yours can be, too!

one

Exploring Your Feelings

On the third day of Advanced Intimacy Week, before Doug revealed his infidelity, all the participants were taken up to the Alps for the night to celebrate Tony's birthday. During the evening Doug started to relax and was more like his old self. When we got back to the hotel, Tony had told us how great the sunrise was over the Alps, so the whole group decided to get up to watch the sun come up over the mountains.

The next morning, for the first time since we had left home, I felt connected to Doug as we stood huddled under blankets together watching sun rise. Shortly afterward Doug went off for a walk with Steve, another coach. At the time I thought that it was great that he was finally going to talk to Steve, that things were finally in place for us to move on in our relationship. Little did I know my world as I knew it was about to change forever.

That morning Doug walked into the seminar room, took my hand and said, "I need to talk to you". I had never seen him act with so much certainty as he took my hand and led me upstairs to the hotel lobby. I had never seen him look or behave the way he was behaving in the 25 years I had known him. With a very numb expression on his face, he proceeded to tell me that he had not been faithful to me throughout our 24 years of marriage, that he'd had one night stands, had been with a prostitute and had an affair with a good friend of mine for eighteen months.

At that moment, I was not sure I had heard what he had said. All of a sudden everything around me seemed quiet and still. I looked at him with utter disbelief as the thoughts ran through my head: "Doug would not do this", "He is a good, trustworthy man", "This must be a joke, but somehow I am not finding it very funny".

Then all of a sudden something inside me snapped. I felt as if I could not breathe and that everything was closing in on me. I knew I had to get away from him, but I was not sure where I was going or what I was going to do. He told me that Nicki, one of the presenters and a brilliant coach, had been made aware of what was happening and was there if I wanted to talk to her.

As I walked out into the brilliant sunshine with the fabulous views over the Alps, I was reminded how, only a few hours before, Doug and I had been huddled together under the blanket watching the beautiful sunrise. All of sudden the reality of what he had said hit and I started to shake and cry uncontrollably. I started to run down the path to the back of the hotel. I felt as if I was going to be sick, as if I was being suffocated, fighting for breath. I kept asking myself, "How could this be happening?"

At this point Nicki appeared and took me to a bench looking over the Alps. So many thoughts and feelings were running through me. I don't know how long I sat with Nicki as she talked to me and tried to reassure me that everything would be okay in time.

I spent the rest of that day in a total daze. At times I tried to deny that it was happening and my whole body felt dead, and then the next minute I was crying hysterically. I walked around not knowing where I was going or what I was doing. I was in a complete state of disbelief. When we returned for supper, even though I sat at the table with the others, I did not feel like a part of the group. It was like my body was there, but not my head. I felt so sick in my stomach that I wasn't able to eat. Amidst all the confusion, the one thing I knew was that I was not going to be brought down by this man, after all I had learnt through my coaching and training over the past ten years.

W hen we find ourselves in traumatic situations, we can easily be overwhelmed by our emotions. It is important to acknowledge and explore these feelings, so they do not have negative effects on our lives, consciously or unconsciously. When we shut our feelings down and don't acknowledge them, it can have many negative consequences. When we shut out feelings like hurt, shame and anger, we also shut down love, happiness, enthusiasm and compassion. We are not living in our true energy if we do not let these feelings into our life. Also, when we are not in touch with our own feelings, we are unable to connect with other people's feelings and how we are affecting them. It is easy to become consumed with yourself and not realise how you are affecting your family and friends, something I realised once I was able to acknowledge and accept my feelings.

Hurt

After the initial shock, the feeling of hurt was very intense. It was like my body was going to explode from the pain inside of me. I kept asking myself questions over and over again. How could he have done this to me? Why could I not see after all these years what he had been doing? Was I so stupid? How could my friend have done this to me? Were they all better than me? Was I so ugly? I thought we were close and had shared so much together. How could he have done this? Had our twenty four years together all been a sham? What about the children? How will they get through this? What will people think? What did I do in my life that was so wrong?

I had never felt so hurt in my life as I did right at that moment. Over the years I had been hurt by people, but nothing could have prepared me for this – it was unbelievable.

*W*hat I have found is that pain and hurt are very similar. With both, it feels as if someone else has taken over your body. When I was subjected to abuse by my father and the man who lived in our house as a child, it changed who I was when I came into this world. I look back now and see that I had to grow up very quickly and learn the rules in order to survive. As I mentioned, I became very much a loner and would isolate myself from others. I know now that for many years I carried around with me the pain associated with events from my childhood, which I carried into past relationships and my marriages.

For many years I had locked away all the pain and hurt, hoping it would protect me, but what I found was it led to more pain over the years. I would at times run the 'poor me' mode, playing the victim in my own life.

It was only by going down the path of personal development that I learned how I had been living my life. When you are a child you do not analyze what is happening to you. It is only when you get older that you can look back and see what effect it had on you and how you can deal with the events. What I have found is that it is essential to go through the process of removing pain of any kind that is stored inside you. It is a gradual process and it has taken me many years. It is like an onion. You have to keep peeling away the skin to get to the heart.

What I also found with this feeling of hurt was how low my energy was. Besides not being able to sleep or eat, it was as if my whole body had gone into shutdown. Everything was so much of an effort to do. My head hurt any time I started to think about what had happened. Looking back, I think it is our body's way of protecting us, by slowing us down and giving us time to heal.

Betrayal

Before she had an affair with my husband, my friend and I had known each other for many years and had shared much together. When she was going through the breakup of her marriage I was always there for her, inviting her into our home as one of our family.

When Doug told me of the affair, which had taken

place from early 1997 to late 1998, what hurt me the most was that she had continued our friendship after she and Doug had split up. She had remarried and our families spent many social occasions and holidays together. I had shared with her my deepest feelings, including the challenges Doug and I had been having with intimacy.

I felt so close to her; she was the last person I would ever have thought would have done this to me. She was like a sister to me. When I thought back to all the times we had been together, not only on our own but also socially as families, I wondered how she could have continued to still see me and act like such a great friend.

I still find it hard to believe, but I also understand that it would have been difficult to cut off all ties with me as I would have wondered what I had done wrong.

I will always be grateful for the times she helped me, but betrayal by someone you trusted and loved is a very hard thing to deal with. When I got back from Austria, I sent her an email telling her everything that Doug had told me, not from an angry place but from a sad, lonely and betrayed place. I told her I never wanted to see or hear from her again and, as of today, I have not. At times I miss her, but I know that it would never be the same. I just had to let her go with love. As they say people come into your life for a reason.

Anger

The day after Doug told me everything, I decided to go home. I had not slept, I was exhausted and I wanted to be near my children. Although I wanted to leave on my own, I reluctantly agreed that Doug could fly back on the same flight, as he wanted us to talk to the children together.

What he didn't know was that I had already rung my two older children and told them what their Dad had said, knowing it would hurt Doug. I was starting to feel very angry towards him and wanted him to hurt as much as I was. Our children were very supportive and just wanted me to come home and said that we would all work through it.

From the moment we were seated on the plane my anger exploded. Doug had said he would answer any questions I had if I thought his answers would help me, so, with much anger and venom, I started firing extremely intimate questions about the women he had been with. What they had done to each other? Where they had been? I also directed a lot of anger towards myself in the form of derogatory statements.

I thought I was talking quietly, but later, Doug told me that I had been very loud. I remember at one point, the pretty young stewardess had come along and asked if we wanted anything, and as she walked away, I said to my husband, "I suppose you want to shag her as well?" Now we laugh about that journey, as looking back, it could have come out of a comedy sketch, but that the time, it didn't seem funny at all.

Once we got home, Doug arranged a meeting with the children and shared with them what he had done. I remained quiet, not wanting to show my anger in front of the kids. I did not want to hurt them any more than they would already be hurt by what was happening. They were all very supportive. As far as they were concerned, Doug was still their Dad, he was a good Dad and they loved him, and what had happened was between me and him. I had a fleeting hope that they would turn against him, but deep down I knew that was not what I truly wanted. I was proud of how well they handled the situation and how they supported both of us through this extremely difficult time.

The next few days were very painful and my emotions were a roller coaster. I was crying, hurt, angry, betrayed, confused and depressed. The atmosphere in the house was unbearable. Doug had moved into the spare bedroom and we kept out of each other's way as much as possible. When we did encounter each other, I threw out more angry questions. Since I had learnt the truth, I had not been able to sleep or eat, and when I did attempt to eat anything, I felt sick.

A few nights after we got back I was lying in bed with lots of angry thoughts going around in my head, unable to sleep. Finally, around three in the morning, I decided to go through our photos and remove all of the ones of my friend. I sat on the floor of our lounge surrounded by hundreds of pictures.

Feelings of pain, vulnerability and anger flowed through me, as I worked my way through the photos with tears flowing down my face. I couldn't understand how two of the most special people in my life, whom I had trusted, had done this to me.

When I had them all together, I cut her out of all of the pictures and spread them all over Doug's desk, his computer and the walls around his desk. I even replaced photos of myself with photos of her. I was so angry that part of me felt good, even though it still hurt like hell. The next day Doug did not say anything. He just cleared them all away into the bin. As a final touch, I also insisted that he delete all her email addresses and phone numbers.

*F*rom my own experience and from the clients I have worked with I have learned that anger can manifest in myriad ways. For example, depression, tiredness, irritability, often exploding over small things; spending too much time in front of the television, eating junk food or sweets, sexual disinterest, not really connecting with people and often not being able to look them in the eye; not being able to communicate, abusing your body with cigarettes, alcohol or drugs, and even eating disorders or a serious illness.

If you have experienced any form of abuse in your life, then it is understandable that you will feel anger. We feel anger when we do not get what we want or people around us do not do the things we want. I know for me that when I used to get angry, the only person who would get hurt in the end would be me.

Through the early years of my marriage I would take my anger out on Doug and wanted to blame him for everything. It helped me to think I was in control and protect myself. I have learnt over the years that this is not the case. When you do let go of control, and go into your feminine energy, that is when the magic starts to happen. It is not fair that every man in your life should be punished because others have abused you in the past. As I have found out, any relationship will only stand so much before it falls apart. What I learned over the years is that you need to let the anger out, because if you don't it can lead to much more pain.

Depression and Loneliness

Just after the anger towards Doug, I found that I also had this feeling of being dead, as if I was not actually a part of my own life. I felt numb, in a constant trance-like state. I also found it difficult to concentrate on anything, let alone think what I was going to do now that I knew the truth. I felt empty and constantly sick to my stomach, so I never wanted to eat. I felt so alone and thought that no one would understand what I was experiencing. When friends told me that I was a strong person and I would be fine, I remember thinking to myself, "I do not want to be a strong person, I want someone to understand what is happening." I knew that unless someone had been through something like this, they would have no idea of what it was like.

It was the holiday season and because I did not know what was going to happen with our relationship it was difficult to be excited about Christmas. I walked around shops in a state of numbness looking for presents for my children. I would see something and think, Doug would like that, and then all of a sudden I had to remind myself that we were not together. Not knowing what I would be doing for Christmas was upsetting, as Christmas had always been a special time for us. Doug's birthday was just before Christmas and I always made it special for him, not wanting him to miss out just because his birthday was so close to the holiday. We had been together for such a long time; it was strange to think that year was going to be a lonely time, not only for me, but for Doug as well.

S ometimes being on your own can be a good thing. Doug works from home and on the days when he is out on business or for whatever reason, I actually enjoy the fact that I have the house to myself. If I want to be outrageous or just do the things I want without having to worry about anyone else, I can. The difference between those times and what I experienced when we were separated, is that now I know he is coming back. However, I have found that even when there isn't anyone coming back, as long as you accept loneliness as a process you need to go through, you can learn to enjoy the feeling of peace that comes with it. What it did for me was give me times to be quiet and think of all that had happened.

Depression is one of the biggest problems facing society today. Doctors are seeing more patients with depression than any other illness, and many people with depression do not even consult a doctor. Although some people who suffer with depression have a chemical imbalance or bi-polar disease, which means it is less likely to be related to trauma, my belief is that the main issue behind depression is anger. When we get depressed the feelings have arisen from anger and fear within ourselves which we are choosing to suppress, rather than allowing it to come to the surface and deal with the pain. The triggers are often linked to things like relationship breakdown, illness, loss of a job, bereavement or a new baby. My personal feeling is that when you are suffering with depression that you are not prepared to face up to reality and be totally honest with yourself.

I also believe that when we go into depression we are unconsciously looking for pity and for significance. Many people do not even realise what they are doing or how they are behaving because they are too wrapped up in themselves. I know that I have been there at times. When this happens, we must notice what we are doing and take responsibility for our actions.

One of the things I learnt on the Relationship Weekend is that when we run our life with our logical left brain we live in fear, doubt, and worry. We are programming ourselves to be anxious, frustrated, angry, and depressed and live with constant adrenal stress. We focus on the past, fast forward life and see it with problems. When you run your life with your heart and your whole brain you think positively, you focus on your heart and your breathing, you are more relaxed and life seems great.

Blame and Guilt

For most of my adult life, whenever Doug and I got into an argument, I would always be looking to blame him. I would also get very angry and scream and shout at him. I realise now that blaming Doug was my way of feeling safe and in control. Unconsciously, I had gone through my life with this brick wall around me, as a defense against anyone who could hurt me. When I blamed others it often met my need for certainty, but not in a positive way. While it is perfectly normal to want to blame someone if you feel they have done wrong in some way, I had always been quick to put the blame onto others in my life, rather than take responsibility myself. By doing this I was attempting to protect myself and to feel important.

Even into my thirties I was still constantly blaming how my Dad had treated me as a child for everything that was not right in my life. Although I do not think what my Dad did to me was right, he thought that being strict with discipline was the way you brought up children I could have gone through the rest of my life blaming him for everything that went wrong, but I know that this would not have served me. I would have been constantly looking for someone else to make everything right, rather than looking inside myself and accepting what had happened in the past and moving on.

During the time I was dealing with Doug's revelation, I started to look at how I had been in our marriage. When I looked back, I started to blame myself for what had happened. I asked myself questions about my part in what had happened. Was I a bad wife? Was she better than me? Was it because I wasn't able to communicate as well as they did? Was it because she was younger than me? Was he trying to get back at me for what I had done to him?

I thought back to when I saw a specialist at the Priory Clinic in 1989 for treatment for Bulimia. Doug had come with me to the clinic and waited outside for me. Afterward he wanted to know what had been said. The specialist had asked me lots of questions about my past and past relationships; he then asked me if I loved my husband. His question confused me. I had never thought I did not love him, even though our relationship had been up and down due to my behavior (at this time I was unaware of how he was conducting his life). I wasn't aware that at this time in my life, I did not know what true love was.

When I came out of the consulting room I knew I could not discuss what the specialist had said to me with Doug as at that moment I had no idea what I was thinking myself. I felt more confused and scared than before going to see him. I just pushed Doug away and would not talk to him, which made him even more curious and uncertain. After that I became even more emotionally unstable. It was like I was determined to upset Doug and push him away, like I wanted him to hate me. It was a very frustrating time for him and I know that he was very concerned about what was happening to our relationship, which seemed to be rapidly falling apart.

During this period I had been working behind the bar at a club and helping to organise social events. One evening one of the members started talking to me. He was having some challenges in his marriage and it seemed we both needed someone to talk to. He said all the things I needed to hear and made me feel very special, unlike Doug who had always found it very difficult to show his emotions. Within a few weeks we had agreed to meet up and before I knew it I was totally emotionally involved.

At the time I was convinced I was madly in love and he was the only man for me. During this the six weeks we were together, I continued to make Doug's life hell. I was constantly doing anything to push him away. I was so consumed with how good this other man was making me feel that I had no consideration for what Doug was going through. Over this six week period Doug and I went away on holiday, which had been booked long before the affair had started. I did not want to go and the week away was probably one of the worst holidays we ever had together. Even worse, on the day we left, I missed my period due date which had always been regular and every day while we were away, I kept praying that my fears of being pregnant were not true. All I could think of was getting back home to take a test and to see the other man.

When we got back home I went and got a test and to my horror, I was pregnant. I could not believe this was happening to me. I kept thinking, this happens to young girls, not someone of my age. After everything that had happened to me I was in a complete state of fear. I knew I had to see him and we arranged to meet up in the next few days. I told him the situation and he reassured me that everything would be okay and he would take care of it. I went to my doctor to get confirmation. I could not go to my local hospital in case anyone saw me, so she told me of a private clinic in a neighboring city. I made the arrangements to go into the clinic on the Thursday and he agreed to pay, which I was grateful for as I would not be able to explain what had happened to the money.

When I came back from the holiday he told me that while I had been away, things with his wife had become difficult. She became suspicious and was questioning him and of course he was denying that anything was going on. At that point

I had become totally obsessed and could not imagine him not being there for me. At the same time, Doug was starting to ask questions, too. I remember telling him that if he did not like things as they were, that he could leave. I know now that I was trying to provoke him, to see how much he wanted me and what he would take from me to stay with me, and also to not have to deal with the guilt and betrayal. I was still looking for someone else to give me attention and affection and I was testing him with my behavior. I was at my most controlling, although I did not realise at the time.

The time after getting home from holiday and waiting to go in for the abortion was very challenging. In a way I was relieved when the day came, although I had to do lots of sorting out to cover up what I was doing. The other man drove me to the clinic but was not allowed to come into the main area. I remember thinking how dirty I felt as I was shown to my bed. I was so ashamed. As a mother of three beautiful children, I would never have dreamed I could do what I was about to do.

The experience was very clinical, like a conveyor belt. I felt as if I were just a number waiting to be called. I had the abortion and a few hours later I told them I felt fine and they agreed I could leave. When he picked me up, he kept telling me how strong I was and how I was handling it all so well. I was doing a good job of controlling my emotions, because that was not at all how I was feeling inside.

The next morning I met up with him and he told me that when he got home that night, his wife had gotten her family to tell him to sort his marriage out. I did not want to hear that he was cooling off. I started to think that after what had just happened, he no longer wanted me and he was ready to walk away.

I drove myself over to my best friend's house and broke down in tears and told her everything that had happened. She asked me if I would still want to be with Doug if this man did not want me anymore and I could not answer her, I felt like an absolute wreck.

That Friday night when Doug and I went to a social event at the club, it all came to a head. If I had not arranged the evening I would not have gone, as I knew he would be there with his wife, but as it was I had to be there. On arrival at the club they were already there and he completely ignored me, which I found that difficult to take. An hour later, I had not said much to Doug and he announced he was going home. He said he did not see any point in him staying if I was not going to talk to him and asked if I was coming home with him. I told him I wasn't and at that point I was not even sure if I was ever going home. I was so consumed with my own feelings and myself that I had not even thought about what our children were going through.

Once Doug left I became even more emotional. I began to drink quite heavily, which is not something I often do, and felt completely out of control. I did not care about what was happening to me or what was going to happen with the situation I was in. At one point during the evening I was crying uncontrollably in the ladies toilets and his wife came in and asked me outright if I was having an affair with her husband. I just screamed at her and told her to go and sort out her marriage. He still had not looked at me or spoken to me all evening and after everything he had said to me in the past about how much he cared about me, I felt so alone.

All of a sudden something snapped inside me and I knew I had to get out of the club. The only thing I could think of was to get on the M25 motorway. I did not care what happened to me. At that moment I felt it would be better for everyone if I was dead. It seemed everything in my life had been such a mess and I never seemed to get it right. As I tried to get into my car, the steward of the club came out and physically took my car keys away. I became hysterical, but he was adamant that I was not driving anywhere in the state I was in. Looking back, he probably saved my life that night.

He went back into the club with my keys, leaving me crying by my car. He came back out with the man and his wife and they insisted on taking me home. I was adamant that I was not going home. I was not aware at the time, but they had agreed to take me round to a close friend of mine, who had not known anything about my affair. We arrived at my friend's at around midnight. She opened the door to us and looked at him and could see I was in a terrible state. She asked him if it had anything to do with him. He just said yes, and walked back to his car where his wife was waiting. I remember walking through the door and collapsing into my friend's arms, crying. Over that weekend I was in a complete state of disbelief and uncertainty. I wanted to see him to see what we were going to do.

My friend arranged for him to come round on the Saturday evening on his way back from the club. He was very distant and to the point. He told me that he would not leave his wife but, if I decided not to go back to Doug, he would help me with a flat. It was then that I realised that he had never wanted me. I had just been a very vulnerable woman who made him feel good and given him something that he was not getting from his wife. I knew I was not prepared to just be his bit on the side and be available as and when he was free to see me. During the weekend I did not sleep very much and after seeing him I knew I had to decide what I was going to do. After lots of thinking and talking with my friend, I decided to go back to my house and speak to Doug. I was not even sure that he would still want me after I told him, but I knew I had to tell him the truth for us to have any chance of moving on. My friend had said I should not tell him about the abortion and so at this time I did not. I now know that if you really want to be at peace in your life, you need to let go of everything and be totally honest.

Before Doug would let me say anything, he insisted he wanted to tell me something. He then proceeded to tell me that whatever he had gone after in his life, he had always succeeded in getting, for example great results in his school exams, passing his driving test first time and any girl he wanted. Then he told me the reason he had asked me to marry him was that he saw winning me from the other man I was seeing as a challenge, but once I accepted, he was not sure if he really wanted me. During our first year of marriage he had constantly pushed me away whenever I attempted to get intimate, saying he was tired and to wait till the weekend. He also found it difficult having a child around, as by then he had not had children of his own We had many arguments over not being able to do things because of my daughter. What he told me was a bit of a shock, but I felt it was not as bad as what I had been doing to him over the previous six weeks.

When I told him he was very calm. He said it would be ok and that we would get through it. I could not believe he was taking it all so calmly and thought what a great man he was, as a lot of men would have thrown me out. I did not know at the time that he had been cheating on me ever since we got married.

The next year was very difficult as I lived with the guilt over what I had done and how much I had hurt him. I also lived with the fear that he would want to get back at some point with an affair of his own, although deep down I never thought he would.

About three months after the affair had finished, Doug came in from the club one Friday evening and started to question me. How honest had I had been? Had I told him everything? Finally after he kept pushing I told him everything. When I had finished, he walked out of the room and closed the door behind him. I suspected that he might be going to the other man's house but was not completely sure. When he turned up a few hours later, he was very calm and was even smiling to himself. I asked him where he had been and then he told me that he had been to the other man's house and had basically kicked their front door in and attacked him. His wife had screamed and shouted for Doug to get off him or she would call the police and in the end she did. In the fight Doug's contact lens had come out and he had to crawl around the floor looking for his lens, all the time his wife was telling him to get out. Doug said he was not going anywhere till he had found his lens!

Many times before the affair I talked to Doug about going back to work. Doug was not happy about it as he felt the woman's place was in the home and being there for the children. As I was still controlling our relationship (although I didn't realise it at the time), I told Doug that I was going back to work and that was just how things were going to be. So I went back to work part time and as Doug said he was not going to give up his social life to be always looking after the children, I made arrangements for us to have an au pair. Our life changed, but it was still not the marriage I wanted it to be.

When I went back to work I became close to a work colleague who was also facing challenges in her marriage She was a great listener and she became a great support to me and helped me in my down days. She was also going through a breakdown in her marriage due to her husband's infidelity and I was there for her to keep her positive through the dark days. It seemed we had been brought together to help each other see another point of view.

I introduced her to my family and we started to mix with her family socially and became very close. It was obvious from the beginning that she and Doug got on very well together and seemed to be able to talk very easily together. As her marriage deteriorated I invited her round to our house more often and she became very much part of our family. I was pleased that Doug got on well with her as I find it is always easier if your husband gets on with your friends. I thought that we were both supporting her through a difficult time, although at the time I did not realise how much my husband was supporting her.

One evening a crowd of us went out together and my friend and her husband and a few others stayed over at our house. Everyone except my friend and Doug decided to go off to bed. As our bedroom is above our lounge you can hear conversations, although not always clearly. I remember waking up and hearing all this laughing and chatting going on between long periods of silence. I did not go down and see for myself what was happening but after my friend had left the next day I confronted Doug and at a later date told my friend what I had been thinking. They were both extremely angry that I would even think such a thing. Their denials made me feel guilty for even thinking that they were having an affair.

I believe that when people have affairs it is because at some level they are not getting their needs met and it is not always the need for sex. For a lot of people it is the need to feel significant and connected with someone. I am not proud of what I did to Doug. Although at the time I did not stop to think of his feelings, deep down I had always thought that he was the one person I could trust. I remember having a discussion when we were first married about how some of his friends had been with other women. I asked him if he had, and he said he had not and would never do such a thing.

As you can see from our story, the other person is not always the one to blame. We also need to take responsibility ourselves. Even if you have never had an affair yourself, it is important to look back and see how your behavior in the relationship might have contributed to what happened. The purpose isn't to make you feel guilty, but rather to become aware of potentially harmful behavior so that you can change it in the future. I know from my own experience and from talking to others, that carrying guilt around is very destructive. It can lead you down many unhappy paths. We have to take responsibility for our actions and learn from our mistakes, without beating ourselves up with guilt in the process.

We have to let go of the past because you cannot do anything about what happened. What you can do is look forward to here and now and enjoy every minute of it. We all encounter obstacles along the journey of life. That is all part of life, but it is what makes us grow stronger and helps us to appreciate the great times even more. At the end of the day, it is not what happens to you but the way you respond to what happens that matters!

Physical Illness

Besides the importance of dealing with your emotions to learn and heal, I believe that the consequences of not properly dealing with negative emotions can lead to physical illness. There is growing scientific research to support this theory and I know that there have been occasions in my life where I am convinced that not letting my feelings out or holding onto past traumas in my life led to physical illness.

One example was an illness that resulted from my inability to properly deal with my emotions around my first marriage. In 1980 I finally decided that I could not continue. We had been married for five years at this point and in that time he loved being a father to our daughter, but seemed incapable of being a husband and a family man.

We lived in a flat above the shop where he worked and after work he would disappear to the pub along the road. Often he would not come home until very late, in a drunken state. On several occasions he was even found lying in the road and had to be brought home.

I had gone back to work when our daughter was three months old because money was tight and I wanted to be able to give her things, but there never seemed to be enough because my husband had an addiction to gambling and tended to gamble whatever money he could lay his hands on. Over the later years his drinking and gambling became so intense that I could not go on any more. When I spoke to my Dad and Mum, their answer to how I was feeling was, "You made your bed so lie on it."

As we lived in a rent free flat which went with his job and I did not have much money of my own, I went to see the council about getting housed. We divorced in the October and the council did not house me and my daughter until the following March. During this period he became more abusive and was constantly putting me down and accusing me of all sorts of things. During much of this time, I stayed very quiet around him and did not show any sort of emotion.

One day at work something snapped inside me and I started to cry and shake hysterically and was totally out of control. My boss thought I was on drugs and ran downstairs to get one of my work colleagues to come and talk to me, but due to the state I was in, I could hardly speak When I saw my doctor, he said that I had finally had a breakdown because I had held in my emotions for so long.

Previously, I had always been a very emotional person, weeping at sad films or stories, so after all the time without an outlet, something finally had to give. The next three days I slept and when I finally came back to reality, it was as if I had finally let go and felt strong enough to move on with my life. Two weeks later I was offered a flat by the council. It was great for me and my daughter to move in, without worrying about how my ex-husband was going to be or what state he would be in when he came home.

On another occasion, I became ill even when I thought everything was going well, but underneath, I had not dealt with my past issues and they resurfaced in the form of another physical illness. In 1986, Doug and I moved into our dream house with lots of space and a lovely big garden. We were excited at the prospect of having our first child together. When our son was born in the September I could not have been happier. I had the little boy I had always wanted. Doug's business was doing well. It seemed like we had everything we could have ever wanted.

After having our son I thought I was happy and life seemed good. Without trying I had lost a lot of weight very quickly and people were starting to mention how good I was looking and how slim I was. When my son was six months old I became aware that I was beginning to put on weight. I think that because I had been getting comments on how good I looked, something inside of me unconsciously triggered my low self-esteem and lack of self worth. I had always loved food and I still continued to eat as normal but as soon as I had eaten something I would beat myself up, feel guilty, then go back and have some more. Then I would go to the toilet and throw it all up and so the cycle would continue. I thought I was hiding it from my family and friends but now I know I was not that clever.

Once I started on this pattern it became a stronger desire in me. It started off being only when I had eaten a larger meal, but soon I was sick after everything I ate. At the time I had no idea of the abuse I was putting my body through. Many times I wanted to stop, but I couldn't. I hated the thought of putting weight on, even though I was losing weight. Over the next six years being bulimic completely took over my life and I felt as if I was living a roller coaster of emotions.

Whenever Doug attempted to talk to me or confront me, I would get very angry and deny it vehemently. One minute I would feel happy, the next I was like some angry dragon! Finally Doug convinced me to get help, but it wasn't until much later that I came to terms with everything that led me to my illness.

*M*any people who have been sexually or physically abused have weight issues as our emotions play a large part in the reasons why we have these issues. What I have realised, after all these years, is that I spent most of my adult life wanting to be in control of any situation. It was my way to feel safe, but the truth was quite the contrary, as I soon learned to my detriment. I have finally learned to love my body, with all its imperfections, although it wasn't easy. To love a body that has been through abuse is going to be much harder, but it is essential that we accept and love who and what we are. Once you can do this, you can more easily break free of past abuse. I found that the abuse I had received as a child led to my low self esteem, lack of self worth and self confidence. It had affected most areas of my life. I know now that we decide how we want our lives to be, for example what we do and do not want in our life. It has taken me many years to feel great about myself. I must say, at times it was not easy but, if you want to get through the feeling of low self-worth you can, as I found out.

Mirror Exercise

How often do we look in the rear mirror rather than looking forward? One exercise that was very helpful for me in developing a healthy-self image is called the Mirror Exercise.

Stand in front of a mirror either clothed or unclothed, but if you can do it with no clothes on it is even better.

Look in the mirror at your whole body and say, "I love my body" out loud.

Working from the top of your head down to your feet, pick out every part of your body with a positive statement as you look in the mirror. Say something like, "I have beautiful hair", "I love my brown eyes and how they sparkle;" and I am sure you can come up with lots of other positive affirmations about your body. It is also great to include affirmations around loving yourself, how beautiful you are inside and out.

I recommend doing this daily for as long as it takes for you to start feel good about yourself. I have affirmations for all areas of my life which I say every morning, even now.

From Confusion To Clarity

During the period that Doug and I were separated, I was very confused, not knowing which way to turn or what to do. I continued to ask myself questions. Why had this happened to me? Why had he waited so long into our marriage to tell me? How had I been showing up in the marriage? I knew that I had not been an easy person to live with and had made Doug's life pretty awful at times. As I had been put down for much of my early years, I had very low self-esteem and found it extremely difficult to accept compliments, especially from men. I never believed what they were saying. How could I when I had only ever had the fun taken out of me, been criticised or emotionally abused?

A few weeks after Doug's revelations, I learned that Kevin, a good friend of mine, was going out to Tampa for a NLP Master Practitioner course. He suggested that I make enquiries about coming out as a coach to give me some time away to think. I wasn't sure how great I would be due to my state, but the organiser understood and agreed that it would be good for me to get away. My older son suggested he come out to Florida for a few days and once we were there, I was pleased to have him with me. Having him there helped take my mind off the situation and it was also good to spend some quality time with him, but when he left Tampa to go back to Miami I felt very alone. I was not sure if I was doing the right thing, being so far away from home.

I felt better later that day when Kevin arrived with his brother. They were both a great support to me through the course. Kevin was a very easy person to talk to and as he was a coach as well, he could be detached in what he was saying to me. Just having him there through my up and down days was great. At registration the next day, I also found that there were many people I knew attending the course, which was also very comforting.

Over the next three weeks, I had days when I actually felt quite normal mixed with days I felt low. It helped that the hotel I was staying in was situated on a beautiful sandy beach and in the mornings I could get up and run along the beach listening to my iPod which I found very relaxing. It gave me time to switch off from all the pain and hurt. When the other coaches saw that I was not doing great, they would advise me to take time out.

During the first couple of weeks part of me did not want to speak to Doug but part of me did. I was very confused because even after all he had done, I still felt that he was a part of my life. On one occasion I rang home to speak to my youngest son hoping that Doug would answer the phone, but he did not. My son told me that Doug wanted to talk all the time and I explained that this was his way of dealing with what he had done and that he was, at some level, looking for forgiveness. Doug knew I was in Florida, but did not know where I was staying, so I finally gave in and sent him an email telling him where I was if he wanted to talk to me.

During some of our subsequent talks I became very angry and frustrated with him. Doug was brilliant and he never allowed himself to return my anger. He was very calm and gave me lots of certainty which is the main thing a woman needs. He was by no means behaving like a lap dog, just very calm and reassuring about how he wanted things to be. He was very understanding; he knew he had hurt me deeply and only wanted the best for me. Although at times it was very frustrating, I knew he was doing the right thing, as this was what we he had been taught on our Relationship Course. On some of our calls I found that I was beginning to be more at peace and starting to heal inside. I still had no idea what I was going to do, but I knew it was a process I needed to go through to feel completely okay with myself.

During my time on the course, a lot of what was being taught helped me to look at the situation in different ways. The course material was the same I had learned on my NLP Master Practitioner course and it was great to have it reaffirmed. One particular exercise was called 'Leap of Faith', which requires participants to ride thirty feet up in a crane and then jump off and land on your back on a huge air bag. The coaches were expected to do it as well and I really wasn't feeling up to it as the day before the jump had been a particularly bad day for me.

On the morning of the jump I felt slightly better, yet still very apprehensive due to my fear of heights. Shortly before my turn I was faced with another hurdle. The crane's hydraulics had become too slow and they needed to get all the jumps done before the sun completely set, so they brought a ladder for us to climb. The only other time I had climbed a high ladder, I froze when I had to come back down, but surprisingly, I managed to climb the ladder without too much difficulty.

When I stepped onto the edge, ready to jump, all the fear kicked in. As I held onto the sides I was shaking. I tried to let go but something just kept holding me back. As it was quite a windy day, the trained stuntmen were only letting us jump when the wind was still and just as I thought I was about to go, they stopped me. It felt like I stood on that platform for hours. I kept saying to myself, "You can do this," and I could hear all the people supporting me from below saying, "Come on Chris, you can do it, just let go!"

Finally, something inside me snapped and as I took the leap out, I felt as if I had let go of more than just that platform. When I rolled off the bag, I was met with hugs and support from many of my friends who knew how difficult it had been for me. I cried with happiness for the release I felt, not only for what had happened with Doug, but for all the significant painful events in my life. For the rest of that day I felt great! I was happier than I had been since Doug told me the news. I sent Doug a text and a picture of me celebrating, which he could not have been happier about. I was finally starting to look at myself and to feel better.

The remaining few days were good, but part of me was ready to go home. I felt strong enough to deal with any decisions I knew I would need to make. I had also missed my children and my grandchild very much. I know that I made the right decision to get away. While some people had said that you cannot run away from your problems I did not feel I was running away; I just needed to get my head around all the confusion of what had happened.

Once back home, I felt a lot calmer and was better able to communicate with Doug, although I still did not know what I was going to do. He was very supportive and said I could take as much time as I needed, as he could appreciate this was a difficult decision for me to make. He also told me that he was not prepared to go back to the relationship we had before. We both agreed that we wanted the ultimate intimate relationship and if that was not going to be with each other, then it would be with someone else. Neither of us wanted to have just an okay relationship any more. One thing I knew for sure was that whichever path I chose was not going to be easy.

Just a week after getting home, I was off again. As I had previously agreed to coach on Andy Harrington's NLP Master Practitioner course, I had another two weeks away from home. During the two weeks through Andy's talks on relationships, I found more pieces were fitting into the jigsaw puzzle. Although I had heard his talks many times before, I realised that previously I had not wanted to really hear what he was saying. I did not want to face what was really going on with me. So often it seems that when things are not going well in our lives, we can be given advice but unless the timing is right, we don't truly hear it.

During the course, Tim, one of the trainers, asked if I would be willing to be a demo subject for a session he was doing the following morning. The demo was going for a therapy known in the NLP world as 'Change Personal History', which assists people to look at a past significant event and see it differently. When Tim asked me, my first reaction was to agree as I had been through this process before and found it very beneficial, but I was not sure what event to work on. I did not feel I was ready to go through what had happened with Doug in front of all the participants so we agreed to deal with the death of my father. As we went through the demo, I began to realise that the emotions I felt towards my father were the same sort of emotions that I had felt with Doug and it was more emotional than I thought it would be. At the end it was a release, not only from my father, but also a release of my negative feelings towards Doug.

Later that day, during one of the breaks, one of the candidates came up to me and asked if she could share something with me from what had happened during my demo in the morning. She told me that she helps people who have animals and by looking at a picture of an animal and knowing how old they are, she can tell you what they are feeling. She then proceeded to tell me that she did not tend to work with spirits of humans, but one of her relatives had died and had come through her to let her family know she was okay.

She then told me that, during the demo, as I was talking about my father, he came through her and kept telling her that he was okay and that I was to let go and that all the time I was hurting, so was he. As she was talking, I started to cry, but also felt for the first time in my life that my Dad was actually there for me and did love me.

In the latter part of the course, I attended a session called, 'Clean Language'. During the workshop we broke up into groups of threes to go through the clean language questions. In this exercise, participants come up with statements which the facilitator feeds back to you in the form of questions, leading participants to gain a deeper understanding of an issue.

During my session, I made the statement that I had never given my heart completely to anyone. My facilitator then asked me what it would look like if I did. I described a picture of Jessica Rabbit with a big red heart with a key, which when unlocked, started pumping very fast. It reminded me of a funny cartoon, yet it was very powerful for me. Although not at the time, it became a huge factor in my decision to stay with Doug. I finally realised that moving forward was all about letting go!

When I went back to the Master Practitioner course with Andy, I felt calmer and was ready to talk to Doug. I called him from the hotel and asked him if it would be possible for us to go somewhere, away from the house, so we would be on neutral territory to see where we were. Over the next couple of days, we continued to communicate and Doug made arrangements for us to go down to Brighton when I was due back from the course.

I realised when I saw him that Tuesday evening, how much I had missed him. I was apprehensive, but also looking forward to going away and being able to talk through everything in a constructive way. On the Wednesday morning when I woke up, I felt very peaceful and I knew what I needed to do, I walked into his office, which is in our home and looked him in the eye and told him I wanted to see about moving forward together. At this point he broke down in tears and just hugged me. Deep down I thought to myself, "We can get through this."

two

Looking At Yourself

Significant Events

Some of you may be asking why we would want to look at ourselves when things that happen to us are caused by other people. The truth is, sometimes we can see things more clearly when we take the time to take a look at ourselves. Through my training to become an NLP Master Practitioner, we learnt about how we process our experience.

External events that happen to us go through three filters in our brain: **delete,** which means by not paying attention to everything consciously we **distort** events by choosing a meaning through our imagination, and **generalise** by evaluating how much like a similar experience it is. This becomes part of our **internal representation** of the event, which then effects our **state** (internal emotional feelings in response to external events) and **physiology** which leads to our response to external events.

Our decisions are our choices based on what this event means to us and how we choose to react to it. This leads to our **actions** – what we do in the real world in response to external events; and finally **results** – the ultimate feedback to our choices in life.

One of the frames in NLP is 'Perception is Projection' which means what you see outside of yourself and see in others is what you see in yourself, which is so often what we don't want to see. Another frame is 'Cause and Effect' which simply means you are often blaming others or situations for what is going on in your life rather than taking responsibility. Also when we ask ourselves quality questions, we find that we get a better answer to what is happening in our life.

We were also taught about Archetypes, which are ancient universal patterns of behaviour embedded deep in our unconscious mind and sustained through universal myths and stories. The six Archetypes are:

The Warrior: The warrior within us calls us to have courage, strength and integrity to make goals and stick to them. Warriors call us to action.

The Lover: The lover within us calls us to be more open, trusting and vulnerable; it is the part of us that wants to connect and to share our bond with others.

The Sage: The sage within us has little or no need to control or change the world, they just want to understand it. This Archetype is about becoming wise.

The Jester or Fool: The fool takes life lightly and is adept at changing someone's focus or turning a serious situation into a humorous one.

The Sovereign: The sovereign displays certainty and majesty and takes responsibility to lead.

The Magician: The magician has the power of insight by trusting his instincts. The magician also knows that everything is connected to everything else.

We also learnt about 'Shadow-Self Psychology', which is our fear-based behaviours in response to external events.

These are:

Blamer: Looks externally for the cause of results. Low self esteem so will often lower others to give the illusion of being worth more than others. Typically loud and fast talking when stressed. Often attracted to a mate who is a Placater. Greatest fears are failure, being controlled, not being enough or being poor.

Placater: Tends to blame themself for everything that goes wrong. Low self-esteem so looks to please others to gain acknowledgement and appreciation.

Unable to set and enforce boundaries. Has little or no purpose and finds it hard to make clear decisions. Greatest fears are abandonment, conflict and the unknown.

Computer: A computer self will evaluate and make decisions based on their intellect and distrust their emotions or instinct. Tend to be very much in their head. Greatest fears are being wrong, failure and being poor.

Distracter: When self esteem is low they will look to keep busy and ignore or distract themselves from reality. When being given advice will often laugh things off. Workwise they will start lots of things but soon loses momentum. They are usually the life and soul of the party. Greatest fears are being judged, commitment and rejection.

W hen I look back at the events in my life and whatever pain, cruelty or infidelity I have experienced, I now know that it has made me the person I am today, although I did not realise this at the time. As I mentioned earlier, my childhood was not a happy one. During my early school years, I always felt very much the outsider and would spend many a break time on my own. I still managed to get into trouble though and I remember getting angry and not always being very nice to other children. I did not know at the time, but I realise now that I behaved that way because I wanted to be liked and feel connected to people. I believe that when children behave poorly, it is to get attention, although not always the right sort of attention.

I mentioned in the introduction to this book that my father was a very strict man and also, at times, physically abusive to me. On one particular occasion, in my early teens, he really did go too far.

One night after my friends and I attended a party, it seemed something had gone missing from the house and for some reason someone seemed to think I was involved. When the headmistress of the school informed me that they would be coming to see my parents in the evening, I was terrified.

When I got home from school my Mum had already received a call from the Headmistress so she suggested that I go up to bed, out of the way of my father, which I was happy to do. I was lying in my bed when the Headmistress and Deputy Head came round and listened as my father shouted at them, finally telling them to get out of his house. Then I heard my father coming up the stairs very quickly; each step he took sounding like a loud drum. He burst into my bedroom, dragged me out of bed and started kicking and hitting me, all the time shouting abuse. As I was struggling on the floor, he put his hands around my neck and started to strangle me, all the time shouting and screaming at me. I had never been so frightened or scared in my life. Luckily my Mum was there to pull my Dad off me or I am convinced I would not be here today.

Over the next year my Dad and I hardly spoke to each other and on the occasions we did, it was either to ask or to tell him something; we did not have any friendly conversations. I do not think he knew what to say to me. The following Christmas he brought me a radio as a surprise present to replace the one he had thrown at the wall and smashed into pieces when he burst into my room that night. We just looked at each other with many thoughts running through our minds, and didn't say a word. He was never able to say that he was sorry.

Although I eventually forgave him, I still did not know how to be fully at ease with him or even what to say to him much of the time. When my children were growing up, he would shout at them if they had done something wrong and even, at times, run them down. As their Mum I know I should have stood up to him, but he made me feel as if I was the intimidated little girl again. I always felt guilty for not standing up for my children. Fortunately he never physically abused them and I would like to think that if he had, I would have done something about it.

It was not until I got into my late thirties that I started to look to deal with what had happened in my childhood and the effect that it was having on me. I always thought at some point I would need to talk to my Dad about the effect it had on my life and to tell him that, whatever he had done, I had forgiven him, but I never got around to talking to him about it and he passed away at the beginning of 2006.

I always remember thinking to myself about how I would feel when he died. Would I be relieved? Would I feel guilty? Would I be upset? Did I ever love him? I had gone through many different feelings over my Dad through the years. There was a time I just wanted him to love me and give me the affection he showed to my sister, a time when I hated him and a time when I did not know how I felt about him. If he had not been my Dad, I often thought I would not even have wanted to see him.

The week before he died, Doug and I went down to see him in the hospital. My Mum and my sister were at the hospital when we arrived and my Dad looked terrible. He had lost a lot of weight as he had not eaten or drunk anything properly for about three weeks. My Mum and my sister were sitting either side of him and he seemed to only want to talk to my sister. He had been suffering with Alzheimer's for nearly two years and had been getting progressively worse, although at times he still remembered things. I remember my Mum saying to him, as she looked at me, "Do you know who this is?" When he answered that I was his sister, my Mum got quite cross with him and said, "No, it is your older daughter." He then replied, "I do not have another daughter. I only have my baby who is sitting next to me."

After all I had been through he still managed to upset me. Even with Doug telling me in my ear that my Dad did not know what he was saying, I was not convinced. When I went up to kiss him goodbye, he looked at me and said, "I have been horrible to you," and I took that as an apology for everything. He looked so vulnerable and afraid, so I told him he had not and to just concentrate on getting better.

The following Thursday Doug took a call from my Mum late at night to say that Dad had died. When Doug walked into the bedroom, I took one look at his face and I knew. I started to cry uncontrollably, overwhelmed with mixed emotions.

The next week leading up to the funeral I felt very alone. Although Dad and I had never been close it was certainly a lonely feeling that he was no longer here. I also had this great feeling of loss, because no matter how difficult things had been at times, he had always been there for me. Dad's death had made me more vulnerable to other people's feelings. I do not condone what he did but through it all I have learned you have to forgive and let go, or you end up carrying all the pent up emotions in your body. You cannot have a great relationship with anyone if you are holding onto your past pain and bitterness.

My Dad was a very angry and violent man. Although I do not condone what he did to me, I know now that my behaviour contributed to his anger and if I had not caused so much trouble, I would not have had as many beatings. I believe that I could have avoided what happened the night when he attempted to strangle me, if I had been able to tell him the truth. However, I do feel that no person has the right to beat or emotionally abuse you, no matter what you have done.

My Mum has often told me that I began testing my father's patience early as I was not an easy toddler. Toddlers are still very innocent and do test their parents to see how much they can get away with and it is an important time for children to be shown what is acceptable and what is not. Being firm while still showing them how much you love them is by far the best way of handling them, rather than using emotional and physical abuse.

As I was growing up, I felt different emotions towards my father: love, confusion and fear; wanting him to love me, not understanding why he only seemed to want to hurt me, and fear because of how he treated me. In all the years my Dad was alive, I never answered back or had an argument with him, as underneath I was afraid of him. I cannot remember a time when he ever hugged me or showed me signs of love. I know now that when I got into trouble, whether at school or home, a lot of the time it was my way of trying to get attention from him, although this would often lead to more physical abuse. This desire for connection and love caused me to get into some difficult situations in later years.

When it comes to sexual abuse, I do not believe anyone has the right to sexually abuse another person, but I do believe that there are situations that can more easily lead to such abuse, and that it is important to be aware of them. Many victims of abuse are seeking something – love, affection, praise, attention – that they are not receiving from healthy sources. Many people who abuse others have suffered abuse at the hands of others. Being a victim of sexual abuse at a very young age can destroy childhood innocence and make victims feel guilty, something I learned from personal experience. It was only as I grew up that the pattern and program of abuse became clear to me.

As a child, your innocence is a beautiful, positive vulnerability and can easily be taken advantage of in situations of abuse. As I mentioned earlier, the man who abused me was living in our house and initially drew me to him by being affectionate and loving. I later learned that an abuser will often target a child who is needy of love, affection, praise and attention – all things I was not getting from my own family. The pain and guilt from this abuse had a huge impact on my life.

Through talking to some of my clients who have experienced sexual abuse, I have found that victims of sexual abuse tend to share similar behaviors and ways of thinking. I found that we all tend to want to please people. These are some of the common thought and behavior patterns:

- *Not feeling that you are good enough inside, while trying to be everything to everybody outside.*

- *Not being able to say no to people.*

- *Having the belief that you do not deserve to receive good things or to be treated well.*

- *When things do seem to be going well, unconsciously trying to sabotage them.*

- *Talking to yourself in a destructive way.*

- *Feeling responsible when things go wrong that have nothing to do with us.*

- *Not being able to accept compliments, favors or gifts.*

While you are never to blame for the actual abuse, you can take responsibility for your emotions, your reactions and your future. As you become an adult, you gain perspective. At some point you have to look back, see the event for what it was and move on. The party that led to my father being violently aggressive towards me was a party for boys and girls, and knowing that he was likely to say I could not go I told him it was a group of girls getting together. I know that if I had been upfront with him about the party and not lied to him, the outcome would have been very different. I spent much of my time as a youngster attempting to lie myself out of situations which only made things worse. Even if I had told the truth, though, he probably would not have let me go anyway.

Following the abuse of my father and our neighbour, I began to seek out male attention in the form of romantic relationships. During this time, I had a lot of sexual encounters, many of which I did not want. This was partially because I was afraid to say no, not knowing how the person would react and partially because part of me wanted the sexual encounter, as it was a way to feel loved and needed. When I look back it seems strange that I had an underlying fear of men, but continued attracting them into my life. If I was ever anywhere men were arguing, I would start to feel very frightened, physically sick and the urge to get away from the situation as quickly as possible, but I continued to attract them into my life.

When I look back now, I realise that the vibes I was giving out to men were not appropriate for my age, but I continued to act that way into my later teen years and even when I was married to my first husband, who was fourteen years older than me. Because I was so much younger, his friends made a lot of fuss over me, which made me feel good and I became a terrible flirt. I realise now that I acted this way because it made me feel like I was in control. I thought I could not get hurt. It was my way of testing men to see how much they liked me and how much they would take from me.

I have since learned through my relationship coaching that it is not unusual for women to behave this way after suffering sexual, physical and emotional abuse as a child.

When you look back at the significant events in your life, what would happen if you asked yourself, "What has this cost me to date?" Your first answer would probably be: lots of pain, hurt, challenging relationships and, for some, even depression. When I took the time to look past the negative feelings, I could also see where there were lessons to be learnt. I was able to see that many of the significant events in my life made me stronger, helped me see what I would and would not accept, and also helped me to see my true self.

A client of mine had been through a challenging childhood. Her parents were unable to show their feelings. Although she was close to her father and tended to put him on a pedestal, at times he would get angry and physical with her. She did not get on with her mother and would often say that if it was not for the fact she was her mother, she would not want to have anything to do with her. My client did not start dating till she was in her middle teens and once she did start dating, she went from one relationship disaster to another.

When she told me about her past relationships, I noticed a pattern running through all of them. My client had a very strong character; She was smart and felt she was able to look after herself. She felt that if she behaved in this way a man would love her. Also, once she got into a relationship, after a short time she was bored and always seemed to be looking for something outside to make her feel happy.

She had been engaged three times, married twice and divorced twice and had numerous affairs in and out of her marriages. She wanted a connection with another person and to feel loved and significant, but was going about it in the wrong way. When she came to see me she was suffering with depression and had a habit of negative thinking. She blamed everyone else for the bad things in her life. Through our coaching sessions, I pointed out her pattern of controlling behavior in the relationships. At first she was skeptical, but after spending time talking about her relationships, she could see her behaviour more clearly and how it kept attracting the same sort of men into her life.

What prompted her to come and see me was an event that had left her feeling guilty and resulted in a downward spiral of depression. Falling back on a destructive habit of drinking to block out negative thoughts and failed relationships after a recent break up, she had a sexual encounter with a close family member and was living with the guilt of what she had put the man's wife through. She blamed the man for telling his wife the truth, because of how it affected her relationship with her family. After working with her through this, I explained to her that she had to let go of the guilt and the anger she was holding onto because the only person she was hurting was herself. If she continued on as she had been, she would end up going even further down the path of depression.

How would it be if you looked at significant events in your life as the teachings of life? As if each event is a test to see how you are doing and to make you a stronger person? I do believe that the universe will not send us anything that we cannot handle, although at the time we may think we can't. Life is about us growing and sharing our experiences with others.

The following NLP exercise, 'Perceptual Positions', has been crafted to allow you a chance to challenge conflicts or disagreements that may be present with others. Be prepared to experience the conflict from a different angle and the perspective of the other person involved. By doing this, we can relive the experience with different information available to us, enabling us to reflect on the impact of our own words and behavior towards other people and how they may have felt about our actions.

This process can be slightly tricky to do on your own, so it would be greatly beneficial, and a more constructive experience, if you can find help from someone else who you can trust and feel comfortable with to honestly express what comes up.

In general you will have three positions:

- **First position:** you are in your body, seeing it through your eyes, hearing what you heard, feeling what you felt from your point of view.

- **Second position:** you are standing in some-one else's shoes – the person you were in conflict or disagreement with – looking, talking and hearing from his or her eyes.

- **Third position:** you are looking at the situation as an observer or fly-on-the-wall, accessing the view or comments as a neutral party.

The Technique

Before you start, ensure that you are in a state where you can do the process fully, being honest and honouring emotions that may come up. Even though the process may bring up strong and painful emotions, the idea is to resolve them so you can move on from the challenges connected to them. Prepare a quiet room where you will not have any interruptions. Into the room bring three chairs (or more, depending on the number of people involved in the situation) and set them up facing each other. If doing this on your own, to make it as smooth as possible, I advise you put the questions for the exercise (below) onto cards so that they are more readable and easily accessible. The idea is to move to the next chair as you change perception (position). Either ask yourself, or have the person facilitating the process for you to ask, the following questions for each position. Answer honestly and out loud.

Move into the first chair, first position.

1st Position – Associated in Problem Scenario. Think back to the event.

a) How are you behaving?
b) How are you feeling?
c) What do you believe about the situation?
d) What's important to you?
e) What is there for you to learn?
f) How has your perception changed?

Now move to the next chair, therefore next position.

2nd Position – Associate into other person/persons.

"I want you to tell me as if you were 'that person' (*insert name here*)."

g) How are you behaving?
h) How are you feeling?
i) What do you believe about the situation?
j) What's important to you?
k) What is there for you to learn?
l) How has your perception changed?

Move into the last chair, last position.

3rd Position – Associate into a fly-on-the-wall/ observer position.

"I want you to tell me as if you were an observer to the situation."

m) How are they each behaving?

n) How are they each feeling?

o) What beliefs do they each appear to be acting on?

p) What's important to each of them?

q) What is there for them to learn?

r) How has your perception changed (as an observer)?

Come back into yourself bringing your new learning and perceptions with you.

Go back to **1st position** and ask again:

a) Now, how are you behaving?

b) How are you feeling?

c) What do you believe about the situation?

d) What is important to you?

e) What is there for you to learn?

f) How has your perception changed?

Now we take a vital step of the process – the test and future pace. In other words, we must check how we now feel about the people involved and the previously unresolved emotions. Go back to the past experiences and look into the future; if you can see positive changes, then the process has definitely been beneficial. If at the end you don't feel any change, my opinion would be that either you did not allow yourself to become the other person and feel what they would be thinking and saying, or maybe the person asking the questions is not giving you the time to feel the feelings.

*I*t is understandable that some people who have been affected by infidelity would not even want to stay with their partner. Regardless of whether or not you stay, it is important to look at yourself in the manner covered here. Because I went through this process, I know that if Doug and I had not stayed together, that my next relationship would have been very different. If you do not learn from these significant events in your life, then you just tend to keep making the same mistakes and you will keep having dysfunctional relationships.

To end this section, I would like to share with you this story which I received through my Daily Insights. It really illustrates the importance of learning from the significant events in our lives.

Life in the Manure Pile
by Marsha Jordan

The husband once aspired to be a self-sufficient, back-to-the-land pioneer. He bought a windmill, oil lamps, beehives, and a couple of pigs, which we named Lois Lane and Clark Kent. This dirty duo caused me headaches from the day we took them home. We tied them in gunny sacks and secured them in the back of our truck; but the Houdini hoglets somehow freed themselves, tumbled from the vehicle, and headed for the hills. We eventually got the slippery little buggers safely home, but only after a wild skirmish in the woods.

The adventurous and clever Clark soon discovered his alternate identity as Super Pig. He learned to climb atop his roofed shelter and leap over the fence to freedom. Lois, not to be outdone, was never far behind. Motorists on the highway near our home reported seeing wild pigs darting between cars. I also received some angry phone calls from horrified neighbors who were shocked to find the pair digging up their flower beds. Perhaps, rather than Lois and Clark, they should have been named Lewis and Clark, due to their propensity to explore.

These two heavyweights usually embarked upon their adventures while the husband was at work, so I was the designated pig herder, responsible for bringing the troops home after each rendezvous. How does one lure two full-grown hogs to follow you? It takes courage, determination, and a slop bucket full of swine delicacies like apple cores, potato peel, and moldy bread crusts. More than once, I trudged through waist-deep snow, dropping a trail of leftovers behind me.

I've never liked animals that were too big to sit in my lap, but these humungous hogs were more than intimidating. They were man eaters! While leading them home like the pied piper, I had to run to stay one step ahead as they followed close behind, nipping at my heels. Yes, pigs BITE – at least these two did. They were scarier than attack dogs.

Once Lois and Clark tasted blood, they preferred it to their usual diet. That diet consisted of truckloads of stale doughnuts, sour milk, and assorted restaurant scraps. Keeping the porkers fed was a big job. They ate a lot, and you can imagine what else they did – a LOT. The manure pile grew into a mountain, which remained long after Lois and Clark were laid to rest as pork chops in our freezer.

The following summer, I planted a garden that I faithfully weeded, fertilised, and watered. At the end of the season I was shocked to discover that my prized vegetables were dwarves in comparison to the giant tomatoes and cucumbers that had sprung up from the manure pile.

You may wonder why I'm telling you more than you care to know about pigs and manure. It's because I've found that where there's manure, there's sometimes a lesson buried under it.

Like you, I've known sorrow, loneliness, and disappointment. At those times, it often feels like I'm living smack dab in the middle of a mountain of manure. However, things that stink aren't necessarily bad. Sometimes, what we think is awful right now may end up being good for us. Ask anyone who took castor oil as a kid!

Just as the garbage in a compost heap makes gardens grow, the garbage in our lives can enhance our personal growth. Trials can result in strong faith and character. The stuff that stinks the most is usually the best fertiliser for healthy spiritual development. Even stinky manure, after a time, turns into healthy and clean smelling soil.

Gardens go through seasons. Spring is the season to plant and fertilise. Summer is the season to weed and cultivate. Fall is the season to harvest. Winter is the season for the land to rest. Our lives have different seasons too. Some of them are more difficult than others. But if we endure 'for a season' without giving in to short-term thinking, we will reap a harvest. When your heart is broken, it may feel hopeless; but there's always hope, even in the dung heap. Open your eyes to see beyond the pig pies to how good -- and growth -- might come from this situation. Blossoms of blessing often come from manure. The smelly, disgusting manure that our lives sometimes become can bring forth prize-winning, life-giving fruit. Celebrate the fact that we don't have to climb that manure mountain alone. Believe and keep the faith, then grab a shovel and start digging. There's a harvest on the other side.

Communication

After looking at the significant events in our lives and how they have affected us, the next step is the look at our own behavior. One of the biggest issues in my relationship with Doug was communication. We talked, but we were both unable to talk about our deepest feelings, and certainly not about intimacy.

Just as it's often said that the secret to successful property investing is Location, Location, Location, the secret to a successful relationship is Communication, Communication, Communication!

When we look back on all the problems we faced in our marriage, we realise how much a lack of communication contributed to them. So often it was easier to brush an issue under the carpet than talk about it, particularly delicate topics that we were uncomfortable with.

A small issue brushed under the carpet might not seem much at the time but if you keep doing that, over time you end up with a whole pile of dirt under your carpet.

If either of you has an issue, however big or small, you must bring it out into the open so that you can discuss it together. If it's something you can't agree on then at least amicably agree to disagree rather than leaving it unsaid and to fester.

Often it's very apparent from talking with my clients that they and their partners are not communicating very well, if at all. And often it's a chicken and egg dilemma. If they are not communicating how can they start to communicate that they need to communicate?

I met Doug for the first time at a football disco in 1980 which I went to with a friend from work. At the time he was with another girl so I did not really take a great deal of notice of him. About a month later, my friend asked if I would like to come out for a drink with her and her husband. I thought this was a bit strange at first, as I did not really know her husband well at that time. I remember saying, why the three of us? She then said, "Oh no, Doug will be coming too." I said, "Who is Doug?" I did not remember him from the disco. When she reminded me I agreed, as I had nothing else to do.

I arranged to drive to my friend's house. When I arrived at the house, I recall walking into their lounge, seeing Doug sitting on the sofa, and thinking, he looks so young! As my ex husband was fourteen years older than me, I was used to being with an older group of people. We all went down to the pub for a drink, on to a Chinese restaurant, then back to my friend's house for a coffee. As it was so many years ago, I have no idea what we talked about that night, but I do remember wondering why I was there, as I did not feel an instant attraction to Doug.

We both left our friends' house at the same time and Doug asked me if I wanted to go back to his place for a coffee. Before I knew it, coffee led to us ending up in bed. That first night I just laid there and did not give anything, which is probably where our lack of communication began.

In the morning he arranged for me to follow him back to a place which was familiar to me and when I got home I felt that I should not see him again, as something was not right. Nevertheless, over the next six months, Doug and I did go out together. I felt he was a good, kind person and everyone seemed to like him. I enjoyed his company and we got on well together, but I did not feel particularly close to him. We never talked about our deep feelings or how we wanted things to be in a relationship. The intimate part of our relationship was very basic and I felt that I never let myself go with him, nor he with me. Also, at times I was not particularly kind to him. When the other man I had been seeing was available, I would make some excuse not to see Doug. You could say that we just drifted along. We were not unhappy together but it was certainly not a great love story.

After a while Doug started to get suspicious that I was seeing someone else and confronted me about it. I told him about the other man and he said that if we were to continue, I had to finish with him. I told Doug I would end my other relationship, but I couldn't and continued seeing them both. Finally, it all came to a head as these things do and I was getting to the point that I could not deal with the situation anymore, so I decided to finish with both of them.

Being the coward I was, I sent Doug a letter telling him it was over. When he received the letter, he rang me up to tell me he would not accept that the relationship was over and was coming over to talk. I had a feeling that he was going to ask me to marry him, so I rang up my best friend in a state of panic to ask her what to do. Her reply was, "Of course, you do not have to say yes." When Doug arrived, he started telling me how he knew what he wanted and that he wanted to marry me. It was not romantic; it was all very practical and logical for Doug. I said that I did not know and would need time to think.

A week later we were at a disco dancing to a slow record and I looked up at him and told him I would marry him. When I look back, I know I felt happy saying yes, although I do not think that it was true love. I thought, "This man is good and kind and is willing to take on a stepdaughter and provide us with a home." Intimacy was not that important, it was more about him being kind and considerate. I thought that he loved me and really wanted me, unaware that he asked because he had always got what he wanted in his life and was not prepared to let someone else have me. I also did not realise that he was looking elsewhere to meet his sexual needs. I know now that if we had been able to open up to each other completely and honestly from the start, we would have avoided a lot of pain.

One of the things we have learnt is the importance of being honest with each other and being honest about what you truly want and are willing to accept in a relationship. The following exercise will help you to write down exactly what you do and do not want from a relationship. It is one I have shared with many clients who have found it extremely useful.

Relationship Check Exercise

1. What must I have in a relationship?

2. What must I never have in a relationship?

3. a) My vision of how I want my relationship to be. *(This question is mainly for women, as they are more likely to have a vision rather than a specific purpose.)*

   b) My Vision and Purpose for life. *(This question is more structured towards a man as it is more about the masculine energy of where a man is coming from and what his main purpose and vision in life is. A woman is more attracted to a man who has a definite vision and purpose to his life.)*

4. My ultimate partner's must haves in life are...

5. My ultimate partner's must never haves in life are...

6. Who do I have to be or become to consistently have 'the ultimate relationship' with this person?

If you are in a relationship, evaluate your relationship fit. Be totally honest. The truth is where the secret lies in this test. As they say, the truth will always set you free. Discuss and compare your findings as to whether you are the person, or could become the person, who could meet your ultimate partner's must haves and must never haves lists. If you are not in a relationship, use these answers to look at your must and must never haves closely. Then as you enter a relationship, be open and honest. Be prepared to share this checklist with your new partner early in that relationship. It could save you time, energy and pain. I certainly wish I had known about this many years ago!

In our case, I had been looking for significance and love, while Doug was looking for a sexual connection. Doug was sexually abused as a young child. He did not share with me about his sexual abuse till twenty years into our marriage, and it came as quite a shock. He had not told anyone before, so this was quite a revelation for him. It also explained why he had difficulty in showing his emotions, and how sex, to him, had been a non-emotional act. I encouraged him to speak to a coach because I felt that people need to deal with issues like this, not just push them under the carpet and say, "That was in the past and does not matter." In Doug's case it had obviously had a huge impact on how he handled relationships and sexual intimacy.

Also it is strange that so often people who have been abused, end up attracting people who have been through the same issues. With many of my clients I have found this to be the case, whether it has been a sexual issue, drinking, drugs or eating disorders.

Now Doug and I both feel that if either one of us is behaving in a way that is unacceptable, we can be honest with each other and talk about it. It is so often the case that we hear or say something and, for whatever reason, we interpret it in a completely different way to what is meant.

Another great communication exercise is called 'Magic Moments'. At the end of each day you take turns sharing what your magical moment in the day was. It helps you to focus on the good things that happened each day and not things that may have had a negative effect on you. It is also wonderful to be able to share your thoughts with your partner at the end of the day. You may find that you also start to appreciate the little things that happen each day. We have had many laughs and emotional moments through sharing our magic moments.

Taking Responsibility

So if what we want is the perfect relationship, why is it that we are not prepared to take a hard look at ourselves and see what we truly want and how we are behaving in the relationship? I know through our years of marriage, I would keep saying to myself that it was a good marriage, except for our lack of intimacy. When I look back now, I think I was looking for Doug to sort it out and make it right.

On occasions I would be jealous when I heard friends talking about their great intimate relationships. While they were laughing and joking about their sex lives, I would often keep quiet because I did not want to feel inadequate. With certain friends I would talk about our lack of intimacy, putting the blame onto Doug, rather than taking some of the responsibility. But as they say, it 'takes two to tango,' and I needed to start looking at my part in the problem.

When I started to look at events in my life around relationships, I realised that it was not up to Doug to sort it out, I had to deal with my past hang ups about intimacy. I had been running my controlling pattern by blaming Doug, and not wanting to take responsibility for who I truly am. I was so afraid of completely letting go with anyone, for fear of being hurt. I shut my true feelings behind a brick wall many years ago, and although I felt safe, unconsciously I was actually bringing more pain into my life than I had realised.

For much of my life, I always seemed to be looking outside myself to find happiness. I was often jealous of what anyone else had, whether a great relationship, money or material things. I also found it very hard if a close friend of mine suddenly started spending more time with one of her other friends. I desperately needed to hold on to and control circumstances around me. When I was finally able to totally let go, I found that I now just feel grateful for what I have in my life and pleased for whatever others have.

*A*fter looking at your past behavior and how you could have contributed to some of the significant emotional events in your life, the next step is to take responsibility. For many years I just kept blaming my childhood on the way I was. So much that I know Doug got fed up hearing it. All the time I was blaming my childhood, I was unconsciously holding onto an excuse, a reason for why I could behave in the way I did at times. It gave me a feeling of control. At some level I wanted people to feel sorry for me and to feel significant.

After Doug had told me about his infidelity, I started to ask myself a lot of questions. Some were helpful and some were not so helpful. The following questions can *help you to gain more insight into your actions.*

- *What do I want?*
- *What do I need to do?*
- *Will I be able to trust again?*
- *What am I holding onto?*
- *What did I do that was so wrong?*
- *How was I being towards the person?*
- *How would it be if I was honest with myself?*
- *How could have I contributed to this happening?*

I was very grateful to my coaches for the coaching they gave me through the difficult time. When they asked me great questions like those above, it helped me see the bigger picture and what I truly wanted in my life.

As you read my story, you have probably realised that the period from when Doug told me, to when we got back together, was relatively short. For others it may take a lot longer to get to the level of relationship that Doug and I are experiencing now. There is no specific time needed to heal. Everyone should take as long as they need. It is better to know exactly what you want than to go back into a relationship half-heartedly and still not know what you really want.

Because I had been through both NLP and relationship training, I had a great deal of knowledge and understanding of what a great relationship was all about. I know that I was not prepared to settle for anything less. Neither was Doug.

When I think of that period, sometimes I still find it hard to believe how far we have come in such a short space of time. He told me about his infidelity in the October of 1996 and we were back together in this great relationship by mid December of that same year. Wow!

Another great exercise showed to us at the Relationship Weekend was called the 'Happy Test'. This simple exercise will allow you to compare where you are in your life verses where you want to be. You will be able to see where your life is unbalanced and see what areas you need to work on to have more balance. It also helps deal with areas of stress which could otherwise affect your energy.

Happy Test Exercise

Using the circle below as a model, draw a similar one representing your life. If another category, e.g. your spiritual life, is more important than one of the categories suggested, then make a replacement.

Using a scale of 0-10, where 0 is absolutely hopeless, 10 is everything you ever dreamed it could be, score yourself in each category on where you are now. Note the first number that comes into your mind and draw an arc in that category on your circle to represent the score out of 10. Remember that you are setting your own standard. Someone else's 10 for physical fitness is not the same as yours. If you are not in an intimate relationship, it does not mean you are a zero in that category. If you totally believe a great relationship is on its way, feel ready and are in a great space about it, you might score yourself very high.

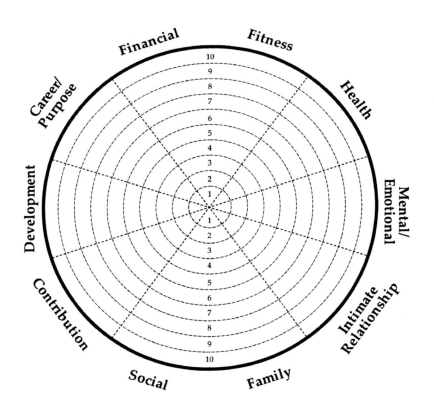

When you are finished, add up all the scores to get a score out of 100 and see what colour in the chart below you are in terms of life balance:

Score Colour Indication

0-69	Red – Danger
70-89	Amber – Caution
90-100	Green – Doing Great

Now see where the greatest imbalances are and decide which low score you need to bring up in order to balance out the wheel. If you try to take it to a 10 straight away, this will often negatively affect other areas of your life. In the lowest areas, ask yourself what needs to happen to take me to an X? For example, what has to happen to take my health from a 5 to a 7?

Becoming Conscious of Your Behaviour

Through my self-reflection, I learned that I was not conscious that the way I was behaving in our relationship was affecting Doug. I had become more masculine and always wanted to be in control. I would make all of our social arrangements. I organised our holidays, although we did discuss together where we were going to go. Over the years I would often say that if I did not arrange anything, we would not have a social life. Whenever we went anywhere I wanted to drive

Since then, I have learned that when a woman takes on the role of a man, her partner immediately becomes disempowered. The result is a lost connection, less attraction and relationship challenges.

If a man allows his woman to take control in the relationship it is because she hasn't had enough certainty from her man. The reason a woman would take control is that they are feeling insignificant, fearful of being rejected or being alone and feeling a lack of trust in the relationship.

In the past, our arguments were nearly always over the same thing, intimacy. During our arguments, I would generally blame him for the problem, wishing he would see my point of view. I would always use the same tactics and kept getting the same result! We both found that since changing our habits, we actually get a different result if we do have something to argue over, which I must say is very rare now.

In relationships there are certain patterns we run that lead to disconnection. One of the biggest mistakes in a relationship is using negative criticism and women tend to do this more than men. Sometimes it can feel they are just giving helpful advice, but men take it that you feel they do not know what to do. This feels like a huge criticism and also a massive rejection. It also makes him feel that he is not lovable and that he will not be able to make you happy. Also he feels you do not respect him and that you never will.

Another mistake couples make is showing contempt, where you appear to feel superior to your partner and give advice from a superior position.

A common response to criticism and contempt is yet another relationship mistake – defensiveness, when one of you is feeling attacked and goes into a defensive position. In our relationship, I would always try to justify why I was behaving the way I was and blaming Doug, because I did not want to be wrong. A fourth mistake is that of stone-walling, which is when one partner stops talking to the other as a tactic to get their own way or as a way of trying to make the other person feel bad.

While it is important to be conscious of your behavior in these areas, it can also help to become aware of your general mode of behaving or your core energy. The following exercise can help you to identify your core energy. It can help you to analyze your role in all relationships, not just intimate relationships, but also relationships with family, friends and work colleagues.

In my experience, for 99% of people, their core energy matches their gender. You can confirm the results by asking questions like the following: Do you find yourself wanting to spend time focused on building and conquering (masculine) or do you want to be protected and spend time nurturing (feminine)? Which energy do you spend most of your time in?

What percentage of the time are you spending in your core energy and how much in your secondary energy (if masculine is your core energy, then feminine is your secondary energy and vice versa)? What difference might it make if you changed the balance? Where do you think it would need to be for you to have the relationship of your dreams?

If you are in an intimate relationship, where is your intimate partner's core energy? What masculine-feminine energy dynamics do you see in your current or past relationships?

Core Energy Exercise

First, answer the following question: On which level is your current (or past) relationship?

Level 1: Neither person is getting their needs met or, at best, one person's needs being met in a dysfunctional manner.

Level 2: Both people are getting their needs met individually.

Level 3: Both people are understanding each other's 'must have' needs and knowing how to meet them: "Your needs are my needs"

Now, to find out which core energy you are living in, take a moment to consider the words below in relation to the way that you currently operate. When you are ready, circle nine words that would characterise you and how you operate.

Owning	Accommodating	Pleasing
Surrender	Focused	Fearless
Powerful	Decisive	Protective
Purposeful	Dominant	Nurturing
Acknowledging	Non-demanding	Leading
Driven	Allowing	Total Strength
Letting Go of Control		Trusting

Now take a moment to look at the words that you have circled and map them onto the following chart. What is your current predominant energy?

MALE		FEMALE
MACHO/AGGRESSIVE	off the scale (unhealthy)	
Dominance		Dominance
Fearless	masculine	Fearless
Total Strength		Total Strength
Purposeful		Purposeful
Owning		Owning
Focused		Focused
Powerful		Powerful
Lead		Lead
Driven		Driven
Decisive	neutral	Decisive
Protective		Protective
Nurturing		Nurturing
Trusting		Trusting
Pleasing	feminine	Pleasing
Acknowledging		Acknowledging
Letting Go of Control		Letting Go of Control
Allowing		Allowing
Non-demanding		Non-demanding
Accomodating		Accomodating
Surrender		Surrender
	off the scale (unhealthy)	VICTIM/PASSIVE-AGGRESSIVE

MALE	**70%** Male Energy	**30%** Female Energy
FEMALE	**70%** Female Energy	**30%** Male Energy

Now ask yourself the following questions:

Where on the chart has your partner in your current (or past) relationships spent most of their time? Where on the chart do you spend most of your time? Where on the chart below do you tend to go to? What is the impact on your relationships of you doing this?

When Doug and I did this exercise, it revealed how I was living more in my masculine energy, always wanting to be in control. It also showed how Doug was more often living in his feminine energy. Once you recognise how you are showing up in your energy, you can choose to change. You are probably asking why is it important to change. The answer to this is that if you don't, you are on a slippery slope to break up.

This is what we both looked to do and Doug is doing brilliantly. I still have my moments when I slip back into my masculine, but I am getting much better! It also helps that he gives me so much certainty now. I hope you will find it as revealing as we did.

Meeting Partners' Needs

If you find your relationship is drifting apart, then the good news is you can do something about it.

Begin by putting yourself into a loving space and

then apply the following:

What men are looking for is the **Three As:** *Appreciate, Acknowledge and Adore*

When you start to use words that say how much you appreciate and acknowledge what he does, it will make him feel great and will help him to feel loved unconditionally. You will also find that the more you make him feel good, the more he will want to make you feel good.

What women are looking for is the **Three Cs:** *Certainty, Compliment and Cherish*

All the women I have talked to about what a woman wants agree that the number one thing they desire is certainty. We want to know that this man is going to take care of whatever is thrown at us (to help with this, it is important to let him take care of things and not question if he is doing it right or wrong, because if you do it feels like a criticism). We also want to be cherished as if we are the most precious thing he could hold in his hands and to be complimented on how we look and what we do and say.

Doug and I found that by applying these As and Cs to each other that our relationship has changed dramatically. We found it was easy to use the Three Cs and the Three As when we were both living in the right energy. Once Doug stepped into his masculine energy and I went into my feminine energy, it was like this great magnet attraction. The more masculine he was, the more certain and trusting I became and our relationship got better. I found when I moved into my feminine nurturing energy, I was more trusting and free of fear. I was also less stressed and felt happier than I had ever been. I was finally able to totally let go.

In those months after Doug revealed his infidelity, he never went back into his feminine. He stayed in his masculine and gave me heaps of certainty, which I know helped me through that painful time. If he had argued back, which at times I am sure he felt like doing, I am not sure we would have gotten through it together. I discovered that if you look more at giving to your partner than looking to receive, you feel so much happier and have everything you want. The most important thing to remember, for couples who have experienced infidelity and want to stay together, is that both partners need to examine their part in the relationship, how they contributed to the current state of affairs and be committed to a change.

I had a client whose husband had been unfaithful to her. After he told her, she of course was feeling very hurt and angry, but she wanted to stay in the marriage even though she was finding it hard to trust him. Her husband was doing everything he could to make amends – wining and dining her, doing anything to make her feel good – but he was doing them more out of guilt than a true desire to make things better. What they needed to do was look at why this had happened and both take responsibility. If my client had been giving him the Three As, he would not have needed to go out to feel significant. She did tell me that she had always been the more masculine one in the relationship and had arranged everything. As mentioned previously, you can see how the man being in his masculine and the woman being in her feminine has a great impact on the relationship.

Every one of us behaves the way we do moment to moment because we are always trying to meet our needs. Whilst we have many different labels or words that describe these they can be summarised in six headings and all fall into four broad categories:

The Six Human Needs

Certainty (Comfort)

The ability to be confident that we can predict in advance what is likely to happen and the experiences we are going to have. The base level of certainty is the ability to be able to experience comfort.

Uncertainty (Variety)

If we get too much certainty we get bored and do not grow or move forward in our lives. This is our need to experience change, difference, excitement, surprise, challenge, spontaneity and fun.

Significance (The Search to be worthy of love)

This is our need to feel that we stand out from the crowd, that we are different, special, talented, and unique. It makes us feel valuable and, we hope, valued by others.

Love/Connection

This is our need to be with, and bond with, other people. Here we relax the boundaries of I and become WE. We all have a need to feel a sense of belonging – that we are wanted and share things in common with others. This is also where our need to be loved unconditionally is found.

Growth

The need to feel that our lives are growing emotionally, physically and intellectually.

Contribution

The need to feel our lives have purpose and meaning beyond ourselves. Our greatest and most lasting fulfillment comes through contributing to other people and feeling good about ourselves.

Everyone has to find a way of meeting their needs in any way they can. The only question is how to meet them. Our needs can be met in ways that are either empowering, neutral or destructive. It is important to know if the way we have chosen is obtainable and sustainable in the long term and its overall effect on other areas of our life and on other people. It is also possible that an area of our life is not, or has not been, working well because we do not have effective ways of meeting our needs in this area. When we find alternative and more effective ways of meeting our needs this area of our life can improve.

An easy way to think about how to best meet our needs is to use the following colour strategy. The six human needs can be met when you are in the *red* (using your head) or in the *green* (using your heart). If you are meeting them in the red you are reacting based on fear, past circumstances and stress. When you are in the green, you are reacting with love, truth and trust in the moment.

The Four Classes of Deepest Needs

CLASS 1: It feels good, is good for you, is good for others and serves the greater good.

CLASS 2: It does not feel good, but is good for you, is good for others and serves the greater good.

CLASS 3: It feels good, but is not good for you, others or the greater good.

CLASS 4: It does not feel good, nor is it good for you, others or the greater good.

Intimate Relationship Needs Assessment

(Scoring 0-10) – How are you getting your needs met? Everyone has to find a way of meeting the first four Deepest Needs (certainty, variety, significance and love) in any way we can. The only question is how, specifically? Is the way we have chosen obtainable and sustainable in the long term and what is the overall effect on other areas of our life and indeed other people?

- How much CERTAINTY do you get from your partner?
- How much VARIETY do you get from them?
- How SIGNIFICANT do you feel to them?
- How much active LOVE/CONNECTION do you receive from them?

- How much are you GROWING in your relationship?

- How much CONTRIBUTION are you making to the relationship?

- How much CERTAINTY are you giving to your partner? (How and when)

- In what ways do you get CERTAINTY in Class Three or Four ways?

- How much VARIETY are you giving your partner? (How and when?)

- How much UNCERTAINTY are you giving your partner? (How and when?)

- How SIGNIFICANT are you making your partner feel? (How and when?)

- In what ways do you make your partner feel INSIGNIFICANT? (How and when?)

- How much active LOVE are you giving your partner? (How and when?)

- In what ways do you NEGATIVELY CONNECT with your partner when you really need LOVE/CONNECTION?

- How much is your partner GROWING in the relationship with you? (How and when?)

- How much CONTRIBUTION are you making to the relationship? (How?)

Forgiving Yourself and Others

When we forgive someone, it is also a great gift that we give to ourselves. If we do not totally forgive those who have hurt us, then we will never be truly free. Forgiveness is the ultimate letting go in a healing process. All the time you hold onto the anger and hatred towards the person who has hurt you, you only punish yourself. The person who has hurt you does not even have to know you have forgiven them. I know that when I wrote the email to my friend who had an affair with my husband, it gave me a feeling of freedom.

Forgiveness is not just about saying, "I forgive you". It is actually a state of being. It is a feeling and there is no mistaking it when we feel it. When you forgive yourself and others, it has to be unconditional, for you to feel totally free. When we forgive ourselves, which I feel is more important than forgiving the person that has hurt us, it also allows us to forgive any hurt we might have caused other people. I strongly believe that whatever happens in our life is for a reason. It helps us find out who we are and helps us grow stronger. Thinking in this way, can help us to see difficult situations as opportunities for growth and learning and perhaps even to be grateful for the "teachers" responsible for the lesson.

Forgiveness Exercise

The following exercise can help you begin to forgive those in your life in need of forgiveness and let go of all the negative emotions associated with the person and/or even. First, take a piece of paper and write down the following information:

- The name of the person you want to forgive

- Exactly how that person has wronged you

- Exactly how you are feeling about the event or situation (identify all your emotions here)

Then copy the following:

I accept that I own these emotions, that I am in control of them; that no one can make me feel anything I do not want to feel and that I can choose to let go of them whenever I please. Even though I have no idea why or how, I acknowledge that this situation has been created in order that I learn and evolve into a greater being.

I forgive _____ (name)

for_____ (act/event/situation)

which made me feel_____ (emotion).

Finally: say out loud:

"I am making a decision now to forgive

_____ (name)."

Say it with real meaning and with love and make sure it's coming from your heart. If you want, put your hand across your heart as you say it.

Take a match to the piece of paper and say goodbye to all the negative things you wrote down as you watch them disappear in smoke.

Now, celebrate!

Loving Yourself

I know that loving myself was something I had never been able to do. For many years I did not even like myself. I know now this was all part of the process of letting go, to get to the real me inside. This is important to do because only when you truly love yourself, are you able to love others unconditionally. I am not saying that you do not have feelings of love for your friends and family, but to love others without expecting anything back from anyone, you have to understand that all you need is within you and you do not have to feel love from anyone else.

For the longest time, I was unable to love myself

and was constantly looking to the many partners I had to make me feel good and lovable. I also looked for connection through my friendships. I was always offering to help so that people would think I was a loving and caring person. Sometimes I would agree to do things I did not want to do; I felt that I would be missing out if I was not part of the occasion. Underneath I always had been a loving person, but for many years, I had unconsciously acted even more so, searching for a connection of love and significance.

When I did finally let go and knew that all I needed was in me, I attracted more people into my life. I believe that when you are being your true self, people see the true you and accept you totally for who you are.

*W*hen *you can let go of looking to others to make you happy, you have found that true love inside yourself. While you do need people in your life, you should not need them to make you feel loved!*

It is not always easy to let go of past pain and all of a sudden to start loving yourself. You may not feel that you can love yourself, but there are small steps you can take to start. The mirror exercise I described earlier in the book is one of them. If you have negative people in your life who are bringing you down, let them go. Tell yourself daily how much you love yourself. Even if you do not feel it at the beginning, the more you say it, the more you will feel it. I believe that we all came into this world with love and it is only events through our lives that have clouded our vision of what we are. For me there is only one thing and that is LOVE because without the ability to love ourselves and others we are empty shells.

One of the things I was told to do, quite a few years ago, is to have an incantation. This, for me, has been so helpful in feeling good about myself. When, for whatever reason, I miss my incantation, I notice how my daily thoughts are not so positive. I've included my incantation here as an example. I suggest you write your own, for what you want and how you want your life to be. I also find this is much more powerful if I say it when I am exercising. You should say it out loud if possible and with conviction. Remember, if you are female, please do it in your feminine, which means your voice is light and girly and your movements are sensual. For a man, in your masculine – you need to be strong and certain with strong movements; no half-hearted voicing or actions. The key, when you write your incantation, is to believe that whatever you want and how you want your life to be, has already happened.

My Incantation

I give myself unconditional love which flows to everyone I meet. I trust and let go to the process of life. I am in a happy, intimate, ultimate relationship with my adorable, handsome husband who gives me certainty and cherishes and compliments me daily. I am fit and healthy and I have a beautiful slim body which I love more and more each day. I am financially free through my coaching, book, film and musical which are spreading hope to millions around the world. I am an outstanding coach and I help people move from a life of pain and fear to a life of love and peace.

three

Taking Action

Acknowledging and Accepting

The first thing I had to do to begin my healing process was to acknowledge the patterns of my life and how I had been showing up in situations. I had to let go of wanting to control others and not letting anyone in and concentrate on my challenges and pain I had experienced in my life. This meant that I had to be willing to take responsibility and acknowledge all that had happened in my life. I had to understand that all the pain and hurt I had received had brought me to where I am in my life now. At times I used to say to myself, I would rather not have had these experiences, but I now know that the universe was testing me to show me the way back to my true self!

For many years I blamed others for the unhappiness in my life. I was not willing to accept my faults or to see that I had choices. When I looked honestly at the events in my life and my past behavior, I also recognised my good points and all I had achieved. I had been carrying around lots of guilt from past events in my life, but since I have let go of the blame and taken responsibility for my life, I feel free and, as they say, it was like having a weight lifted from me. I have also begun to do other things which, in the past, I would never have had the confidence or belief in myself to do. I would never have believed I could write this book!

For some of you, it will be hard to accept painful events that you have experienced in your life and to believe that you can move on. You do need to accept what has happened because only when you are willing to accept, can you move on to the healing of yourself. Once you accept who you are, you can do and become who you want to be and start to create the life you truly deserve.

O *ne of the things I found useful was to write a journal of all the events in my life, both good and bad. I found, as I was writing, that I saw a pattern running through the years. I also asked questions about myself and how I had been behaving. I was truthful with myself as I answered the questions. As I did this, I found it to be quite painful to acknowledge that at times I was not a particularly nice person.*

The questions I asked myself were:

- *How much did I love myself on a scale of 1-10?*

- *What do I do when I treat myself in an unloving way?*

- *What would it be like if I was able to say no to people when I wanted to?*

- *What would it be like if I stopped running in fear?*

- *How would it be if I believed I deserved to be happy?*

- *When will I stop thinking that I am not good enough?*

- *When will I be happy and accept what I have?*

When writing your journal, keep a daily record of your feelings, what is great about the day and what has not been so great. I found the more I did this, the more happy, positive days I had.

Keeping a regular journal can also help to change negative language and body language. As you can expect, this takes time and will not happen overnight, but if you can catch yourself when you are being negative and turn it around to positive, over time you will notice your language will change.

Talking About It

After I had had my affair, Doug and I went to see the counselors at the Relate Institute who were helpful. Things went great until they started to talk more about intimacy. At that time this was one area I found extremely difficult to talk about. Although I kept saying I wanted to address it, unconsciously I was still holding back. I decided to stop going and we continued to avoid the topic of intimacy in our marriage, a decision that played a big part in our future challenge.

After the revelation of Doug's infidelity, I talked to a few different people, the first of which was Doug. One of the things I learnt through my NLP training is that if you have an issue with someone, then that is the person you need to discuss it with. In the past I would rather have talked to someone else than to have a direct confrontation. Additionally, my family, friends and my children were also a great support and helped not only me but also Doug.

*S*ome people find it hard to talk about significant emotional events in their lives for a variety of reasons. One reason may be that they are ashamed or feel guilt for what has happened. Other people want to just push it away and pretend it did not happen, which is what Doug had tried to do, not realising how it impacted his views on intimacy. Regardless of the reason, I have found that if you do not talk about the past or current significant events in your life, you will never feel completely at peace or be able to have a healthy relationship. It can be very painful, but once you have shared your thoughts and feelings with someone, you will feel better and be able to live your life in a more positive way.

If you are ready to talk to someone about your challenges, you will feel so much better when you start to release all those negative emotions inside of you. Who is best for you to talk to depends on the challenge you need to address, then there are various people and this would also depend on who you would feel comfortable with. Over the years I have seen many different types of people, from counselors to coaches, hypnotists, healers and spiritual people. At some level, all of them have had an impact on where I am today. Talking to someone is most effective if you are ready to accept your challenges and are willing to do whatever it takes to free yourself of all the negative feelings you are carrying around.

Relationship Exercise

The following exercise can help you to see where you are in your relationship. When you have finished answering the questions, share them with your partner. You may both find it. Remember as you do it to be honest, otherwise there is no point in doing the exercise.

- What are your top two needs in a relationship?

- In which area of your life are they met most?

- For the two needs to be met, what has to happen in your relationship?

- What do you respond best to? For example, giving compliments, certainty, making decisions, organising events etc.

- On a scale of 1-10 (10 being high and 1 being the lowest) for each of the 6 human needs, put a number against each one for how you are meeting your partner's needs.

  (Reminder of the six Human Needs: Certainty, Significance, Love/Connection, Growth, Contribution and Variety.)

- What do you believe your partner responds best to?

- What could you do on a daily, weekly, monthly basis to meet your partner's needs?

- Ask your partner how you can meet their needs (see the list above of the 6 human needs).

- How can your partner make your heart melt?

- How can your partner make you feel special and how can you make him/her feel special?

Asking For Help

If you are ready and willing to ask for help here are various paths you can go down. If you are in a relationship your partner is a good person to speak to, especially if your relationship is not what you thought it should be. This a great start in communicating honestly with each other.

With all I have learnt over the last 10 years, I found that training to be a Neuro Linguistic Practitioner (NLP) Practitioner and working with other NLP coaches was what led me to deal with my past issues. NLP explores the relationship between how we think (neuro), how we communicate, both verbally and non-verbally (linguistic), and our patterns of behavior and emotion (programming). I've included an article from *The Model* magazine by The British Board of Neuro Linguistic Programming (BBNLP) written by Paul Jacobs in the appendix to further explain NLP.

What you will also find is that many people who have done NLP training have gone on to specialise in particular areas, which led me down the path of Relationship Coaching. Doug and I would not be in the great relationship we are now, if we had not had the lessons from Tony and Nicki's Relationship Course. It was how they lived their life and how they helped others that prompted me to train as a relationship coach. For me, nothing is more gratifying than see my clients change their lives.

Another course I took was hypnosis, which I found fascinating as well as very helpful to use in various areas of people's lives. You can bring in hypnosis to some NLP processes, which together can have a powerful impact. I know that some people believe that if you are hypnotised you are out of control. This is definitely not the case. Any trained hypnotist can explain this to you and put you at your ease.

Many years ago, long before I trained in NLP or Hypnosis, I went to see a hypnotist to give up smoking and I have not smoked in the 22 years since, so it does work as long as you have the desire to give up. The hypnotist cannot stop you from smoking, he can only give you the tools to help you do what you want to do. Like anything, you have to want to change.

If talking to your partner and/or friends isn't enough, or you would feel more comfortable talking to a professional, you can seek out a therapist or a coach. A therapist is often a mental health professional, trained to help people deal with difficult life challenges. Therapists have many different approaches and it is important to find someone you would feel happy with. Coaches are trained to assist with different challenges in your life. A life coach or mentor is a bit like having a coach at the gym, someone to keep you on track and to also help you with past challenges.

If you feel you are not ready to talk to someone, then there are many books on the market which offer help and advice on overcoming past or present difficulties, as well as your personal development.

When reading books, I find that there will be certain things that will jump out at me and I highlight them so when I need to, I can go back to the book without having to read all of it and find what is important to me. I do sometimes read them again as well, especially a book that has had a great influence on me. Nowadays you will find many different books in audio format, which is helpful for people who learn better through listening. I have included a list of helpful books in the appendix at the end of this book.

Another way to look to for help is to attend a seminar. There are some great speakers who can help you without you having to speak to them personally, if you do not feel ready to talk to someone on a one-to-one basis. I have included a list of recommended seminars in the resource appendix of this book.

When you attend a seminar, I feel it is important

to know what your outcome is from attending. I like to make notes which I can refer to at a later date for reference. At some seminars, the speaker advises against taking notes, but if you find taking notes to be beneficial, I recommend that you do what is right for you. I have attended seminars where I only came away with one thought, but it was what I needed at that time.

The good thing about attending seminars is that you will find like-minded people and can make new contacts. Not only will you have someone to speak to about the seminar, but you may also find a new circle of friends. Since I began attending seminars, I have a complete new list of friends who I am able to call whenever I feel I need some support.

Choosing To Stay or To Leave

When I told Doug that I wanted to see about us moving forward together, we agreed to go away to talk. He booked a hotel in Brighton right on the seafront and arranged for a twin room, conscious of the fact that I might not want a double bed (although I later upgraded to a double when given the choice).

As we left home, I was apprehensive, although I felt it was the right decision to get away from our familiar surroundings to be able to talk openly. In general, if ever you need to iron out any challenges in your relationships it can help to get away somewhere different.

I had deliberately let Doug take care of everything as this was how I wanted things to be in our new relationship. I had finally let go and was not attempting to control the situation. Once at the hotel, we spent the afternoon just talking. It felt so good to be able to speak completely openly and honestly with each other. We discussed how we wanted things to be different in our relationship. We knew that we both had to let go of all the past negativity if we were going to have the relationship we wanted. It was like sitting with a completely different man and not the person I had spent the last twenty seven years with.

In the evening we went out for dinner and continued talking and laughing. I felt closer to Doug than I ever had before. I still find it hard to believe how completely I let go. For the first time in my life I felt love, not only for Doug, but more importantly, for myself. I was not afraid because I knew that if things had turned out differently and I was on my own for the rest of my life, I was happy with the person I was now.

After dinner we made our way back to the hotel. We were both feeling a little unsure about getting into the same bed after all that had happened. It felt a bit like the first time you are with someone new and are not sure what is going to happen or what it is going to be like. Initially we just cuddled and held each other. I had not planned what happened next and for the first time in my life I finally knew what making love was all about. I completely let myself go with Doug and him with me. It was pure magic. It was not about sex, it was about two beings becoming one. Here was my knight in shining armor!

The rest of the time we spent in Brighton was so special for both of us. We talked, loved and had fun being together. Every time I looked at Doug, he had a great big smile on his face – not a smile that said, "Well I got away with it," but one that showed he was genuinely grateful to have me in his life. Now I know that he loves me and that I am the most important thing in his life. Before, beside his business, golf was top on the list! We agreed that if ever either of us had doubts or worries, we would talk to each other. Even if it may not be what the other one wants to hear, we agreed to always be honest with each other.

I made the choice to continue with my marriage, but I know some people could not even imagine staying with someone who had behaved as Doug had. After our relationship sessions, we both knew that whatever happened, the relationship had to change from how it had been in the past. We knew if we stayed together with the relationship as it was, it would never be what we both truly wanted from a relationship and would be doomed to fail. We also knew that if we split up and not come to terms with how we had been showing up in our relationship, we would take the same behavior into future relationships. I knew that if Doug and I were going to have any sort of future together we both had to change old patterns and we both agreed that we were ready to let go of our past issues and history.

Choosing to stay is also about having the will to change. I had one particular client who rang me up in desperation saying she could not go on any more because she was so depressed and angry all the time. I agreed to see her that day and she came round in the evening. When she had finished venting all her anger and blaming her husband for everything that was not right in their marriage, I explained to her that she did have a choice in whether she wanted to stay or go.

I knew her husband as well, as I had spoken to him on several occasions and I knew that this was not only about him – it was about her as well. I felt that if these two people had any chance of making a go of their marriage, they both had to be willing to change and to come to terms with how they were behaving in their relationship.

What she could not come to terms with was that she would have to give up her home, her social life, and move away from her family and friends if she decided to finish the marriage. Married, she was a well to do lady with the opportunity to have the good things in life which included lovely holidays in faraway places. As I talked to her I asked her what was more important to her, her happiness or to still be able to have the social life, nice house and good holidays? Who was to say that she would not meet someone else in the future with whom she could have the kind of life she desired? Or perhaps, if she found the ideal partner, she might find that all those things were not so important to her after all.

What was certain was that if she stayed in her current relationship with all the bitterness and anger she was feeling, she would go through the rest of her life not truly being herself or being completely happy. She would be staying just for the fringe benefits of being with this man. I also found that deep down she was not ready to change herself. She felt that her husband was the only one who had to change. With this mindset, even if she decided to leave her husband, she would still end up attracting the same sort of partner in the future.

Even if you decide to leave your current relationship, it is still important to be willing to change, as in the case of two of my clients, who even though they decided to leave their marriages, still held on to all the bitterness from what their husbands had done to them. The first client had not been able to come to terms with her husband's infidelity and so attempted to drive a wedge between the children and her husband. Many years later, her ex-husband had remarried but she never had another relationship. It was sad to see that after so many years, she held on to all of the anger, hatred and bitterness. The second client's ex-husband had constantly put her down through their marriage and was very condescending. Whenever she mentioned him, it was always with so much anger and hatred. I understood her feelings but feel strongly that holding on to such negative feelings can have negative effects, and can even manifest into illnesses and other health ailments. This client is now terminally ill with cancer and I feel sad knowing that this could be related to her holding onto her past emotions.

My mother made the decision many years ago to stay with my Dad. I questioned this at the time when he was treating her so badly. He constantly criticised her and ran her down. She would say, "What else can I do?" With two children to look after and not very much money, she felt it was better to stay put, even if it meant she was not truly happy. Also, at that time divorce was not as accepted as it is today. I am sure that being constantly put down put a huge strain onto my Mum and at a certain level she shut down emotionally. I am sure she loved my father even after all he put her through, but since he died, my Mum looks much younger and is definitely more relaxed. For so many years it was as if her face was carrying all the pain and stress from the way he had mistreated her. Now she has found a friend who is giving her the sort of attention from a man she has never experienced before. She is finally being treated like a princess and it is so great to see her happy.

I know that if Doug had made the decision that our marriage was over, then I would have been ok on my own because by letting go, I finally had found the love in me. If that is all I had, I know I would be happy as all I needed was within me.

*I*f *you decide to leave a relationship, whether it is because of infidelity or for some other reason, then I do urge you to be willing to look at yourself and also why your husband/partner was behaving in this way. I have several clients who have left their partners through anger and bitterness and have either carried the same patterns into another relationship, or continue to be unhappy on their own, still blaming their past partners for why they are not happy. In the final analysis, please do what you feel is right for you and remember that life is for living. All I want for everyone is to be happy and at peace.*

When Doug and I got back together, I had friends questioning if it was what I really wanted. How did I know that I would be able to trust him again? I explained that I had to just let go and trust that I was doing the right thing. When I made the decision to stay, I never felt so at peace and certain of anything in my life. I knew that whatever happened down the road would be for a reason. My life would be about what was happening 'now' and not worrying about the future, as none of us know what the future is going to bring.

An NLP exercise that helped me to get to a place where I could just trust and let go is called 'Clean Language'. This exercise uses the metaphors at the heart of your own unconscious thinking, rather than asking you to 'pretend', and helps you to generate new ideas that will help you to make lasting change. It also allows you to come up with the answer to your own challenges, without someone else putting thoughts into your mind. Clean Language can be done on your own, but is best done with a trained NLP practitioner if possible.

The exercise consists of nine questions that build upon each other. As you answer each question, a follow-up question will contain your answer to the previous question, allowing you to go increasingly deeper into the matter. A qualified practitioner would also pick up on your body language and might go back over the questions a few times until you have achieved the result you are looking for, but it is also possible to do the exercise on your own. Below I have listed the nine questions and followed them with an example from a session with a client in relation to his relationship concerns. As you can see, I had to go back over the questions a couple of times to get clarity, which is fine to do.

Clean Language Exercise

The exercise begins with a question about your purpose for needing assistance, such as "What would you like to happen?" (with your problem/concern), or, "For what purpose are you here?"

Once the issue at hand has been stated, the following questions build on your answers to each of the questions.

- And is there anything else about.........
- And what kind of......... is that.........
- And that......... is like what.........
- And where is.........
- And whereabouts.........
- And then what happens.........
- And what happens next.........
- And what happens just before.........
- And where could......... come from

Example:

In this instance, my client was looking for clarity in his relationship.

Q. And is there anything else about the clarity, thinking of what you have to do? (1)

A. Direction and a course of action

Q. And what kind of direction is that course of action? (2)

A. I need to know what I need to do right now.

Q. And what is that "knowing what you need to do right now" like? (3)

A. A clear path to follow.

Q. And whereabouts is that clear path? (5)

A. In my heart.

Q. And then what happens in your heart? (6)

A. When I am in my heart it makes it easier for me to follow.

Q. And what happens next if you follow your heart? (7)

A. Everything will be fine.

Q. And what happens just before everything will be fine? (8)

A. There will be some challenges.

Q. And where could these challenges come from? (9)

A. My partner

Q. What happens next for you to overcome your challenges with your partner? (7)

A. I need to follow my heart as that is where I will find the right answers.

Q. And what is that path to following your heart like? (3)

A. The key that unlocks the door.

Q. Where is the key that unlocks the door? (4)

A. Within my heart.

Q. Whereabouts within you is the key? (5)

A. Within my faith and beliefs

Q. And then what happens with your faith and beliefs? (6)

A. For the key to unlock the door my faith has to be consistent and I must trust myself.

Q. What happens next if your faith is consistent and you trust yourself? (7)

A. I live with truth.

Q. What happens just before living with truth? (8)

A. Everything falls into place.

Q. And where could everything falling into place come from? (9)

A. From me.

Q. What happens next for it to come from you? (7)

A. I make a decision

Q. What happens just before you make the decision? (8)

A. I look inside of me and find what I really want

*A*s you can see, my client did not reach his goal *(clarity) with the first round of questioning, so I continued through a second round in order to get him to his goal. You can continue each round of questioning until you feel you have met your goal. It may mean you have to change the questions around at times, to get the outcome the client is looking for.*

Once Doug and I decided to move forward together, we found that lots of magical things started to happen. When you both live in your hearts and are content in giving rather than receiving, your needs will be met without you even noticing.

Moving Forward

In January 2007, a year after our initial trip, we went back to Austria to attend a Vision and Purpose Week. Doug had booked the course and I went along to support him, and also because I wanted to go back to Austria. I flew out a few days earlier to talk with Nicki and Tony about sales training as I was helping them with their sales. I was so excited about spending time with them and supporting Doug on his Vision. As I sat on the plane looking out of the window I thought to myself how the last time I had been on the plane back from Austria, I had been screaming at Doug like someone possessed. Inside I had to laugh to myself and I felt great about how far we had both come.

Tony met me at the airport and when I arrived at their house, it felt just like home. This had always been a magical place for me and when Doug had told me about his infidelity, I was afraid I would never want to come back. I was happy to find that this was not the case. It felt so good to be back in this great house with my two special friends. When Doug arrived a few days later with the rest of the participants, I was so happy to see him I was like a little girl. I knew that the next 8 days were going to be very special for both of us.

On the first morning I wanted to go out for my run, which I always did when I was at the house. It is not a long run, but it takes you past this great big oak tree with a bench underneath it, over-looking a great landscape of rolling hills. On my first visit to Austria in April 2006, I had spent a coaching session kicking the hell out of the tree as a way to let out all my emotions towards my Dad (it is surprising how you can feel so much better when you are prepared to let out your feelings!).

Being in a much better place this time, when I got close to the tree I remember saying to my Dad, "Everything is ok now. I have finally found peace and know what true love is all about. I know you are now at peace and I love you, miss you, and forgive you. One day we will be together and will be able to hug and love each other like never before." I smiled to myself as I continued running and all of a sudden I had this warm feeling down my left side and felt as if someone was running beside me. To this day I am sure it was my Dad and I continued to have this great talk to him as I ran. It was such a magical experience that when I got back to the house, I could not wait to tell my colleagues what had happened. I can honestly say it was the first time I had felt totally connected to my Dad.

When you go to Austria you never know what surprises the hosts are going to have up their sleeves for you and where they are going to take you and that morning was no exception. At breakfast Tony announced that we would all be going out for the day. We set off that morning, not knowing where we were going and when we arrived at the first stop I could not believe what we were seeing. It was a huge rock that looked like a person's head. Tony had us climb one-by-one up the rock and stand on the ledge overlooking all the tops of the trees. As I stood on the ledge, I was amazed to realise that I had really let go, not only of my fear of heights, but of all my previous fears. As I was standing and looking out at the amazing scenery, I became very emotional thinking to myself how free I felt.

Our second stop was yet another large rock, but this one was shaped like a heart. There was a very narrow passage right through the middle of the heart which we had to crawl through on our stomachs. As we got halfway through, we had to shout any negative thoughts we might have had to the heart. Being in such a great space, I found that I did not have any negative thoughts to shout, so I just thanked the heart for bringing me to the place I was in my life.

On the first night of the course they always ask what you want to get from the course and why you are there. I initially thought I was there to support Doug and to be able to spend time in Austria, but ended up working on the most amazing vision and purpose, one that led me to write this book (and not just talk about it). When I read my Vision and Purpose out to the rest of the group, it was clear to me that nothing was going to stop me in following through with my vision.

My vision and purpose was about me writing a book which was going to spread around the world assisting people in overcoming challenges in their lives. Then I saw it becoming a film and then a musical. As I had always had a passion for musicals and singing in my vision, I was having singing lessons with Tony Wade, better known as Dr. Voice. Together we wrote a song which was also about moving from pain to peace. I would sing this on the opening night of the musical and it would be featured in the musical. I also talked about my successful coaching practice and my family, who are the most important people in my life.

When you write your vision it is very personal and is about what you want in your life. The idea is to make it as big as you can and believe that it will happen. If you have a big enough vision, why, then nothing will stop you!

When Doug and I got back from Austria I was determined to get going on my vision. I contacted Mindy the Book Midwife, who provided me with guidance in how to go about writing my book and has been my coach during the last 7 months, keeping me on track. During our first meeting she took me through a visualisation about how the day of my book signing would be.

She had me visualising leaving my home, what I was wearing, touching up my lipstick in the mirror then walking out to the car and being aware of how I was feeling. I pictured the queue at the door and she asked me to picture one person and describe what she was like including her age, what she was wearing, and her coloring and height. Then going into the bookshop and seeing the table all set up with my books and lots of pens waiting for me to use to sign my book. I felt such a feeling of achievement and pride knowing that my book was going to help so many people.

Visualising is a very powerful tool that anyone can use. All you need to do is close your eyes and picture how you want something to be. When I have had days where I felt uncertain about the book, I put myself back into my visualisation and it put me right back on track. I found this extremely powerful and it helped me finish the book. I also contacted Dr Voice. I am in the process of having singing lessons and he is assisting me in the writing and production of my song.

A week after getting home from Austria and setting up dates to see Mindy and Tony Wade, I received an invitation to attend a four day master class workshop with the production team of 'Mamma Mia'! On the last day I would do my own master class at the theatre where 'Mamma Mia' is running. I was completely blown away by this because that show was my all time favorite. I had seen it around seven times and had always visualised myself as the mum in the show. Even though I couldn't attend the initial workshop due to knee problems, I am down for next year and I can't wait!

When you keep in touch with your vision, or for a man his vision/purpose, you remain open to things that come into your life and keep your energy at a higher vibration. As everything is energy, the more we can resonate at a high frequency the more the universe listens and sends us what we are wanting to attract in our lives. Sometimes they may not show up in exactly the way you have written in your vision, which may mean things could change or you may follow a different path. I am a true believer in that everything happens for a reason and to trust and know that everything is coming to me just as it should. Since writing this book my vision has changed slightly, but the underlying vision is still the same.

four

Keeping It All Going

It is now August 2007, almost one year since the beginning of my healing journey, and I want to reflect on the life I have chosen. If you are wondering, do I have days when I feel doubtful, the answer is, of course. Nearly every day there is something that will remind me of what has happened. At times I have been known to dwell on it a little longer than I need to. Yet most of the time, if I have a negative thought I just remember what we have together now, especially the weekend when we got back together and how magical it was. We also now have the kind of relationship in which I can always go to Doug and tell him how I am feeling. As he is in his masculine energy and very certain of himself, he makes me feel great about myself and our relationship.

There are times when I see that I am starting to slip back into wanting to take control. Once when Doug confronted me about it I accused him of not giving me enough certainty, or supporting me. This was the worst thing I could do, as men do not want to be criticised. I was also looking to blame him for the way I was feeling. Even after all our training, I don't always handle every situation as well as I should. Even though I have the knowledge it is sometimes hard to 'see the wood for the trees', as they say.

The day after one such slip, I was due to go to a meeting with our friends from Austria about a seminar they were hosting. As I left Doug said, "I recommend you talk to them," and my reply was, "I intend to." At the end of the meeting, I spoke to Nicki about how I had been feeling and how Doug had responded. She said that what had been so great when Doug and I had gone through our challenge was that I had been very honest with him and was prepared to speak my truth. She suggested I do that now and if it meant venting my feelings, then I should do so, as he needed to know how I was feeling. I went home that night feeling much better, although I was a little apprehensive about talking to Doug.

That evening Doug and I sat down and talked. After we had finished telling each other exactly how we had been feeling, we realised that if one of us goes into the red (living from our head), it sends the other person into the red as well. What we needed to do was go back to the Three As and the Three Cs, which is what we have been doing since.

*W*e have learned that even if you are in a great relationship, there will be times when you will have challenges and it is important to communicate and find your way back to where you want to be. It is these challenges in life that make us stronger. As Ronan Keating sings, 'Life is a rollercoaster,' and it is so true! For me, having a coach I can go to when I am riding on that rollercoaster is invaluable. If you think about it, anyone who wants to excel in their lives, whether sportsmen or business people, more often than not they have a mentor or coach to help them through the challenges they face at times.

I would like to close this section with the following hypnotic script which you might find helpful to keep yourself motivated on your healing journey. You can either have someone to read it to you while you have your eyes closed or record yourself reading it and play it back when you have doubts.

Closed Eye Process

As you sit there listening to my voice, notice your breathing and the warmth of the room.

You are ready to open your mind to the possibilities of your success.

Success means you are comfortable in your life

and life is for living amongst the shooting stars... and a star you are.

Being that shining star you can see that it's better this way and everything will become easier and easier as you find the shorter path to follow your dream.

And dreaming is good, isn't it? Helping you create deeper understanding, profound insights into the powerful you.

I know you think I'm wondering and it's good to wonder, because today you have learned many things and you will change when you are ready... now... that you are feeling that power and it's better that way.

So – do you think you can make the changes you want?

You know the real voyage of discovery is not in seeking new landscapes but having new eyes.

I f you would like more information or wish to contact me then I recommend you take a look at the website Doug and I have put together to help others with relationship challenges:

– www.askdougandchris.com

…where you can also sign up for further updates to help overcome your past challenges and create your own ULTIMATE relationship.

five

Doug's Thoughts

In December 1998, Chris finally got me to go to the Intimacy Weekend at Happy House with her. I'd managed to get out of it in January, so off I went to please her this time.

Being someone who shoots from the hip, I declared to the group on the first evening (the 'Why am I here' session) that I didn't really want to be there, that I'd been to too many seminars and not followed through afterwards and that above all, I'd rather have taken my golf clubs with me and left the rest of them to get on with it. Fair enough!

Anyway I decided to play full out while I was there, actually had a lot of fun and ended up signing up for us to come back for some more courses, again (to be really honest) largely to please Chris. Obviously the 'accommodating' bit hadn't sunk in. But did the weekend improve our relationship? To a certain degree yes, but as time went on things drifted back pretty much to normal.

However, what only I knew was that there was a darker side to me which I didn't like that was holding me back. I'd gotten into a rut in most areas of my life, including my relationship with Chris. Everything was okay, and probably by a lot of people's standards more than okay, so I thought, "Why rock the boat?"

Looking back now, I can see that my thinking about everything was inside out. I thought, "When I sort this out, when I sort that out, then everything will be great with me and Chris." Not that things were bad between us, just no real spark, but after all we had been married for twenty four years.

Chris didn't see it that way though. She was on an amazing path and knew there was more to life than mediocrity. We openly talked about our relationship and agreed it was okay and while I was prepared to live with that, she wasn't.

So, come October last year, *déjà vu!* Here I am back in Austria, this time at the Advanced Intimacy week, declaring to the group on the first evening why I didn't want to be there. Chris in the meantime had declared to the group that she wasn't prepared to accept a life or marriage that was just okay any more. No pressure then!

I was in a space I had never experienced in my life before and one that I found very difficult to describe. My emotions were like a rollercoaster and I didn't really want to talk to anyone, which is unlike me. It was like some outside, alien force had taken over.

This time I found it difficult to play full out because of my state. Then something happened that I will never forget. We were watching one of the films, *Meet Joe Black*. In the film Anthony Hopkins plays a father who is concerned about the man his daughter is about to marry and gives her a wonderful lecture on what true love really is. I realised there and then that I had never really experienced true love in my life, that I had never let go and that I had never been with someone who made the hairs on the back of my neck stick up just by walking into the room. Right then, I decided that I was not prepared to deprive myself of that any more.

I knew that I had to talk to someone and in my heart I just knew that that someone was in the group of participants. I had already struck up a bond with a man named Steve Clark because I admired his openness. I knew he was a trained relationship coach and I just felt he was someone I could talk to, which is what I did.

To cut a long story short, Steve made me realise there was only one way forward – as Tony Robbins says, "the truth will set you free". The rest is history, as they say. I decided to live my life in truth from that moment on which wasn't easy because it meant I had to come clean with Chris and dump on her some truths that, to put it lightly, I knew she wouldn't want to hear.

Needless to say things got a lot worse before they got better. Tony and Nicki gave us tremendous support both individually and collectively and Tony gave me some dynamite advice on how to deal with the situation personally. He told me not to blame myself for anything because everything happens for a reason; to work out the worst case scenario of what could happen and work out how to deal with it; then to put that to bed and focus on the outcome I wanted because what you focus on normally happens. That was when I realised that my previous thinking was inside out. Once I sorted myself out and my relationship with Chris, then everything else started to fall into place.

Just two months later, just before Christmas, I took Chris away on a weekend that I will remember and treasure for the rest of my life. We were really as one for the first time, the hairs on the back of my neck really were standing up just by being in her presence and we both completely let go to each other.

And that's how it has stayed and will always be because we now have the wonderful tools at our disposal to understand, and retune, our relationship and our love, if necessary.

At one of the seminars Tony had told us that if you can accept the three 'uns' then you will live your life at a different level.

These are:

- unconditional love
- unconditional acceptance
- unconditional forgiveness

That's what we have done and that's the reason why we're where we are. Of course it was so much more difficult for Chris, being on the receiving end of what I threw at her, but we made a commitment to each other and life has just got better since then.

In January this year we both went back for the Vision and Purpose week. It was great to be there in such harmony, given the acrimonious circum-stances in which we had left there previously (apparently we're the only ones ever to have left half way through an event)! It was also great to share how we intend the course of our lives to go and to each write our own blueprints to follow.

We've recently moved into a lovely brand new house, the house of our dreams. In May we went on a Caribbean cruise to celebrate our 25th Wedding anniversary which, after all that had happened, was even more special to both of us.

Now, after reading Chris' book, I have to say that I've been absolutely blown away reading it. At the end of the Vision and Purpose week in Austria, we all had to take time out to write down our vision, a blueprint for the rest of our lives, then to present it to the rest of the group. Chris had gone on the course mainly because I'd already committed to it and she wanted to be there with me, yet also knowing about the presentation at the end. She told me before we went that she had no real idea what she would come up with, as she had never given much thought to committing to a life plan.

What Chris came up with was amazing. What is equally amazing is how she reads it every day, has totally committed to make it happen and totally believes that it will. The first part was her decision to write a book, something she'd occasionally mentioned in the past she'd like to do, but never believed that she would ever have the ability or commitment to do. Seven months later here I am being asked to write a bit at the end of it!

Bearing in mind Chris decided to go public on the events on her life because she wants to help others, I suggested to her that she should reproduce the Vision that she wrote and presented in Austria word for word at the end of her book, and I'm really pleased that she's decided to do so. It demonstrates the power of taking time out to assess your life, decide what you want to do with it then commit it to paper. As Walt Disney said, "If you can dream it, you can live it".

Reading the book really helped me to refocus. I think there's so much to learn from it. My belief is that there is no Holy Grail and that you have to keep permanently working on yourself, your relationships and your life because if you don't you don't just go sideways, you actually go backwards. It's also so easy to slip into the red and let your head rule your heart. This book certainly helps put you back in your heart where I've found life is so much more pleasant.

Do Chris and I now have a 100% perfect marriage?

No.

Are our lives now a permanent bed of roses?

No.

Do we have our ups and downs?

Of course.

However our marriage and our lives are infinitely better than they were before and so much better than either of us ever thought possible. The great thing is that we now have a tool box at our disposal that we can open when something goes wrong, confident that inside we'll find just the tool we need to carry out the repair. And then if we can't find the appropriate tool, we have people who we can call upon to help us. We've learnt how to really communicate with each other and, above all, we've learnt the power of unconditional love.

Another thing Tony taught us was never to say, "I'm sorry." So you may be surprised to know that I never once said sorry to Chris, either when I made the confession to her or since. He taught us that instead of apologising, we should tell the other person what we have learnt from the situation. That is so much more powerful as it's much harder to do and is so much more meaningful.

So what did I learn? After I'd confessed to Chris in Austria, I took myself off for a walk, in a numb state I find difficult to describe. I remember looking across at the peak of one of the mountains thinking to myself that I'd just done the equivalent of leaping off the top without a parachute and trusting that the Universe would land me safely. I had no idea what course my life would take from thereon in. Yet at the same time I had an inner peace and kept drawing comfort from what Steve had said to me, "The truth will set you free". What I've learnt from all this that it is so much easier to live your life in truth. Whatever your situation, whatever you're holding back, one way or the other the truth really does set you free. You've just got to trust and let go.

When we got back from Austria I set about telling everyone close to me what had happened and all about my past, no holds barred, as I thought they might as well hear it from the horse's mouth as Chris was gunning for me and certainly would have told them anyway! Some couldn't understand why I didn't just decide to draw a line in the sand on my previous behavior, embark on a reformed path and keep my mouth shut. I knew where they were coming from, but also knew that in doing that I wouldn't have given Chris a choice. On reflection, if I had kept quiet I would have saved my family a few months of undeserved grief, and I suspect Chris and I would have stayed together in our okay marriage, and Chris would never have written this book which I'm sure will help many people improve their lives and maybe not make some of the mistakes that we made.

— **Doug Young 1/10/2007**

six

Chris's Vision

As I drew back the curtains and looked at the brilliance of the sun glistening on the sea, I felt an inner feeling of warmth for all the beautiful things in my life. What an amazing evening it had been last night.

I am blessed with a strong, handsome, adorable husband who cherishes me and compliments me daily and give me the certainty that whatever I do, I know he is always there for me. I love his passion and energy for life and being by his side, supporting him in his life's purpose, makes me very proud.

We travel around the world first class seeing all the great places there are in the world, not only for the experience, but also to spread my message of life's possibilities. I have lots of laughter, fun and love with Doug and together we grow daily through our experiences. I live my life in a healthy and invigorating way.

We have three beautiful children who we are so proud of. They all have a great uniqueness and passion for life. They are all living in great relationships, experiencing the same love that Doug and I have.

The times we are all together as a family are most special to me and sharing my time and love with my six beautiful grandchildren, who keep us young and alive, is incredible. Through my learning I have been able to give them the greatest gift, knowledge of what true love is all about. I know that this will be passed on down through the generations for years to come.

I am blessed with so many wonderful things in my life: family, great friends and a beautiful large house with windows overlooking the sea from the back and out to the mountains from the front. My door is open for anyone wanting to spend time in a loving, caring, warm environment and needing some guidance. I welcome them into my home as my guest.

We have a peaceful sanctuary in the house which has a feeling of serenity. When you are there it gives you a feeling of inner peace. This area in my home is where I run my successful coaching business.

I am privileged to receive so much praise and love from clients and for me nothing is more gratifying than seeing someone overcome the fears that have held them back in their life. I split my time with face-to-face clients and telephone coaching.

I had been on a journey of discovery and I had overcome one of the toughest challenges of my life. Funnily enough, what had been my toughest challenge turned out to become my greatest strength. Taking from all the lessons I had learned, I wrote a book which enabled me to share my story with others and to show them that no matter what pain or cruelty they have had in their life, it can be overcome. I am very proud of my book, which has a brilliant gold cover with white sparkling diamonds on it. The book has now spread around the world in different translations. I love the feeling that I am helping people see there is a way out of the darkness.

What else came from writing my book was the opportunity to go on television and share my story with millions. I have been to America and spoken on television and traveled around the country talking to groups about my journey. The exciting part of going to America was that I was approached by a film producer, asking if I would be willing to have my book turned into a film. I was very excited at this prospect, as it would be able to touch even more people's lives.

I had always had a passion for singing and I thought it would be great if I could put my story into a song. So I went to see Tony Wade, an amazing man who not only helped me to sing, but also helped me write a beautiful song. The first time I heard myself sing the song I could hardly believe it was me, the feeling was indescribable.

Last night was the premiere of the film. I was excited and proud as I sat in the front row with Doug by my side and all my family and friends around me. It was truly a magical feeling. At the end of the film, as the lights started to go up, I could hear all this noise and realised that it was all the audience applauding and crying as they were getting to their feet. I had never felt so much at peace knowing the effect this film was going to have on people who saw it and how it would change their lives.

There was a party after the film and, unbeknown to me, Andrew Lloyd Webber was there. He approached me saying how much he had enjoyed the film and that he had also read my book. I was then taken aback when he asked if I would be willing to have my story made into a musical. I was speechless, as this was beyond my wildest dreams. I had always had a great love of musicals and to have my story put to music would be amazing. He had also heard about the song that had been written and asked to use it in the musical. He asked if I would be willing to sing it on the opening night. I knew this would be the proudest and most emotional time for me, as I would be singing the song to just one person and he would know who he was!

Walking away from my window, I smiled to myself and thanked the angels for all the beautiful things in my life and looked forward to seeing the musical which was due to be out within the year. The opportunity I had been given to stand up on stage in front of a large audience and sing my song, was the greatest gift I could give to everyone, as I would be singing from my soul and my truth.

Appendices

Ask Doug and Chris

You will have noticed references in this book to our Ask Doug and Chris products which are focused exclusively on dealing with infidelity. For further information please go to *www.AskDougandChris.com*

Work with Christina

For information about the work Christina is doing helping women to re-ignite the flame inside them and live their life with love and connection please go to *www.ChristinaYoung.co.uk*

What is NLP?

I would like to thank Toby who granted me the permission to use this insert from the BBNLP magazine (at the time of writing this he was the owner of the BBNLP).

> *"At the heart of NLP is a wide range of methods and models it offers for understanding how people think, behave, learn and change. It offers a flexible approach which brings about positive, fast change in individuals and empowers them to adapt in an ever-shifting world.*
>
> *Within NLP, as well as being able to coach, you also have the ability to take people through various*

therapies, some of which I have described in the book.

It is often said that we were born with the most amazing computer in the Universe – the Human Brain. The only problem is, nobody gave us an instruction manual on how to work it. Now with NLP, we have our first handbook for realising the potential of our mind. NLP is the wisdom of research over the past 25 years into how the human mind works. It was developed by Richard Bandler and John Grindler in the early 1970s.

NLP goes a long way to showing you how to run your brain, how to control how you feel, how to be a more effective human being, how to improve your learning and communication skills and how your mind influences your health.

NLP enables people to overcome limitations, conflicts, fears, anxieties, and many physical problems with relative ease and achieve an increased level of personal success in a greatly shortened period of time."

Personally I am available for telephone or face to face coaching. It depends on the location of my clients and what is best for them. If you would be looking for more therapy work, then this is much better done face to face. One of the courses I offer which has helped my clients to let go and move on in their lives, is My VIP Program. For more information go to www.christinayoung.co.uk

Recommended Courses

In NLP there are many different processes which can help people deal with past events in their life. If, as you read this you feel you could do with some help in coming to terms with events in your life, I would recommend contacting a NLP Practitioner to learn about available courses.

My personal recommendation would be Gemma Bailey who is not only an NLP Trainer, she is also a Master Hypnotherapist. Her website is:

— www.gemmabailey.com

She has also set up NLP for kids. If we could train kids at an early age in the benefits of NLP, they would not have to go through so many challenges later on in life.

— www.nlp4kids.org

Besides NLP there are various other ways of dealing with issues. The Journey with Brandon Bays (www.thejourney.com) is very powerful and my clients have found it very helpful.

Another type of course I would recommend is a hypnotherapy course. Hypnosis can help with many different types of challenges in your life, anything from stress, smoking, phobias, and confidence as well as many others. (See my recommendation above for Hypnotherapy)

I do believe that if we are ready to put the time and effort in, then whatever challenges life has dealt us can be overcome, as long as we *want* to change.

Recommended Books and Seminars

Books

How to win friends and influence people – Dale Carnegie

Women who love too much – Robin Norwood

The Journey – Brandon Bays

The Power of Now – Eckhart Tolle

The Dynamic Laws of Healing – Catherine Ponder

The Dynamic Laws of Prosperity – Catherine Ponder

Multiple Orgasms with Ease and Elegance – Tony and Nicki Vee

The Richest Man in Babylon – George S Clason

Seeds of Greatness – Denis Waitley

The Big Leap – Gay Hendricks

Destiny of Souls – Michael Newton

You Can Heal Your Life – Louise L Hay

The Secret – Rhonda Byrne

Seminars

Power To Achieve – Andy Harrington
(formerly *Fire Your Desire*)

Unleash the Power Within – Tony Robbins

The Journey – Brandon Bays

Relationship Seminars – Tony and Nicki Vee

Dr Voice (Immersion Day) – Anthony Wade

The above seminars are ones I have attended and can endorse personally. If you look on the internet you will find there are many more seminars available. Some are even free.

About The Author

Christina Young is an inspirational mentor who helps people, especially women, to free themselves from negative emotions and painful, challenging experiences which hold them back from finding true love and connection,  not only with others but more importantly with themselves.

Christina is a certified NLP Master Practitioner, (Neuro Linguistic Practitioner), Certified Hypnotherapist, Relationship Mentor and Inner Power Therapeutic Coach.

She has overcome many adversities in her life and, based on her own personal experiences and training, now spends her time helping others to overcome their challenges.

As a child she was abused physically, emotionally and sexually. After 24 years of marriage, her husband Doug admitted to her that he had been continuously unfaithful to her throughout their marriage.

As they were often told at the time, and are continually reminded now, that would have signalled the end to most marriages. But, despite the huge challenges that lay ahead of them, they managed to survive it and stay together.

Soon after Doug and Christina got back together again, they were approached by a journalist about featuring their story in a national UK newspaper. They didn't feel entirely comfortable about exposing the inner secrets of their marriage to the public but agreed to do so in the hope that they could inspire others that surviving infidelity is possible.

That led to an ongoing string of features and interviews in the UK national press and on TV and radio. When a celebrity is thrown into the spotlight around infidelity issues they are usually contacted for their views and advice by the media.

Doug is a NLP (Neuro Linguistic Practitioner) Practitioner and Professional Relationship Coach. When couples are going through challenges in their relationships he and Christina work together and have found this very effective in helping their clients achieve the results they are seeking.

Whilst Doug mixes his coaching with other business interests Christina devotes all her time to mentoring and helping others. She particularly enjoys working with women either on a one-on-one basis or via her workshops.

Lightning Source UK Ltd.
Milton Keynes UK
178180UK00009B/1/P